D0866629

Reshaping Religious Education

OTHER BOOKS BY MARIA HARRIS
PUBLISHED BY WESTMINSTER JOHN KNOX PRESS

Fashion Me a People: Curriculum in the Church
Proclaim Jubilee! A Spirituality for the Twenty-first Century

RESHAPING
Religious Education
Conversations on Contemporary Practice

MARIA HARRIS AND GABRIEL MORAN

Westminster John Knox Press
Louisville, Kentucky

Book design by Jennifer K. Cox
Cover design and illustration by Alec Bartsch

First edition
Published by Westminster John Knox Press
Louisville, Kentucky

This book is printed on acid-free paper that meets the
American National Standards Institute Z39.48 standard.

PRINTED IN THE UNITED STATES OF AMERICA
98 99 00 01 02 03 04 05 06 07 — 10 9 8 7 6 5 4 3 2 1

Library of Congress Cataloging-in-Publication Data

Harris, Maria.
Reshaping religious education : conversations on contemporary practice / by Maria Harris and Gabriel Moran. — 1st ed.
p. cm.
Includes bibliographical references and index.
ISBN 0-664-25738-6 (alk. paper)
1. Christian education—Philosophy. 2. Catechetics—Catholic Church. I. Moran, Gabriel. II. Title.
BV1464.H36 1998
268—dc21 97-38735

Contents

Introduction

OVER THE YEARS

MARIA AND GABRIEL: Since we met in 1966, we have been exploring issues of religious education in local, national, and international settings. We have taught in large and small schools, parishes, and congregations, in almost every U.S. state, many Canadian provinces, and cities as diverse as Brisbane, Australia, and Seoul, South Korea. In every instance, we've received far more than we've given, and the gifts bestowed on us have deepened and expanded our understandings of what it means to educate religiously.

At the same time that we've changed, the religious and the educational worlds have changed and brought their own influences to bear on us personally and professionally. In this introduction, which serves as an introduction to both us and this book, we reflect on some of these changes. We hope our readers will find this interesting; we also hope they will consider engaging in a comparable exercise with one another by using the same or similar questions.

Q: What do you remember as the religious education situation in the mid-1960s?

MARIA: In the mid-1960s, I joined the religious education staff of the Catholic Diocese of Rockville Centre, New York, where my major work soon became in-service education with directors of religious education—DREs. In 1967, our diocese had four DREs. By 1973, influenced largely by the Second Vatican Council, that number had increased to 178, and today those women and men fill every conceivable ministerial role. Back then, however, especially in Catholic circles, the majority of people in individual parishes were only at the start of a world-shaking awareness of new possibilities for being "Spirit in the world"—a phrase of Karl Rahner's. Women and men were signing up for master's programs like the one our diocese was initiating and were reading Rahner too; and the laity were crowding the many educational programs we were running because they were experiencing a new kind of community. They wanted deeper theological understanding for themselves and yearned for non-rote teaching and a broader religious education for their children.

During those same years, having finished an M.A. in catechetical theology, I began doctoral studies in religious education, which eventually led to a degree granted jointly by Union Theological Seminary and Columbia University in New York. In those contexts, I came into regular contact with Protestant and Jewish religious educators and discovered several sets of religious education traditions of which, until then, I'd been only marginally aware. I also met a number of men and women who were pursuing the study of religion in public education, which led me to become interested in the many ways of educating religiously that complement the practices of more overtly religious communities.

GABRIEL: I was studying for my doctorate during the four years of the Second Vatican Council (1961–65). In 1965 I became director of a master's program in religious education at Manhattan College. Under the leadership of Brother Luke Salm, the program had three hundred people from the New York area coming to class every weekend and in summers. I was surprised that my dissertation, published as two books,[1] was so well-received; people were looking for support for what they had discovered in practice. And at that moment the Council encouraged Catholics to rethink their relation to other religions and to modern culture. Similar to the political upheavals in the United States of the late 1960s, this moment of great religious hope is often dismissed as romantic illusion. True, by the early 1970s it was becoming apparent that the road to a reformed Catholic church was going to be a long one. But the hope initiated in the 1960s still provides much of the impetus for Catholic church reform.

Q: How would you describe the situation today?

GABRIEL: I am very cautious about pronouncing on the contemporary scene. No one has a picture of the whole. However, the general religious scene in the world is fascinating to me. Maria and I attend the International Seminar on Religious Education and Values every two years, which has given us a sense of religious education worldwide. The 1994 meeting, held in Germany, was especially revealing; its theme was the fall of the Iron Curtain. It was an amazing experience to listen to colleagues from St. Petersburg, Prague, East Berlin, Johannesburg, and Tel Aviv on the centrality of religious education to what is happening in all those places. I am less encouraged by the kind of religious movements we have in the United States. In this country, any connecting of the words "religion" and "education" is still unimaginable for many people.

MARIA: I find the contemporary situation immensely more complicated than that of the mid-to-late '60s. I think that the U.S. Catholic church, in particular, has gone through a period of growing up, with all the ambiguity and mystery and loss that entails. Many more laity are now involved as a matter of course in local religious education, and are taking ownership of that education. But that has made for a strange paradox. On the one hand, there's a focus on the local parish—something that has always characterized U.S. Protestantism. But on the other, there's a growing awareness of other religious traditions, a worldwide consciousness not only of solidarity with, but of genuine and sometimes awesome differences between them. These are differences that too often work themselves out in the brutality of war, and so, in my view, religious educators have much to contribute to the realization that we don't and can't live in isolated religious compounds, and we must find ways to live together.

Q: What religious developments have been significant during this period?

MARIA: There are a great many, but here let me name three. First is the growing centrality of justice as a constitutive dimension of the gospel. That's had an enormous influence in eroding a purely privatized and individualistic spirituality. In Catholicism, education for justice resurfaced a long tradition of concern for justice that was present in the church's social encyclicals. Today it would be a rare curriculum that did not integrate outreach and works serving justice with the learning of doctrine and religious history, a rare curriculum that didn't assume and present the biblical traditions of justice that shape the religious lives of so many of us.

Second has been the ecological movement, a profoundly religious development that seemed new to many of us until we realized that ecology also draws on traditions important in past centuries. In religious traditions, ecology has renewed sabbatical and sacramental sensibilities, has affirmed Native American practices, and, in the churches, has rediscovered traditions kept alive in religious orders such as the Benedictines.

Third, especially in the U.S. and Canada, a sense of identity as adult religious educators has developed—of education *for* adults as well as *by* adults—

with an accompanying awareness of our responsibilities to and for one another, to and for our world. Devotion to lifelong education in adult life has been emboldened by the conviction, "If not us, who, and if not now, when?"

GABRIEL: I would second what you say of the ecological or environmental movement. I think it is not exaggerating to say that ecology is the primary religious movement of the late twentieth century. Generally, this development has been a positive challenge to every traditional religion. Ecology provides a meeting ground for worldwide religious discussions. A few years ago when I had to address an audience of Buddhists in Pusan, South Korea, I was worried that they would not know what I was talking about. I was pleasantly surprised to find that the Korean Buddhist speakers were citing the same ecological literature that I was.

The other great religious movement of the twentieth century was Marxism, whose collapse has left the world with little restraint on the money market as religion. The cry on behalf of the poor has to be taken up by the "old time" religions. The United States Catholic bishops have distinguished themselves here. Ecology as a religious movement is unfortunately not strong on the political and economic side. Emphasis upon person, community, and justice is a legacy of Jews and Christians that the contemporary world, including the ecological movement, still needs.

Q: What educational responses to these developments would you cite as positive in nature?

MARIA: I noted the impact of justice above. Two educational responses that have been a direct result of this emphasis are the attention religious educators now give to diversity and the attention we now give to privilege. We still have a long way to go, but with reference to diversity we are much more attentive to the vast range of approaches people make to the same religious story. For example, as the U.S. Christian population is increasingly Latino, those of us who are not Latino are becoming bilingual. We are also becoming sensitized to the many facets of Latino worship, culture, and priorities. And as this happens—and this has implications with reference to African- and Asian-American communities too—white religious educators are examining white privilege and power. We who are white are learning—or trying to learn—our own biases, and working more carefully not to assume that our way is the right or only way.

One way of addressing the question is to say that our educational responses seem to be experience-based. Our starting point is no longer some fixed and immutable list of "truths" that everyone must learn, and (especially) learn in the same way. Our starting point, instead, is a reverence for the many ways human beings approach and have been approached by the Sacred, the Divine, the Holy, and as a result of that reverence have learned to name and to celebrate the diverse forms of teaching and learning that are ours as human beings. Today, education at its best is concerned with—to draw on Howard Gardner—multiple forms of intelligences[2] and a multiplicity of approaches.

GABRIEL: One of the central elements in the upheaval of the 1960s was educational change and experimentation. Many new schools were started at that time; most of them did not last long. A more permanent change was in the colleges, which expanded in the number and diversity of their students. People of any age can now study for a degree and no one thinks that to be peculiar. The ideal of a lifelong education has been realized as much in this expansion of the college population as in the fifty million participants in adult education programs. Schools for children are generally more humane places than they were before the 1960s, but trying to maintain academic standards in any school has become more difficult. The chief educational force, for better and worse, has been television, now in the process of merging with the Internet. Many evangelical Christian schools and Jewish day schools originated in this period. Catholic schools are fewer in number, although better in quality, than in the past. The movement to have parish directors of religious education has flourished in the Catholic church but has run up against institutional and financial limits that Protestant congregations experienced earlier in this century.

Q: What responses have been disappointing?

GABRIEL: I am disappointed that "religious education" is still not a common language spoken by Catholic, Protestant, and Jewish educators, as well as public school teachers of religion. Catholics did not much use the term "religious education" before the 1960s, but I think Catholics are its major users now. We ought, however, to speak of religious education in a way that invites participation by others. The venture of "catechetics" remains almost exclusively Catholic, which is not a bad thing so long as people realize it when they are using an intramural language.

MARIA: As we became a global village and realized our connectedness, I assumed we'd be having much more interreligious conversation, which in turn would influence our religion curricula. For example, it still surprises me that Christians know so little about Judaism, not only the

Judaism of the Hebrew Bible, but the living, breathing, contemporary Jewish tradition that so influences the practice of those of us who are Christians. It also distresses me that those of us who are Christian educators do not study the Holocaust, not only as a fact of Jewish history, but as a facet of our own, including our people's involvement and contribution to the conditions that made the Holocaust possible.[3] From another perspective, I'm disappointed that as educators in religion, we know so little about Islam or Buddhism. I'm also saddened, frustrated, and resistant to what I see as sinful and intransigent attitudes toward women and toward sexuality, especially homosexuality, in the churches. Not only do these attitudes demean women—and men—who keep the churches alive, they also create an unhealthy climate that precludes important work in sexuality education in some cases, while in others it sours and destroys the work we do try to do.

Q: How has your own work changed?

MARIA: I've always been intrigued by the shapes and forms and images of things—my doctoral dissertation was on the aesthetic dimension of religious education.[4] Over the years, I've become far less defensive of that work, far less apologetic in the face of views of it as peripheral, or "fluff." The artistic isn't an add-on, it's an essential component. So I've become more celebratory, more up-front about the impact of imagery, ritual, and nonverbal elements on our learning. When I observe educational and catechetical situations, I'm distracted regularly by the power of the *implicit* curriculum (what's going on beneath the surface of what's going on). I'm intrigued by how things are designed and framed and fashioned and how that influences what we do even more than what we say does. For example, attending to form often clearly reveals the ways that power is shared or not shared: who speaks, who gets heard, who's in on decisions.

Another change for me is that I regularly work with Protestant traditions and communities. For more than a decade in the '70s and '80s, I taught at Andover Newton Theological School just outside of Boston, where for years I was the only Catholic on the faculty. That gave me an invaluable and treasured ecumenical education that continues to this day. Similarly, teaching throughout the world makes me see the U.S. church through eyes other than my own, and helps give a worldwide dimension to my work.

GABRIEL: My own interests have remained fairly constant over the decades. The setting in which I work, the School of Education at New York University, is the biggest change for me. I continue to be interested in religious education as a test of what education is. I also teach courses in the history and the philosophy of education. Both have helped me better understand religious education, just as my religious education background gives me some extra insight into the history and the philosophy of education. I feel that my recent book *Showing How: The Act of Teaching*[5] was possible only from the combination of my interest in religious education and my involvement in the history and philosophy of education.

Q. Why did you choose *Reshaping Religious Education* as the title of this book?

MARIA: In answering this question, I will comment on the idea of "reshaping," and Gabriel will comment on "religious education."

Reshaping (and its corollaries such as reforming, refashioning, and redesigning) has always been a central impulse for both of us. We have long been interested in the shapes and forms of things, and the ways in which the activities of forming, shaping, and fashioning help to determine outcomes and end points. For us, each of these is an aesthetic category, and we have consciously drawn from the artistic wisdom that form shapes content, indeed *is* the shape of content. So you will find both of us alluding regularly to such subjects as the forms power takes, forms of teaching, and social and economic forms.

Because we live in time, however, we are always receiving forms from the past and then molding and remolding, reforming and refashioning them so they will "fit" better in the present and the future. This reshaping is a work of the creative, artistic imagination, and we believe that new forms and shapes come into being whenever we take the risk of becoming artists and creators ourselves. So an essential dynamic of this book is a summons to the reader to take this risk, especially as she or he considers our main categories of foundations, development, spirituality, and the implications of living in the wider world of the twenty-first century.

GABRIEL: Since the 1960s, both of us have used the term "religious education" to designate our work, always with the awareness that the term may not have the rich connotations for the reader that we intend. Despite the term's limitations, I do not know a better term in English to refer to all the possible relations between religion and education. These relations are explored in chapter 2. We adopt the term religious education, but we are also trying to change it, that is, to reshape its meaning.

Is such a change possible, let alone likely? Anyone who thinks a book can change the meaning of a term is naive about the complexity of language. Terms do change their meanings, usually in the course of decades or centuries and because of repeated use by thousands or millions of people. Nonetheless, one can try in the company of others to contribute to the reshaping of language. In this case, "religious education" is a relatively recent term whose meaning is not fixed. We are not trying to invent something entirely new or oppose something that is completely established. We are taking shapes and forms that exist and trying to reshape them in a way that would open up a much larger conversation about religion and education.

Q. What can the reader expect to find in the chapters to follow?

GABRIEL: I will comment on the contents of the chapters. Maria will speak to the equally important issue of format and style. The content of this book reflects our convictions about the nature of religious education. While the reader will easily detect the stylistic differences Maria and I have, I do not think we have any substantive differences about content. Both of us understand religious education to be that part of education concerned with religious attitudes, ideas, and practices.

Such an area is extremely broad. No one is an expert in every aspect of this developing field, and we frequently acknowledge the limits imposed by our personal histories. We do think, nevertheless, that we have a distinctive contribution to make by combining contemporary educational theory and practice with the knowledge and practice of a rich religious tradition. The bias in what follows is toward a Christian, and often more specifically a Catholic Christian interpretation of religious education. Where it is appropriate, we explicitly note the bias or take steps to compensate for it.

The chapters are grouped into four parts: (1) foundations, (2) development, (3) spirituality, and (4) a wider world. These four themes provide a rough guide to our interests and to what we hope are also interests of the reader. All twelve chapters may not be of immediate relevance to every reader, but each of them touches on an issue of historical value or contemporary practice that is already contributing to the reshaping of religious education.

In part 1, "Foundations," we lead off with an exchange on the meaning of curriculum. As we often do, we move here between the universal and the particular, drawing upon both secular educational writing and church practice. The broad and deep meaning for the curriculum of religious education provides a backdrop for all the subsequent chapters. Chapters 2 and 3 are a paired set of essays. In the first, I describe two distinct aims for a field of religious education, one that is internal to a religious group and one that arises from comparing religious groups. In chapter 3, Maria responds to my proposal, showing how one of those aims is embodied in the changing structures and practices of catechetics, mainly, but not exclusively, in the Catholic church.

Part 2, on the theme of development, traces how this modern ideal has interacted with religious and theological ideas. In chapter 4, Gabriel traces the origin of "development," and Maria gives special attention to the economic side of its meaning. In chapter 5 the development of the individual and the influence of gender in that development is played out in our exchange on the education of girls and boys, women and men. Chapter 6 is on death and mourning. Developmental theories do not usually include death and mourning as stages. We argue that a religious way of approaching lifelong development must include mourning the deaths of those closest to us as well as the small deaths within our own lives. Although each person's death does not appear until the last step in life, one's attitude to that death structures each step along the way of life.

We have called part 3 "Spirituality." Similar to the pattern that we used in the first two parts, chapter 7 provides an overview of this theme. We examine the history and nature of spirituality and its surprising prominence in the present era. Our concern is to keep spirituality related to our historical religious tradition, rooted in the challenges of biblical tradition and the ethical problems of today's world. The two chapters that follow are paired around the ideas of justice and jubilee. In chapter 8, we explore the tension between the Greek philosophical ideal of justice and the biblical tradition of justice. In chapter 9, Maria summarizes the work she has done on Jubilee, and I respond with comments on the importance of the Jubilee for the ethics of the New Testament. The theme of Jubilee provides the basis for a way of life—a spirituality—that is as relevant at this century's end as it has ever been.

Part 4, "Toward a Wider World," points beyond the limits that generally exist in any one group's discussion of religious education. In *Religious Education as a Second Language*[6] I argued that religious education has to be interinstitutional, intergenerational, interreligious, and international. These last two qualities are addressed in chapters 10 and 11: a Christian dialogue with Judaism and a United States dialogue with one of our international colleagues. We view these two topics not as esoteric concerns but as reminders that a Christian-Jewish dialogue ought to exist within Christianity itself and that an international dialogue should be present even within the borders of the United States. Chapter 12 acknowledges some of the obvious things we had to leave out. The previous two chapters in this section have offered modest examples of where the future might lie. Without trying to predict the future, we take it as part of our task to indicate some possible directions for the future. These are areas where we hope to work with others who are interested in developing the theories and practices that will contribute to reshaping religious education.

MARIA: When we decided to coauthor this book, we did so out of our experiences of team-teaching throughout the world. In that teaching, we tend to develop our class sessions and presentations in a variety of ways. Sometimes, where one of us is particularly experienced and has had a much greater involvement in a topic, that person takes the lead and the other is a primary respondent. At other times, in contrast, we are both so involved in the theme that we have the kind of lively conversation that is punctuated by breaking into one another's speaking or ending one another's sentences. At still other times, we invite a third person, or several people, or the entire group to join in the conversation.

In using these different processes, we have discovered one constant: the dramatic difference in power relations. When two or more people team-teach, power is routinely shared. Instead of a lone "expert" at the front of the room, two or more people model a shared authority, and their conversation invites others into that sharing. This becomes especially true for groups that are of diverse race, gender, or ethnicity.

In coauthoring this book, therefore, we have chosen forms that mirror the diverse characteristics of teams involved in teaching. These forms, we hope, will serve to empower the reader. Obviously, writing differs from classroom teaching in that the teaching act embodies actual physical presence, whereas writing is generally solitary. Still, as this work evolved we found ways that we could continue to share power with one another and invite the reader to share it with us. This led us to use six different forms.

First, we use conversation where our questions and our responses are relatively brief. This form begins and ends the book. Second, we use a form that is almost but not quite the opposite: each of us wrote a chapter completely on our own, although the topics are interrelated and thus interface with each other. This is the form of chapter 2, on aims, and chapter 3, on catechesis as an embodiment of one of these aims. A third form, bringing together complementary perspectives on a theme, is a going back-and-forth twice in the chapter; we use this form in our writing about curriculum (chapter 1), spirituality (chapter 7), and justice (chapter 8). In a variation on that, we write a chapter in two equal parts with each of us providing major input, as we do in writing on "the roots of development" (chapter 4) and on gender (chapter 5).

Two of the chapters take a fourth form to shape the input. These are the conversations on death (chapter 6) and on Jubilee (chapter 9), where one of us has written the major part of the chapter and the other has provided a briefer response. For death and for Jubilee this form seemed most appropriate, since for twenty years Gabriel has taught courses on death and dying, even as I have spent almost a decade teaching the spirituality of the Jubilee.

Our fifth form is to include a third person in our conversation when speaking to an issue where an additional perspective is essential. We do this in chapter 10, which is concerned with what Christians can learn from Jews, where Sherry Blumberg is our partner, and in chapter 11 on international religious education, where Friedrich Schweitzer joins us.

And finally, by appending questions to each of the chapters, we explicitly use a sixth form where the reader also delves into the issues we raise. It is our hope that in offering this plethora of forms, we are making a contribution that is itself significant in reshaping religious education.

FOR REFLECTION AND RESPONSE

1. What do you remember as the religious education situation of the 1960s (or '70s or '80s)?
2. How would you describe the religious education situation today?
3. What religious developments have been significant during the period you chose?
4. What educational responses to these developments would you cite as positive in nature?
5. What responses have been disappointing?
6. How has your own work changed?
7. What is the role of the national or international leadership of your religious tradition toward other religious traditions? What is your own relation to religious traditions other than your own?

part one
FOUNDATIONS

Chapter 1

THE CURRICULUM OF EDUCATION

Educational Forms

GABRIEL: "Curriculum" means the course that one runs. Although it is a term with ancient roots, the discussion of educational curriculum is mostly a story of the twentieth century. When debates about curriculum arose at the beginning of this century, the assumed context was elementary and secondary schools. If you look up "curriculum" in a library computer, you will find that nearly all the listed material is still within that context. Running the course of education still appears to be a journey from first to twelfth grades.

In his 1997 State of the Union Address, President Bill Clinton gave extraordinary attention to "education," listing a ten-point program. Many commentators dismissed his words by saying that the federal government provides only five percent of educational budgets. They assumed that "education" is equivalent to state-run elementary and secondary schools. However, four of the ten points were not about those schools. Mr. Clinton could have been clearer on the fact that in addition to proposing help for elementary and secondary schools he was trying to indicate a different meaning of "education."

I think that people concerned with religious education have usually had some sense that curriculum means more than elementary and secondary school classes. If someone had asked me in the late 1950s what curriculum meant, I would have pointed to the textbooks I was using in high school teaching. But when I began studying religious education in the 1960s it quickly became apparent to me that there were larger questions I had not seen. The improvement of religion textbooks is a good thing, and certainly today's books are an improvement over what I used as a high school teacher. Nonetheless, the course of one's religious education runs much wider and deeper than any of those textbooks. The problem that I and many others have faced is to find a consistent and effective way to lay out an alternate course.

What I eventually discovered was that the modern problem with curriculum is largely a religious one. This discovery took me more than two decades, and I will return to this point later. But first I want to recount how I initially approached curriculum from within the literature of secular education. In the third part of this chapter I will describe how church language helped me to describe more accurately a curriculum of education.

A work in the early 1960s that many found illuminating and provocative was Bernard Bailyn's *Education in the Forming of American Society.*[1] In contrast to many historians of education who simply recount the story of the public school, Bailyn wondered what had gone on between the founding of Harvard College in 1637 and the beginning of the Boston school system in 1844. Bailyn did not devote much space to the question of education itself. Instead, he assumed an anthropologist's meaning, that is, "the entire process by which a culture transmits itself across the generations."[2] With that meaning, he explored how people actually were educated in seventeenth- and eighteenth-century Massachusetts. Since the Puritans of that time kept detailed records and diaries, Bailyn was able to draw a fairly precise portrait.

The picture that emerged was of four "agents" of education. A child who grew up in that era was likely to be influenced by family, church, school, and apprenticeship. The first agent, family, has always been of obsessive concern in this country. And although as early as 1680 a church synod in Boston bemoaned the complete disintegration of the family, the family then and afterward has exercised profound influence on each child. The church as the second agent of education may seem out of place here, but its role in all education was central. It helped to maintain society and transmit culture, even for people who were not Christian. The third agent, school, was important from the beginning; schools were immediately founded to teach people how to read the Bible. Although schools were widespread in the eighteenth century, attendance was subject to the vagaries of the labor market, especially the rhythms of the agricultural cycle. The fourth and final agent, apprenticeship, was crucial in preparing the teenage boy for his lifelong calling. Interestingly, girls were often sent out for apprenticeship even though they did not learn a specific trade.[3]

Bailyn's description provided encouragement for those of us struggling to find a new language of curriculum and education. When one is proposing something new, it is a great help to know that it has already existed in some form, that one is not just spinning out ideas, that the task is to retrieve what has been forgotten. Of course, one possibility is that education took on a new meaning in the late nineteenth century because the new was in fact better and therefore replaced the old. John Dewey, writing at the end of the nineteenth century, did not necessarily think the new was better; he just assumed that the old was no longer operative—more specifically, he thought that family, church, and apprenticeship no longer functioned as agents of education. That left the school as the only agent still standing, one that now for the first time in history was to be universally available. Dewey's 1900 essay, "The Child and the Curriculum," is therefore about the child as the recipient of education, and curriculum as what happens in primary and secondary schools.[4]

With the advantage of viewing this issue a century later, it should be obvious that Dewey badly misjudged the curriculum of education. The family remains the first and in many respects the most important educational influence on children—and on their parents and grandparents. Apprenticeship is much discussed these days as the part of education that is badly needed but sadly neglected.[5] Other countries, such as Germany, have shown the great value of apprenticeship programs for high school or college age people. Dewey's pessimistic view of the church as educator—in Dewey's experience the small Protestant congregation of his Vermont youth—has proved more accurate. And yet the country remains as intensely religious as ever, and the church is by far the most widespread voluntary organization in the United States.

What these developments suggest is that instead of a straight line of progress from the seventeenth century to the present, the period of about 1860 to 1960 was an educational aberration. The belief that the school could do what was once the work of family, church, apprenticeship, and school was an unrealistic faith in the rational control of life. In the nineteenth century, many reformers were explicit in wishing to replace the church with the school. It is no disparagement of the school to point out that schools are ill-designed to do what churches have done. To this day schools are subject to the mood swings of a public that vacillates between unrealistic expectation and overly harsh criticism.

Bernard Bailyn's book was not a history of education but a snapshot of one place at one time. Puritans of the seventeenth and eighteenth centuries have something to teach us, but they had their own limited view of education. Nevertheless, the pieces of the puzzle they provide can lead us further back in history. They can also give us a lens for our present and future.

What I found unsatisfactory about Bailyn's use of the term "agent" was the uncritical assumption that education is a one-way process between adults and children. For Bailyn, the delivery system was fourfold, but there was still a thing called "education" that adults were trying to get into children. The nineteenth century was confident that it knew what "it" (education) is. At the end of the twentieth century most people, for better or worse, are not so confident. Not even our most highly prized science inspires a trust that the truth is secure and that the way forward is clear. Most of us nonetheless realize that we cannot abandon the quest for truth, the need for order, and some overall sense of what our lives mean. Educationally, this implies a curriculum that has interactive or mutual elements, drawing upon the best that can be found among adults and children, men and women, humans and nonhumans, past and present.

Since the 1960s I have preferred to speak of *forms* of education, rather than agents. The best description of education I have been able to devise is "a reshaping of life's forms with end and without end." Education is lifelong because of the tension between the two different meanings of "end": an end to education can refer either to a purposeful direction that is always intrinsic to education or to a termination point that should always be resisted in education. And if education is to be lifelong it has to be lifewide, that is, a continuing interaction among the various forms of education.

The forms of education are simply the main places where the reshaping of life occurs in relation to human purpose. One could perhaps name dozens of forms, but it is more helpful to choose a set of major forms that are as comprehensive as possible. I began working with a set of four forms that are broadly but not exclusively chronological. Nearly everyone in today's world is born into a family, attends some school, makes some contribution to society by a job, and then enters a period of retirement or leisure. I correlated each of these four places with a corresponding educational aim: family in relation to community; school in relation to literate knowledge; job in relation to work; leisure in relation to wisdom. The curriculum of education is the interaction within each of these four forms, as well as the interaction among all four of them.

In the course of life, nearly all of us move through each of these forms. None is in total segregation from the others. In fact, the four are always in interaction; when one is at the center, the others are present as satellites. When a child goes to school, the family's influence decreases but it does not disappear. When one gets a job, school may not be central but it is likely to remain an influence. When one is retired, family matters may reemerge with more prominence.

The correlations I have suggested between an educational aim and its primary expression not only invite a reshaping of these expressions but also call for secondary expressions. Thus, community is partially embodied in the family, but the family needs other communal expressions to complement it (for example: a neighborhood, a friendship, a bowling team).

Similarly, school is a place for literate knowledge, but it needs help from beyond school. One's job can be a partial embodiment of genuine work, but no matter how fulfilling a job is one still needs other work in life. Retirement is a place where wisdom is especially to be found, but that wisdom needs to be present in quiet moments elsewhere in life.

It may be surprising that the one agent of Bailyn's that I have not used is church. That is not because I think the church is unimportant but because religious organizations, including the Christian churches, cut across the four educational forms and can have a part in each of them. The church's role is more complex than being one more agent for the control of children. How the church has educated and what light that might throw on education is Maria's subject in the section that follows.

The Church as Educator

MARIA: In engaging the themes of this book, any reader who is familiar with our work will recognize how much Gabriel and I depend on and complement one another. This is particularly true with reference to curriculum. I had been teaching courses on curriculum (more often on curriculum and teaching as a pair) for several years when Gabriel began to develop his ideas about forms of education.[6] However, my teaching context was a seminary—in contrast to his, which was a large urban university. My students' interests were ministerial as well as educational. My daily work was inextricably connected with women and men who were planning to become involved in or were already engaged in religious, ecclesial life. We were regularly concerned with life in local parishes and congregations, with dioceses and judicatories, with laity and clergy, with priesthood. More particularly, they—and I—were concerned with birth and death, with gain and loss, with brokenness and healing, with the earth, with humanity and divinity. Educational issues were discussed in an intramural language not always accessible to or translatable in the wider society. Clearly, in the settings where we found ourselves, education was broader than Sunday school or the CCD[7] program, although for lack of better language, the word "education" was often limited to those.

My Andover Newton colleague Gabriel Fackre had often spoken of the work of the church as *koinonia*, *leitourgia*, *diakonia*, and *kerygma.* It occurred to me that Fackre, like Moran, was speaking about *forms*—in this case, forms of church life. I wondered how much symmetry existed between these historical religious forms and the discoveries Gabriel Moran had made in naming the four forms of educational curriculum. I began to articulate for myself, and then with my students, a meaning of curriculum within the church as "the entire course of the *church's* life." I also began to pursue the relations between community, literate knowledge, work, and wisdom and the ancient religious forms of koinonia, didache, leitourgia, and kerygma. But I held on to the holiness of the first set of forms as well, struck by the realization that Christianity refers to God as community, knowledge, work, and wisdom when it uses the names Trinity, Logos, Creator, and Sophia.

The idea of form was particularly congenial to me, since my understanding of art had long been dependent on Suzanne Langer's teaching that art is the creation of perceptible form. I'd learned from the painter Ben Shahn that form is, quite simply, the shape of content. Besides artists, however, I knew that church folk often spoke of their educational work as Christian formation; that administrators of religious orders appointed directors of formation who initiated novices into the work of the order; and that the catechetical office in a Catholic diocese was sometimes named the Department of Formation.

I also knew that Dewey had conceived of education as the "reconstruction" and "reorganization" of experience which enables human beings to find meaning in experience and direct the course of subsequent experience. I believed that "reconstructing" and "reorganizing" the forms of experience could be construed as artistic work—as aesthetic work—and I realized the metaphors of *fashioning* and *refashioning* actually were central to my own understanding of how the curriculum of the church might be described.

To flesh that out, however, I needed to go back to the original New Testament description of the forms of church life that are found in the second chapter of the book of Acts, which is itself one of the founding documents of the Christian church. The central *teaching* of the church (which is also its central kerygma or proclamation) is announced in Acts with the words: "This Jesus God has raised up, and of that we all are witnesses" (2:32). Then the account proceeds:

> And they continued steadfastly in the *teaching* of the apostles and in the *communion* of the *breaking of the bread* and in the *prayers*. And all who believed were together and held all things in *common* and would sell their possessions and goods and *distribute them among all according as anyone had need.* And continuing daily with one accord in the temple, and breaking bread in their houses, they took their food with gladness and simplicity of heart, praising God and being in favor with all the people. (Acts 2:42, 44–47, italics added)

Communion, prayer, care for the needy, the preached word, teaching—the forms were all there, in the treasury of the church. These forms constituted church curriculum, sometimes overlapping with the curriculum of education, sometimes distinct although related to it. I decided to lay out these forms and did so subsequently in the book *Fashion Me a People: Curriculum and the Church.*[8]

In writing *Fashion Me a People,* I made several discoveries. The first is that, from an ecclesial perspective, church curriculum is usually sequential. It begins with the gathered community or koinonia. That community gathers for two main purposes: to worship God through liturgical prayer, and to engage in works that serve justice—the traditions of leiturgia and diakonia. These three constitute the embodiment of the "teaching of the apostles" that is lived before it is discussed or presented. Only when the first three are in place do the curricular acts of preaching the word and gathering for instruction and catechesis—both of which are largely verbal—make sense.

I also recognized that each of the central forms has *multiple embodiments.* Community in the church may refer to everyone in the congregation or to the many small, basic Christian communities that are a contemporary expression of parish or congregational life. Community may also be embodied in age groups, from pre-kindergarten to silver-haired seniors, and may include youth groups, young adults, and working parents. It certainly refers to families, but it also applies to workers for social justice and to self-help, divorced and widowed, and Lazarus groups—the last a reference to those in the local church community who act as mourners and who bury the dead.

Similarly, liturgy in the church refers not only to public worship. It extends as well to the ministries of prayer, contemplation, retreats, missions, meeting for the canonical hours such as Vespers and Compline, novenas, and all kinds of paraliturgical services. Works that serve justice also take innumerable forms—the best-known being the "works of mercy" that are traditionally named as feeding the hungry, giving drink to the thirsty, clothing the naked, sheltering the homeless, visiting the sick and the imprisoned, and burying the dead. These are the works that serve justice, as described by Jesus in the twenty-fifth chapter of Matthew's Gospel with the reminder that "As long as you did these things to the least of my brothers and sisters, you did them to me."

Kerygma and didache also have numerous embodiments. Preaching is generally the best-known and most often used form of kerygmatic speech, but advocacy for the poor and the abused; taking part in processions and demonstrations, especially in the service of justice; and protesting the death penalty in the name of the gospel may also be incarnations of the embodied word that is the soul of kerygma. And didache—the word translates as "teaching"—carries a meaning that allows it to be applied not only to the catechesis of catechumens preparing for baptism but to the mystagogy that follows; to the instruction in practices already being performed, from centering prayer to the celebration of marriage; to the study of the history of how these developed; to presenting the story and the theologies of the church through the ages all the way back to and through its origins in Judaism, with pride of place given to the biblical tradition.

These examples lead to still another facet of church curriculum: each of its forms exists in interplay with all the others. Touch liturgy and the works that serve justice quiver; touch prayer and community is strengthened; preach compassion and knowledge is deepened. It is never possible to separate these forms and, upon reflection, it becomes clear that each abides within the others. Community is within prayer and service, teaching and preaching; the word of advocacy is, similarly, at the roots of worship, community, mercy, and catechetical instruction.

Or, viewed from a somewhat different angle of vision, each of the forms of church curriculum both educates and is itself an educational process. We are educated *to* koinonia (community and communion) *through* the forms of community and communion; we are educated *to* leitourgia (worship and prayer) *through* engaging in the forms of prayer and worship and spirituality; we are educated *to* diakonia (service and outreach) *through* being of service and reaching out to others locally and globally; we are educated *to* kerygma (proclaiming the word of God) *through* the kerygma's practice, especially the speech that advocates living the gospel and the speech that protests injustice wherever we find it; we are educated *to* didache (teaching and learning) *through* using the most appropriate forms of teaching and learning whenever we instruct or catechize or share the traditions that are ours.

Further, should any of these be left out as full partners in the educational work that is the curriculum of the church or should any of them be downplayed, we would not be educating fully. Each of them is needed. And underneath each of them and pervading each of them is the one form that encompasses all of them, and without which they could not come together. That form is, of course, the church itself. The church is present, whole and entire, in each of its forms, although it is not equivalent to any one of them. Instead the church is a community, a center of prayer, a house of justice. The church is an incarnation of the word. The church is, as Schillebeeckx teaches, the sacrament of the encounter with the Christ.[9] And the church as educator makes that encounter possible.

Church, School, Classroom

GABRIEL: The picture of the church's educational efforts that Maria describes shows the variety of ways by which the church has historically formed its own members. Most secular educators assume that the sole form of education in churches is "indoctrination." When they look at the church the only thing they can identify as education is a man behind a pulpit speaking to an audience composed mainly of women and children. Church education is exclusively identified with preaching and homiletic speech. Catechetical teaching in the Catholic church is taken to be a subset of preaching or homiletics.

If this is the picture that modern educators have seen when looking at the church, it is because that element of education is there, and in some local churches there may be little else. But two correctives are needed. First, the equating of preaching or homiletics with indoctrination is an unjustified assumption. Preaching is a legitimate and effective form of teaching—if all the conditions for its use are present. And catechizing has its own distinct place and shape; it is not a subset of preaching.

Second, modern education does not see the variety in the church's education because modern secular education has been tone-deaf and color-blind in recognizing other forms of education beyond "instruction." Secular education, of course, borrowed instruction from the church but changed the term to mean "giving reasons" and "imparting information." Whereas in church practice, instruction was (and at its best still is) a reflection on practices already being performed, in modern secular education, instruction was supposed to provide the information that would explain everything. This meaning of instruction has never been able to carry its assigned burden; it is periodically attacked from both right and left for either failing to control children's behavior or else for exercising too much control over people's thinking.

My suggestion, therefore, is that secular education look again at church practice and the variety of teaching languages within those different practices. In the educational forms that I identified in the first section of this chapter, the church is not one form of education but an institution involved in all four forms. A few words on each of the four will indicate the church's importance here.

The church (local and universal) is composed of families and other communal groupings. By its mode of operation the church is capable of enhancing community life in ways that range from groups meeting in the church basement to a national church speaking out against governmental policies detrimental to the welfare of the poor. In relation to work, the church's most distinctive contribution is its liturgy, worship, and public prayer. In regard to work as an educational form, the church is also home to many of the voluntary service programs in the United States that educate the givers while helping the recipients. The church's academic instruction is provided in church related schools, within the liturgy, and through published statements. Instruction in Christian living is very directive about the meaning of texts that shape church tradition. Finally, the church is a place of retirement or leisure, not only for the aged and dying but for people of all ages who need periodic respite from ordinary pressures. Retreats and contemplative prayer are an educational necessity that the contemporary secular world often gropes for.

Earlier I criticized Bernard Bailyn for describing four agents, thereby accepting a view of education as something deliverable from adult to child, from powerful institution to receptive individual. I proposed instead that we need to name *forms* of education that bring about intelligent control in people's lives by lifelong interaction. Having gone by a circular route, I can now reintroduce the term "agent" as descriptive of the church: an institution that can effectively house all the major forms of education. The agent's main work here is not to *deliver* education but to *provide a place* for the interaction of educational forms. For example, the liturgy can and should be an experience of community, good work, instruction, and contemplative quiet. If some people, including some liturgists, shy away from the word "education" to describe this experience, they should reflect on what they assume education to mean.

Reflection on the church gave me the missing link that I had long sought in trying to understand the confusion in the literature of educational reform. This reflection also revealed a serious flaw in the description of educational forms that I had used for about twenty years. I had used the ambiguous term "schooling" for one of the four forms, trying to include both the instructive element in the classroom and other elements in a typical modern school. This deliberate ambiguity, I finally concluded, was a source of confusion in my own mind and in the minds of others.

By seeing the school as almost exactly parallel to the church in education, the school, too, can once again be seen as an agent of education. Like the church, the school is not an agent for the delivery of something called education; rather it is an institution that houses several forms of education. The school has to try to reshape these forms and provide for their interaction.

The literature on educational reform that tries to see beyond the school usually begins by assuming that education consists of school plus other elements. The attempt to name the non-school parts trails off into innumerable examples, a process which usually returns everything to the school. While Bailyn found three institutions to add to the school (family, church, apprenticeship), contemporary writers find dozens (television, movies, computers, magazines, rock music, sports, malls, museums, and so on). The problem is that in posing the question of "school plus what else?" the school is treated as the obvious part of the answer; naming the other parts of education is thought to be the difficult part. The key for making progress here is to recognize that the school itself is not a form of education. The school, similar to the church, is an institution that can and should house all the forms of education.

Some people predict that the school will cease to exist. They could be right, but schools have been here for centuries and at present show no sign of coming to their end. They are, however, in need of constant and modest reform. We need a simple and comprehensive blueprint for what constitutes a school.

First, schools, like churches, are places that can help or hinder community. How schools interact with parents, how administrators act with teachers, how teachers and students relate to each other influence the community existence of everyone involved. The power of the school in teaching community should never be underestimated. Second, schools are places of work in several ways. Classroom instruction is serious work for a child, even more so for an adult. School prepares people for jobs or helps them to do their jobs better. Schools can also house service work, the voluntary contribution of time and skill, without which a community or a country cannot long survive. Third, school is also a place of leisure (our English word "school" is derived from the Greek word for leisure). The practice of the arts and athletic competition should be part of most schools. These activities are extracurricular in relation to the classroom but integral to the curriculum of the school.

Fourth and finally, there is classroom instruction as a form of education. Instruction can occur outside the classroom, but it is useful to have a particular place and a set time that constitute the form of instruction in literate knowledge. The classroom is not a place to "impart information"; other places and resources, such as books, television, and computers, can do that better. Classrooms are places for a peculiar kind of dialogue that reflects on language itself. If education were confined only to a classroom, the result would be either utter vacuousness or hidden indoctrination. Fortunately, despite some myopia in educational writing, other forms of education have never ceased to exist. And the best teachers in classrooms have usually learned about teaching from the teaching done by parents, artists, athletic coaches, writers, and others, even while reflecting carefully on the possibilities and limits of a classroom for one peculiar form of teaching.

In summary, there is a curriculum of the classroom that ought to be a carefully structured set of readings and exercises on one course of study. That precise and narrow meaning of curriculum needs to be situated within a school. For most young people the school curriculum includes artistic activity, sports, and job preparation, as well as what occurs in the corridors, cafeteria, and counselor's office. Finally, there is the curriculum of education that is not just a larger version of school curriculum. It is composed of the main forms of education and their interaction throughout a lifetime. Both schools and churches can be institutions that house all the major forms of education. To do so requires looking within to see what is already happening educationally and then working patiently to reshape the forms of education.

The idea of curriculum (similar to the idea of development to be discussed in a later chapter) requires a religious element to keep from closing in on itself. When curriculum excludes religious concerns, it becomes a straight line from a beginning to an end point. A curriculum that is adequate for a person's life has to run the course of life and encompass the major formative influences that are as wide as life. The rejection of religion reduces the curriculum to things that an individual can mentally master in search of autonomy. A religious curriculum, in contrast, allows for a playful twisting and turning on a journey supported by the wisdom of the past and the rituals of a supportive community in the present.

The Priestly, the Prophetic, the Political: Ways to Understand the Community

MARIA: The final presupposition Gabriel articulates above, that curriculum requires a religious element to keep from closing in on itself, refers not only to religion's place as a substantive part of any curriculum that is adequate for our times. It refers as well to qualities, characteristics, or aspects of curriculum that contribute to making curriculum whole and complete. In this concluding section of the chapter, I want to name an ancient set of qualities that are not usually associated with curriculum, which, when taken together, make up a set of religious criteria that draw on the wisdom of the past and the rituals of the present. They also draw on the possibilities of the future.

These criteria are the priestly, the prophetic, and the political—three motifs found not only in Judaism, but in the teachings of Christianity too, as ways of understanding facets of the community itself. The priestly dimensions of the curriculum encourage living fully in the present out of the past and draw on the priestly roles of preserving the tradition; remembering in liturgical, patterned ways; and acting as mediators of a great and holy reality. The prophetic dimensions encourage living fully in the present out of the future; refusing to let false words pass; caring for the stranger, the widow, and the poor. The political dimension directs religious educators to shape systems of organization, government, community—in short, polity—that will provide forms that are both lifelong and lifewide and promote forms that are priestly and prophetic.

Viewing curriculum as priestly is a way of reminding the institutions that house education—schools and churches—that their work must never cease to address the bodily nature of education: more precisely, it must take seriously the human bodies of the selves who are participants in education. Put another way, it must be *sacramental.* For even as priestly activity anoints, celebrates, heals, and blesses the body, so too must educational forms be appropriate to human beings during all the bodily changes of life. The need for play, activity, and concreteness on the part of the small child; the search for meaning by the young adult intellect; the battle with disabilities that must be joined in educating those of us coping with sense deprivation or loss of mobility; the slowed down pace of life's later decades: to each of these attention must be paid in shaping the varied curricula of education.

The curriculum must also be understood—as priestly work always has been understood—as inclusive of remembering. Drawing on the religious sense of priesthood as a work of *anamnesis,* re-presenting or re-membering the past in ways that make it real in the now of family and work and literate knowledge and leisure, those who focus on curriculum must always take seriously the heritage that has contributed to making the world what it has come to be. This means that memory must be a companion of both affirmation and atonement. As affirmation, memory celebrates and incorporates the past that has enriched those present settings in which education goes on. It reminds us that the traditions that have become part of present-day life have been received from other persons who have lovingly and sacredly transmitted them to us. As atonement, however, memory acknowledges the mistakes of the past; it acknowledges that with the good of the past has come the evil of the past. As part of priestly activity, both repentance and forgiveness are needed as preludes to reshaping the future.

Keeping alive the priestly dimension of curriculum will therefore be a way of ensuring that whatever is good in the past continues to be studied, held on to, corrected, and when necessary reshaped and transformed. Instead of being thought of as the dead knowledge of those who are living, curriculum needs to be celebrated as the living knowledge received from the dead. In our own times, as those from cultures of silence have reclaimed their voices and added to what may have been forgotten or unknown, we need to remember the truth, wisdom, and importance of our *entire* culture. An adage that exemplifies a dimension of priestly curriculum is found in the caution: "Discard no tradition without examination; it may be right"—even as critical awareness and a hermeneutic of suspicion remembers to "Accept no tradition without examination; it may be wrong."

This caution leads into the conviction that curriculum is also religious when it incorporates a prophetic dimension. This will probably mean that the entire course of life, and all of the forms that curriculum takes, must be studied, in Paulo Freire's terms, with *critical consciousness.* Just as prophecy has historically been a saying "No" to what divides humans from one another, from the earth, and from God, and just as it has been a calling to account on the part of those who wield power, so a prophetic dimension to curriculum will be the continual raising of questions concerning our curricula. These questions may take such forms as "Says who?" and "On what grounds?" and "How do we know this?" and "Who will benefit from doing things this way?" and "Who will lose?" The fact that these questions are asked in the communities shaping curriculum will ensure that the religious dimension of prophecy stays alive.

Although prophecy stems from *speaking*—Isaiah 6:6 reminds us that the prophet was anointed to prophetic utterance when a burning coal was placed on his lips—prophecy will also demand the speech of bodily activity. Protesting prison conditions; taking a stand for children; organizing and taking part in prayer vigils that condemn unfair treatment of the homeless; marching in demonstrations against domestic violence are each embodiments of the prophetic character of curricular activity.

Keeping prophecy alive leads to the awareness that the political aspect of curriculum must also be addressed, and further, that it must be addressed as a religious vocation. In our time, politics often has a very poor press and is rarely understood as a holy calling. But biblically, and in the history of the Christian churches, Jesus of Nazareth who is become the Christ is traditionally referred to not only as priest, not only as prophet, but as Lord—even as *Adonai* as Lord is at the core of the Hebrew Bible. This title, Lord, is a political one, and it is with awareness of its political connotations that I use it here. Those of us who are heirs to the biblical traditions need to keep in mind that the work of lordship is a work of governance and of creating forms that make a body into a body politic. The political dimension of curriculum is related to our using forms that include legislation, and judicial review, and executive decisions, and reallocation of resources. Notably, the political dimension of curriculum reminds religious people that we must address the use of power in our midst.

In his educational writing, Dwayne Huebner fleshes out the political vocation by suggesting that educators "talk about the political tasks of making a more just public world. Talk about it in such a way that the political and economic nature of education can be clearly seen."[10] He proposes three rights as ingredients of this task, rights that are as appropriate to church education as to education in other arenas. These are the unconditional respect for the political, civil, and legal rights of students as free people participating in a public world; the right of access to the wealth in the public domain, which is primarily the knowledge, traditions, and skills that shape and increase a person's power in the public world; and the right of every person, regardless of age, to participate in the shaping and reshaping of the institutions within which they live.

Each of these is a work of curriculum design; each a work of curriculum creation. Understood religiously, the application of such political criteria to the curriculum can ensure the attention to form and the reshaping of life's forms that have too often been ignored in presenting curriculum in the past. For if curriculum is understood not only as priestly and prophetic, but as political too, such ignorance is less likely to be the case as we move into the future. Political intuition and imagination brought to bear on all of the forms that educate will guard the manifold forms through which education takes place. It will help keep alive the religious realization that ultimately, education is the work of God and of God's Spirit, and that we who seek to serve the many forms of curriculum are trusted stewards of these great gifts.

FOR REFLECTION AND RESPONSE

1. What meanings do you give to the word "curriculum"? To "education"?
2. Which of the main forms of education that Gabriel names (family, classroom/schooling, work/apprenticeship, leisure) have been most influential in your life?
3. Which of the main forms of church education that Maria names (communion, prayer, care for the needy, the preached word, teaching) have been most influential in your life?
4. Give an example from your own life of where the forms of education, either in religious settings or in the wider society, are in *interplay* with each other.
5. Why do you think some people resist or even denigrate the word "education"? In the long run, do you think this is productive?
6. Give an example from your own experience of the school or the church housing several forms of education.
7. Where do you see curriculum that can be described as priestly? Where is it prophetic? How is it political?

Chapter 2

THE AIMS OF RELIGIOUS EDUCATION

GABRIEL: In undertaking any work, a first question to ask is the purpose or aim of the work. Sometimes the answer may seem so obvious that the question answers itself before it is asked. The purpose of going on the football field is to win a football game. The purpose of studying history is to understand the past. The purpose of a political speech is to persuade one's hearers. Often there are secondary aims that can buttress the primary aim or provide collateral benefits. But it usually helps to have one's efforts focused on a single, clear outcome.

For reasons I explore in this chapter, religious education is unusual in that it has two distinct and equally important aims. At the end of the chapter, I comment on the relation between the two aims; here at the beginning I wish to emphasize their distinction. The two aims are so different as to be almost contradictory, but it is precisely in the tension between the two that the logic of religion and religious understanding emerges.

The two aims, most succinctly stated, are: (1) to teach people to practice a religious way of life and (2) to teach people to understand religion. The first aim has a singular object: the practice of one, concrete set of activities that exclude other ways of acting. The second aim has a plural object, even if "religion" is written in the singular. The modern use of the term "religion" would not exist except for the recognition of plurality. This second aim of understanding religion begins from one's own religion but involves comparisons to other religions.

Throughout the centuries there have been Jewish education, Christian education, Muslim education, Buddhist education, to name several. None of these names necessarily involves reference to any other religion than that of the learner and the teacher. Today the need remains for Christians to teach Christian practice and Jews to teach a Jewish way of life. The twentieth century, however, has also seen the beginning of another educational enterprise, one that overlaps and transforms Jewish, Christian, and other particular educations. A *religious* education does not simply add something to these educations nor is it their sum. Instead, religious education situates the work of the Jewish or Christian educator in the worldwide conversation of today.

The closest analogy we have to religion is language. People learn to speak a language before they know any of the rules of that language or, more exactly, they learn the rules by using them and only later find that these are rules. A person could learn to speak English (or Japanese, Hindi, Italian) without even knowing that it is a language. Most people do learn one language first and are brought up short when they first encounter another way of speaking with different (and impossible to memorize) rules. If the individual pursues an understanding, mainly by trying to speak the second language, the rules become simpler and less peculiar. The knowledge of the second language also makes one appreciate better the structure and possibilities of one's original language. English teachers who tried to teach the subjunctive mood or nonrestrictive clauses now become understandable. At the same time one's native tongue emerges as "a language," utterly unique and yet comparable to every other language.

Religious understanding progresses in a similar manner. Every child acts out a religious way with a set of beliefs, symbols, and actions that relate the person to the enduring religious questions of wherefrom, whereto, and why. Every child takes up a stance toward the universe as a whole and toward the meaning of life and death, even if this way of life is not one of the traditional religions. Anyone who grows up in an insulated religious world is shocked on first encountering people who, seemingly intelligent and well-meaning, live by a different standard. The individual elements within the other person's religion are likely to seem strange and even bizarre. If one respects the otherness and tries to understand that way of life from within, the religion remains other but the people no longer seem bizarre. Depending on the historical relation of the two religions, light is thrown on one's native religion. For a Christian, Islam and Buddhism have different but equally valuable lessons to teach. For the first time one fully recognizes that Christianity is "a religion," utterly unique but comparable to every other religion.

As in every analogy, one should note the differences. The shock of otherness is much greater for religion than it is for language. A religious way is for the religious person *the* way. Religious teachers do not say "this might be good" or "there are plenty of other ways if this one is too difficult." Religions are about the one way to follow because it is demanded of you. As Baron von Hügel writes: "Not simply that I think it, but that in addition, I feel bound to think it, transforms a thought about God into a religious act."[1] To confront genuine otherness in religion is always a threat to one's world. The claim to ultimate and universal truth is directly challenged.

Language does not usually have the same problem. Plurality first seems strange to us, but it does not undermine our native tongue. The English speaker, on first confronting Italian, may recognize that English lacks the sonorous quality that Italian possesses. But few English speakers give up speaking English for that reason, and no one is likely to declare that English is a fraud or that no language is worth speaking because there are so many of them.

Teaching

A statement of aims is often made from a generalized, abstract point of view but on the issue of the aims of religious education, the question of perspective is crucial. In this discussion I am taking the perspective of the person or people who teach. This choice leads to a recognition that carrying out the two aims requires two contrasting forms of teaching. Before commenting further on the objects that are the aims of religious education it is necessary to comment on the nature and forms of teaching.

Amazing as it may seem, the great unexplored topic in educational literature is the activity of teaching. The great majority of books on teaching are about what (school)teachers do in classrooms. There is usually a gesture in the direction of recognizing teaching by other people in other settings, but quickly that notion is dismissed. In order to take other forms of teaching seriously, one has to resist the assumption now deeply embedded in language that "teacher," unless otherwise qualified, means the "professional educator." Given that assumption, a discussion of "teaching" takes place mainly within that group and refers to what they are the experts at. The standard reference to "parents and teachers," as, for example, in Parent Teacher Association, implies a denial that parents are teachers.

My starting point is that teaching is what every human being and some nonhumans do. Teaching is one of the most important and regular acts that we perform in life. Humans have to learn nearly everything they know; humans learn by being taught. We are shown how to do something, and we respond. In modern educational theory, teaching has been reduced to explaining, giving reasons, or providing information. In most of the rest of history, including today's practice, teaching means to show someone how to do something, a process that may or may not include explanations, reasons, and information.

In its most comprehensive meaning, to teach is to show someone how to live. Teaching nearly always has a moral side to it because it involves an imbalance of power, a fact that makes teaching suspect. Most teaching also has a religious dimension; it shows someone how to live and that eventually includes how to die. The flight from religion at the beginning of modern times entailed a flight from teaching, in all but its most rationalistic form. Teaching became equated with telling things to people who cannot yet think for themselves; thus, the relation of teaching-learning gets mixed up with the authority of adults over children.

Religious education cannot be carried out unless there is a wider and deeper meaning for teaching than providing explanations to children. Religious education, as part of the modern project of education, includes giving reasons and explaining. But it also includes other languages of teaching that have been rendered invisible in the modern philosophy of education. It includes teaching by communities in nonverbal ways and teaching by the nonhuman universe.

Most of the teaching in the world is done nonverbally and even unintentionally. Every religious tradition has known that the way to teach the young is to immerse them in the practice of the group's way of life. Words are, of course, part of the way, but the first words are usually ritual formulas, words that are secret passwords for belonging to the group (savior, faith, limbo, dispensation). Other words are usually direct commands ("stop here" or "walk to the altar").

More complicated lessons are eventually taught by the community as it draws upon its tradition. Teaching in its most complete form takes place in the relation between adults; this relation can gradually encompass the children, who learn from exchanges within a family, community, or social organization. The presence of good and holy teachers does not guarantee that goodness and holiness will be learned; there are counter-teachings always present. However, the absence of good and holy people does guarantee that goodness and holiness *cannot* be learned.

The first need is that people's lives be an example. Not only is intention not the main element in teaching; it gets in the way of some of the most important teaching. Admirable lives do not have to be set forth as examples. The learner confronts a well-lived life and reacts to what is shown in whatever way he or she can. The response to such teaching is not a mechanical reproduction but inspiration to act according to one's best possibilities.

Much of human teaching-learning bears strong resemblance to the way our next of kin in the animal world teach-learn. The teacher has to be patient in demonstrating a bodily skill to a learner, repeating small rituals over and over. Once the learner "gets" it, whether the skill is walking, flying, using a fork, or cleaning a paw, it must become a part of the self by practice, practice, practice.

The human capacity to distance its speech from bodiliness is what distinguishes human from nonhuman learning. That is both the glory and the danger of the humans who can imagine new worlds in their minds but can also coldly wreak violence from a safe distance. Human language can be used for many purposes. For discussing teaching, I distinguish three groups or families of languages. The first two have opposite effects although they both draw their meaning from their bodily surroundings; the third draws its meaning from reflecting back upon the other two families.

In the *first family,* language is used to show someone how to get to an end that is known and can be chosen. Storytelling and preaching are two of these languages, important to every religion. Storytelling may be stronger in Judaism and preaching stronger in Christianity, but every religion has stories about origins and stories that provide support for current practices. Similarly, every religious group exhorts its members to live up to their commitments. If you say you believe *x,* then you must do *y.*

In the *second family,* language is used to heal a fragmented self so that choices are possible. Languages in this set include praise, thanks, confession, mourning. Again there are variations from one religious group to another, but all of them use celebration, disciplines to overcome failure, mourning rituals, and other emotion-laden activity. If the rituals are handed down, then the teaching will emerge from the rituals themselves. Periodic reforms are necessary but the understanding of reformers is always suspect. Do they know what they are tampering with? Do they know that ritual does not have to be immediately intelligible to every curious onlooker?[2]

In the *third family,* language is used to reflect back on the other two families. This family of language includes dialectical discussion (often in the form of debate) and academic criticism. The use of speech for critical understanding is central to the contemporary academic world, but it can corrode a religious way of life that does not have strong underpinnings. A student should possess strong beliefs before those beliefs are criticized. Classrooms are places designed to teach people to be skeptical, that is, to have an attitude of questioning everything. If the beliefs one professes to hold have not become part of one's life, then such beliefs are likely to crumble in the face of challenge. Alternatively, a person may raise a wall of defense to prevent any serious challenge to his or her beliefs. The cost of the latter strategy is that one's professed beliefs become more rigid in form and less able to generate a greater appreciation of one's own tradition.

Teaching the Way

To realize the first aim of religious education—to teach people how to practice a religious way of life—the languages of the first and second families are indispensable. These ways of speaking join with nonverbal forms of teaching to show a person what it would mean to live according to this way. Of course, the learner is not going to learn much if he or she is coerced; the learner has to say explicitly or implicitly "show me the way." Showing a person how to practice one religious way does not guarantee that the person will follow that way. The teacher should do no more and no less than show the way.

A very young child is not able to choose a religious way and yet is being taught from the first moments of life. In learning a religious way the young child absorbs some of the attitude of adults and can also learn external practices. The teaching of the child will be effective if the practices are simply part of the routine of life. The child does religious things because "that is the way we do things here."

A child also learns from what the universe teaches: sunshine and snowflakes, rivers and ocean, mountains and desert, domestic pets and wildflowers, clean air and human-made slums. The meaning of these and other elements is mediated by the stories children learn and the way children are treated by adults. A child who has had a desperately cruel childhood has a special difficulty in hearing the positive side of religion, especially stories of a loving Father who watches over every creature. Such children often do find their way despite much evidence to the contrary. Eventually every one of us has to deal with contravening evidence to our religious interpretation of divine purpose or cosmic order.

Questioning of the family/community story begins as soon as the child can take a different perspective—the child's own perspective. Somewhere between five and twenty-five years of age there is likely to be a severe rebellion against childhood beliefs. The nature and intensity of the rebellion depend upon the instigator in the environment, new friends one has made, the path of studies one has chosen. During this period of life, teaching a person to follow *the* way has to be done with a light touch. Mostly what young people need is the availability of the way of life in practice and an increasing freedom to choose how they are to respond to it.

Eighteen-year-olds today are likely to profess that they cannot believe in one religion, even if they profess an interest in the "spiritual." That is hardly surprising; everything in their lives is being called into question. Many of those who are confused or are in rebellion still practice much of the way they were brought up in. If religious congregations panic over the noninvolvement of the young and put most of their educational resources into pressuring the young, the result is likely to be self-defeating. What the young most need is an adult community continuing to learn, continuing to demonstrate care and compassion, continuing to celebrate a living liturgy.

Liturgy, or worship, is the chief teacher in the religious community. Its gestures and language are necessarily a puzzle to those outside the community. For those who know and value the community's tradition, the liturgy speaks with all its verbal and nonverbal expressions. Some liturgists are wary of talking about the educational value of the liturgy, assuming that teaching means to explain or to inform. It is not that one should use the liturgy to teach but rather that the liturgy is the teacher. The individual is taught by participating. Christian children, with their parents, learn to say grace before meals. Jewish children, with their parents, learn the meaning of Sabbath by participating in prayers that welcome in the Sabbath.

The first family of languages described above is embedded in the practice of liturgical worship. Through this first family, the story of the community is told by the repetition of ancient rites and formulas. Readings from a sacred book make more explicit the story from the past that is to be made present. Preaching reflects upon these readings, directing the listener to acts of compassion and justice. Preaching and the rest of liturgical experience are intended for a narrowly circumscribed group; in contrast, the people to whom acts of love and justice are directed should not be chosen on any principle of exclusion. That is, the Jew, Christian, or Muslim should help the neighbor who is close; anyone who is in need is a neighbor, regardless of their religion. Doing acts of justice is an overflow of prayer. Muslim practice of religion is often summarized in two words, *salat* and *zakat:* prayer and giving of alms, one leading to the other.

Religious rituals also cover a wide range of languages from the second family: songs of praise, confession of sin, giving of thanks, mourning the dead. These ritual languages do not try to explain the world or inform us with new knowledge, but they are indispensable teachings. They show us how to live and how to die in a world that is not always rational. They break the bonds of egocentrism and let us receive the world with its joys and sorrows. By healing the split within us, they provide a beginning experience of what "salvation" means: the health, wholeness, and holiness that religions promise.

The third family of languages has a more limited role to play in the first aim of religious education. Some people get along with almost no academic reflection on the practice of their religious way. However, in the contemporary world nearly everyone asks historical, philosophical, and interpretive questions. In Christian terms, these are the places for doctrinal exposition in catechetical and theological language. Catechizing began as a liturgical act: the preaching of the Christian gospel centered on the life, death, and resurrection of Jesus of Nazareth. Catechisms and catechizing remain oriented to the liturgy. Theology has a shorter history in Christianity; using more abstract categories, it provides a systematizing of Christian doctrines. The leaders within a Christian community have to be versed in these exegetical and philosophical issues. Jewish, Muslim, or Buddhist leaders also need to be able to reflect on conceptual and verbal intricacies of their respective histories, although the study might be more oriented to the law or to esoteric disciplines rather than to theology.

Teaching to Understand Religion

In this second aim of religious education—teaching to understand religion—the third family of languages dominates. That is, dialectical discussion and academic criticism hold center stage while drawing their content from the other two families of languages. The focus is on the single act of understanding but the object is multiple: the phenomena of religion. In trying to understand religion the indispensable starting point is one's own religion. To understand is to compare; to understand one's own religion involves comparing it to some other religion. Theology already makes implicit comparisons to other religions. The study of religion makes the comparison explicit.

One need not assume that the comparison is to every other religion. To appreciate perspective a person might best start with only two perspectives. Trying to deal with a dozen or a hundred other perspectives can overwhelm any one perspective while still failing to reshape it. Without detailed comparison to what is done and said in another religion, the perspective on one's own religion is unlikely to be seriously challenged. By beginning with a dual perspective, one need not deny that there are dozens, hundreds, or millions of other perspectives.

This issue of perspective can seem abstruse and complicated. But any good classroom instructor engages in this practice regularly. He or she conveys two perspectives to the student: I stand behind the truth in what I am now saying, but it is also the case that my formulating of this truth is subject to improvement from other truths. For a Christian theologian, the two perspectives are usually from within Christianity itself. He or she struggles to convey the truest form of Christianity while acknowledging that any one version is not the whole truth.

For a religious educator, the alternative perspective can be another religion or no religion at all. In discussions today, except perhaps in a Christian seminary, the classroom teacher cannot assume that the students' main questions are about the best version of Christianity. Their underlying questions may be not the meaning of a text in Matthew but why a New Testament is needed; not whether the bishop's teaching is correct but whether "God" is a meaningful term; not whether women should be ordained but whether religion is inherently sexist. Even if students do not openly voice such questions, these or similar questions may still be floating about at the back of their minds.

The plurality of religion is often assumed to be a problem in need of a solution. But plurality can also be seen as the answer to a problem: the limitations of human beings and their languages. Each of the world's major religions has always acknowledged that in relation to God or the absolute it is itself not absolute truth or absolute good. At the same time, its own ideal is stated as universally valid. For example, it may be taught that the only way to be saved is by "following Christ" or being a "true Muslim." The harsh language of the alternative (to be cast into everlasting hellfire) is directed at laggards within the religion, not at outsiders. Religions in the past had very little to say about people in other religions (the idea may not even have been formulated).

Somewhere in each religion is the admission that, because religion is only relative, God may have other ways of salvation that are not evident to us. This admission is formulated from within the belief in the supreme importance of each respective religion. The Christian says Christ is the way; therefore, all who are saved are followers of Christ whether they realize it or not. That someone is "anonymously Christian" is the highest praise Christianity can bestow upon the outsider to Christianity. Similarly, the Muslim believes that only the true Muslim is saved. Since "every child is born a Muslim," then all who are saved have not turned away from God on the path they started. Being called a true Muslim is to receive the highest praise.

The recognition of religious plurality solves the problem that each religion had in understanding the salvation of the outsider. That is, no religion can proclaim itself as absolute; it is relative compared to God. Salvation was therefore always *possible* beyond the historical institution; God has God's own ways according to the Bible or the Qur'an. This possibility is now given concrete form with the relativizing of religions toward each other; the *outsider* is now on a distinct but related path. Thus, from a Christian perspective, the salvation of the Jew depends upon being a good Jew.

Today, the most common language being used to discuss the multiplicity of religions is a threefold classification: exclusivism, inclusivism, and pluralism.[3] The argument is that religions have been exclusivistic in their claim to be the one right way; all others were presumed to be wrong. A variation on this stance has been inclusivism, in which a religion recognizes some good in other religions but claims to include within itself all that is good in other religions. Today, pluralism is being offered as the only real alternative, one in which a multiplicity of religions embody a common search; each religion is thought to be a variation of a common theme.

A number of writers have pointed out that in this scheme pluralism itself becomes both exclusivistic (any other view than pluralism is declared wrong) and inclusivistic (all religions are included in pluralism). It may be the fate of all words ending in *ism* to become one ideology among others. Ironically, this pluralism seems to lack plurality. I think that naming the possibilities as exclusivism, inclusivism, and pluralism misses the paradoxical logic of religion.

Every statement includes and excludes at the same time. In human speech the choice is not to be inclusive or exclusive; the skillful choice is to find the best relation between inclusivity and exclusivity for whatever purpose is at hand. If one tries to be all-inclusive, then a statement loses any explicit reference. In contrast, a statement that is too exclusive communicates with only a small circle. In both of these directions lies vacuity. The mark of poetic speech is that exclusive concentration is combined with a high degree of inclusiveness. A line of Shakespeare or a phrase in Virgil might hold a truth for anyone prepared to listen. Similarly, in the nonverbal arts—a sculpture by Giacometti or a self-portrait by Rembrandt—the universal is approached not by abstracting from the particular but by going more deeply into it.

A religion uses logic that is close to this aesthetic principle that the universal and particular are not opposites, but instead go together. The universal can never be stated, but it can be glimpsed in the depths of the particular. In religion, the claim to universality is embodied in the most concrete and particular reality: this group, this book, this ritual. Plurality is not an alternative to the exclusive and inclusive; plurality arises out of the way that the exclusive and inclusive are held in tension.

In Christianity, salvation is believed to be embodied in one person, and even at one moment in that person's life. Is that absurd? Not if Christians see the universal embodied there. Could universal truth be found in the Qur'an? That is certainly possible within the logic of art and religion. Christians sometimes wield their concepts and terms as if there were a system of absolute truths that the Christian church controls. But if statements of the New Testament are testimonies of praise, thanksgiving, wonder, and so forth, they provide no basis for limiting God's action.

Take the favorite and widely proclaimed biblical text: "God so loved the world as to send his only begotten son that whosoever believes in him may have eternal life" (John 3:16). If the statement is presumed to be a scientific explanation of why Christians are saved, then it implies that Muslims are condemned. However, if the statement is one of praise and thanksgiving, then it can logically be complemented by giving praise that God has sent the Qur'an into the world. Indeed, a test for Christians' understanding of the Christ is whether they are able to see religious value in the Qur'an, a book that sustains hundreds of millions of Muslim people. This dual perspective is required for an understanding of religion.

Religious dialogue is most difficult but most needed where one religion has borrowed many of its terms from another (for example, Christian from Jewish, Buddhist from Hindu, Baha'i from Muslim). The biggest problems arise from the later religion borrowing a term with one exclusive meaning, giving it a different exclusive meaning and then giving it inclusive or nearly universal reference. I noted above that if a Christian says to someone "you are saved as a follower of Christ whether you know it or not," the Christian intends the statement as a compliment. A Buddhist, having no special relation to the term "Messiah" or "Christ," might accept the intended compliment (while still believing that finding one's Buddha nature is the way to salvation). The Jew, whose historical relation to the term "Christ" has been an unhappy one, is likely to find the statement oppressive or insulting.

Muslims can do something similar when they appropriate Christian terms. Muslims do with "Jesus" or "gospel" what Christians do with "Messiah" or "covenant." That is, Muslims may presume to understand the Christian words better than Christians themselves do. The Christian listening to Muslim reinterpretations can experience what Jews often feel in hearing Christians use terms that are Jewish in origin. Good intentions are a necessary but not sufficient condition to solve these problems. Long conversations between Christians, Jews, and Muslims that go deep into the words are necessary. Only with patient attention to the exact words of the partner can progress in understanding be hoped for.

For ordinary teachers in religious education the prospect of grappling with these extremely complicated issues is daunting. The good and bad news is that the whole world is still at the beginning stage in the attempt to respect and to understand as far as possible the religion of other people. Until recently the classroom teacher could block out this task and concentrate on intramural problems. Today this is becoming impossible in the majority of classrooms. Teachers do not have to survey all the religions of the world. They do need to explore with sensitivity whatever differences of religion lie within the classroom or just beyond its threshold. An appreciative understanding of other religions redounds to a better understanding of one's own.

Relating the Two Aims

The two aims of religious education come together in the person of the learner. Every human being should have available the opportunity to learn how to practice a religious way and to learn to understand religion. Within the course of a person's life span, one or the other aim is the focus, depending upon age, institutional setting, and other personal factors in the individual's life. Concentrating on one aim need not entirely exclude the other.

In the modern world, there are typical learning patterns correlated with the age of the learner. Religious education, like all education, begins at birth (if not earlier) in the formation of attitudes and behavior. Even the smallest infant joins in the human dialogue and quest for meaning. It would be claiming too much to say that a baby can understand religion. But it is not an exaggeration to say that even the youngest child is shown a way of life and begins to respond to it. The example of adults and the repetition of rituals have a powerful formative influence on young children.

The second aim, understanding religion, becomes a practical possibility as soon as the child has the conceptual and linguistic ability to form abstractions, listen to reason, and compare cases. That ability to understand develops throughout childhood and into the teenage years, when the second aim of religious education might take precedence. Religious beliefs at this stage of life are often thought to be childish. For this newly liberated understanding, the actual practice of a single way of being religious may seem confining and superstitious. However, the maturity of adulthood can bring together the rituals and beliefs of childhood with a faculty of reasoning that is now aware of its own limitations.

The institutional settings for religious education ought to vary appropriately in relation to the needs of age. The first religious and educational formation usually occurs in a family. Parents, grandparents, and siblings are the main teachers who surround the young child with demonstrations of the way to live. The parent teaches by being a parent, not by imitating a classroom instructor. The family setting is the natural place for the first phase of religious education.

A school, or more specifically a classroom, is a place designed for understanding the kind of knowledge available in books and computers. To understand is to compare and, while a six-year-old's range of comparison is limited, the child's growing ability to understand has to be respected. The first classroom instruction in religious education may be an extension of the liturgy, clarifying some of the words used in community prayer. But every six-year-old who can turn on the television has begun to discover radically different ways that people live in this world. Understanding religion is something that has to begin in childhood. By the time of high school it has to be the primary task of the classroom. And throughout adulthood classrooms for teaching-learning religion should be available, places where every kind of question is askable.

If we return now to the teacher's perspective with which we began, the teacher has to be aware of aims in relation to age and other personal characteristics of the learners as well as of the physical and social setting of the teaching. When a parent or a friend is the teacher, the teaching usually has a simple, clear aim. But a professional educator or a religious professional may have a conflict in carrying out the aims of religious education. For example, a teacher of religion in a Lutheran high school may aim at the understanding of religion while the school's administrator may be trying to form good Lutherans. Actually, some conflict in this situation could be healthy, with the recognition that school and classroom might have aims that are not entirely congruent. Obviously, if the disparity is too great and there is little or no communication, the situation will become untenable. In the other direction, a church minister who wishes to do more explaining of religion than appropriately fits within the worship service may have a conflict with the church board and congregation.

Can the same teacher accomplish both aims? Undoubtedly some people do. The college professor of religion may be a reader at the Sunday liturgy, or the presiding minister at the worship service may teach in a local college. A clear distinction of time, place, and learners has to be maintained by such teachers.

Most teachers devote themselves to accomplishing only one of these aims. But they should know that there is another aim, and they should also have some feel for what it is to engage in another kind of teaching. A teacher is helped to teach an understanding of religion if he or she has a sense of what it is to practice a religious way of life. Conversely, one can teach a religious way only with some appreciation for the understanding of religion. This mutual benefaction may seem obvious, but there is a lot of suspicion that people deeply immersed in practicing a religious way of life are thereby obstructed from teaching people to understand religion. This suspicion is tied to the misunderstanding of religious logic discussed earlier. We understand religion not by abstracting from individual cases to general propositions. Rather, we understand religion by developing a deeper appreciation of particular religious ways. Thus, a teacher of religion should not have to prove his or her orthodox belief and behavior in a religious institution but does need to have some experience of belonging to a particular religious way.

The teacher in a religious school has the opportunity to be both kinds of teacher, although such settings are also subject to the greatest confusion of teacher aims. A religious school (especially a boarding school) is set up to accomplish both aims. But unless all of the teachers (parents, administrators, classroom instructors, coaches, counselors, dormitory monitors) first clearly distinguish the two aims, the school will create muddle and rebellion. When there is lack of clarity in the distinction, then on one side the academic inquiry may not be challenging enough and on the other side the formation may not be particular enough. Endless talk about Christianity or Judaism is not religious education. Rather, religious education means teaching people religion with all the breadth and depth of intellectual excitement one is capable of—and teaching people to be religious with all the particularity of the verbal and nonverbal symbols that place us along one path of life.

FOR REFLECTION AND RESPONSE

1. What is an example from your own experience of religious education as teaching people to practice a religious way of life?
2. What is an example from your own experience of religious education as teaching people to understand religion?
3. Can you name something that—like Baron von Hügel who is quoted here—you feel "bound to think" as part of your religious tradition?
4. List at least 10 teachers who/that are not classroom teachers. List 20 if you can.
5. What did you learn about teaching by reading about the three families of languages? How do these families apply to (a) teaching the way, and (b) teaching to understand religion?
6. How is the universal glimpsed in the particular? Give three examples.
7. In which aim of religious education are you most involved? How do you also take part in the other aim?

Chapter 3

TEACHING THE WAY

MARIA: In the previous chapter, Gabriel wrote that religious education has two distinct and equally important aims: to teach people to practice a religious way of life, and to teach people to understand religion. He calls the first aim "teaching the way," and reflects that the way varies among different peoples. The way may be Muslim or Buddhist or Hindu. It may be Jewish or Christian. Whichever it is, however, teaching it means showing people how to live and how to die by embodying this religious "way" through a set of beliefs, symbols, and actions. These in turn connect people to the enduring religious questions: From where do I come? Where am I going? And why?

In this chapter, I am going to describe one way: catechesis. More specifically, I am going to describe it from the perspective of a Catholic Christian, reflecting on its meaning for other Christians, both Catholic and Protestant. Influenced by the approach of the new millennium, I am going to explore this way by asking the questions, In Christian tradition, what is living today? What is dying? What is rising? In doing so, I offer one case study of how Christian religious tradition in this place and time might embody the first aim of religious education. I do so in part because this is "the way" for me. I also do so in the hope that *mutatis mutandis*—the necessary changes being made—others might do the same in their respective religious homes.

The Core of Catechesis

The narrative center of catechesis,[1] for every Christian tradition, has its original expression in the book of Acts. There the apostle Peter speaks to a crowd that he had only recently feared:

> Listen to what I have to say. Jesus of Nazareth, a man attested to you by God with deeds of power, wonder, and signs that God did through him among you—this man you crucified and killed. . . . But God raised him up, having

> freed him from death. [And then Peter repeated it.] This Jesus God raised up and of that all of us are witnesses. (Acts 2:22–24, 32)

That is the essence of the catechesis from which all else flows (or echoes) over the decades, centuries, and millennia. To it in every age, the catechist or religious educator who is teaching this way is called to witness. However, catechists illuminate different facets of this core catechesis depending on their historical context. The context or era in which the catechesis resounds shapes the catechesis as much as the catechesis shapes the era.

As the foundation for this chapter, Peter's original catechesis is the reminder that at its center, the Christian vocation or calling is to a continuing and ever deeper embodiment of the life, death, and resurrection of Jesus of Nazareth, whom Christians believe has become the Christ. The way of Christian communities, and of individual Christians, is never finished and must be renewed continually in each judicatory, congregation, family, school, and heart. For unless the catechesis makes sense in the present, it is in vain. Another way of saying this is that unless the catechesis is lived, manifested, and taught—in all the ways teaching goes on—it is sounding brass. On this point, I find it relevant that when the tradition continues the story that Peter's catechesis initiated, the tradition says that the first apostles "went out and *gospeled* Jesus." Gospeled did not mean the disciples went out and talked and talked. Instead it meant they went out as living incarnations, teaching the way by using all the languages described in chapter 2.

At this point I pick up on Peter's original catechesis by engaging in a simple exercise. In this exercise I ask the questions to which I have already alluded: "Today as we examine our churches—what Christians call the Body of the Christ—what in these religious bodies is living? What is dying? and What is rising? My intention is to put these questions in play, to initiate a conversation about them, and to illustrate one possibility of teaching the Christian way. My hope is that such an exercise will provoke readers to engage in similar probes of their own distinct "ways."

What Is Living?

I will describe three out of the many signs of living catechesis that I find in my own church today. First, we are becoming a church of the laity, including in that term not only adults but youth and children too. Many documents support this conclusion, among them the 1980 document of the United States' Catholic bishops, "Called and Gifted," which names the call of the laity to *holiness, community, ministry,* and *adulthood.* Included as well is the even stronger 1995 revision of that document, which concludes, "We bishops have spoken that we might listen to the Spirit in the midst of the people. We invite your response."[2] This theme is very familiar to Protestant Christians, for whom the Reformation was an attempt to return the sense of ministry to all church members. Documents similar to "Called and Gifted" are found in most Protestant communions and ministries, from the promulgations of COCU (Consultation on Church Union) to independent statements of Lutherans, Methodists, and others with strong commitment to the ministry of the laity.[3]

Signs that today's churches are becoming churches of the laity are not only discoverable in texts. They are also incarnated in individual lives, where ministry and mission—the lived beliefs, symbols, and actions of the Way—rest securely and increasingly in the hands and hearts of the entire people of God: in volunteer corps, such as lay associates of orders like Maryknoll; in the refusal of urban congregations to abandon the cities; in graduates of religiously affiliated colleges and universities who spend a year or two after graduation in pastoral service either abroad or at home. Such persons are living proof of a distinction made early in this century by Yves Congar. Reflecting on the laity as a sign of life, Congar pointed out that the decisive pair that structures the church is not clergy and laity. The decisive pair that structures the church *today* is ecclesial community/ministries.[4] As living catechesis and religious education become more insistent that laity are "the church," and as "the church" ceases primarily to mean "church officials" and simply means "the whole people," the catechesis will resound even more in its proclamation that today's churches are made up of one ecclesial community of many ministries.

A second living sign in the Body of Christ today is a hunger for spirituality. Not only in church circles, but in secular society too, retreat centers across the country are booming. Those who work with young people know that just like adults, their spirituality is alive and well too, although their religious practices may differ from that of their elders. I would lift up the particularly vital, living dimension of today's spirituality and the catechesis that accompanies it as its connectedness, its relational and communal character, which is in contrast to a privatized or individualistic spirituality. The impulse toward connectedness places the practice of justice in a special and privileged place with justice understood as "fidelity to the demands of all our relations."[5] Such justice includes not only our relations to other human beings; it includes our relations to the nonhuman universe as well: to the other animals, the trees, the ocean, the earth, and the ozone layer.

This in turn mirrors a truth of modern physics: the world in which we live, including our churches, is made up of different groups of connections, not of different groups of objects. The poet Antonio Machado suggests that we look for our "other half," "Who walks always next to you / And tends to be who you aren't."[6] In our spirituality, increasingly, we walk next to the Salvadoran peasant, the Dutch physician, the Pakistani child laborer. Philosopher Maria Lugones makes a similar point concerning spirituality today. She writes that those who are different from us, alongside whom we pray, "are mirrors in which we can see ourselves as no other mirror shows us. . . . They reveal to us that we are manifold, they show us parts of ourselves we may not [notice in an ordinary mirror.]"[7] A relational spirituality is at the core of small Christian communities, of house churches, of places like the Church of the Saviour in Washington, D.C., Pendle Hill, and Kirkridge, and of programs like RENEW 2000 and the RCIA.[8]

For sacramental churches like my own, a third living force in catechesis today is *eucharistic spirituality.* Some of my brothers and sisters in the Catholic church do not agree with this, arguing that Catholicism is becoming a non-eucharistic church due to the fall-off of priestly ordinations and the growth of communion services in the absence of a priest. I disagree, however, due to the evidence of sacramental living throughout today's world. For, although eucharistic *forms* are changing, eucharistic *essence* is not. Bishop Jacques Gaillot, who lives with homeless people on the Rue du Dragon in Paris comments on this form-essence point by saying, "There are various degrees [and kinds] of Presence . . . [in] the mystery of religion. Right now, the community of believers needs a [form of] physical Presence for the sacraments. But who knows what the future may bring?"[9]

Several examples support this contention of living, eucharistic sacramentality: the three I will cite are each personal testimonies. I sat with a group of catechists in Australia not long ago, and two of them described a weekend youth retreat they had just led. They told of Sunday morning dawning, and a call from the priest who was to preside at Eucharist. He had just discovered that the rain was so heavy the bridge to the retreat center was impassable and he could not get there. "What did you do?" someone asked. The catechists said they had everything ready, so they opened the scriptures and read the words Jesus spoke at the Last Supper. They shared the cup and the bread. Then one of them hurried on to say, "Of course, it wasn't a real Eucharist," a conclusion that might be debated in catechetical discussions.

My second example comes from a recent conversation I had with a Sister who had just returned from Peru, where she'd visited one of the members of her order. One weekend, she traveled for miles into the Andean mountains with her friend in order to bring the Eucharist to a small Christian community living there. Meeting one of the Indian women, she told me she'd said to the woman, "It must be wonderful for you when Sister brings the Eucharist every few months." The woman responded that it was, and then she added, "But," and finished her thought: "But Sister has taught us that *we* are Eucharist."

Third, I want to recount a report from catechists in Sudan, who in describing their sacramental practice told a priest-missionary who had come to visit them, "Our children go and harvest *dura* (a local grain). The *dura* is ground into flour which is used to prepare some *kisra* (flat, unleavened bread). The elders and the rest of us gather outside the chapel and pray over the *kisra*. We ask God to make it a sign of God's love and God's presence among us. Then we distribute and eat the *kisra* during the prayer service. We know, and the faithful know, that this is not the Eucharist, but it helps us to go on until we will have a priest with the power to nourish us with the Body of Christ."[10]

The implications for teaching the way today through these beliefs, symbols, and actions are many, but one possibility for all Christian catechists and religious educators is the primary role they suggest. The recognition of a living laity, living spirituality, and living sacramentality summons today's catechists/religious educators to the role of *midwife*. Significantly, midwifery and education have been linked throughout the ages, starting with the Hebrew Bible long before Socrates also used this image.

When we reflect on what midwives do, we find that biblically midwives take their cues from Shiphrah and Puah. They work in pairs. Shiphrah and Puah are the two midwives described in Ex. 1:15–22, the wise women who assisted at the births of the Hebrew babies and then helped those babies stay alive by being wise as serpents and simple as doves, risking arrest, overcoming their fear of power by telling Pharoah's police that they had arrived too late and that the babies were already gone, living a new life somewhere else.

We also find that midwives do not administer anesthesia.[11] Alert to this truth, midwife-catechists support people's attempts to live the gospel—to *gospel* Jesus—to strengthen what is living, but they do not suggest such living is easy, and they do not do the living for the people they educate. They do not hand out cheap grace or gloss over the difficult demands of the teaching of Jesus.

In fostering new life, midwives also attend to where "the corn is green." They are like the teacher in the great Welsh play of that name, who had learned *from* her students to recognize new life *in* her students. One of the teenage miners she taught wrote in an assignment that when he went down into the mine, the mine was dark. "But when I walk through the shaft in the dark," he said, "I can still touch the roots of the trees with my hands; I can even touch where the corn is green."[12] Catechists and catechizing communities today are made up of people touching the green places in the spirits of others. They are people learning how to midwife the new life that pulses through today's Christian communities.

What Is Dying?

The second catechetical question that can guide educators in teaching the way asks catechists to search honestly and openly for responses to the question, "In the churches today, what is dying?" Once again, I will offer three examples as catalysts for the reader's response. I will also suggest a catechetical role these examples imply.

First, structures are dying. This is a particularly widespread observation as the century ends, one that church professionals routinely make. A pastor with whom I work told a group I was in that he believes the work of today's pastoral leaders is to stand in the midst of the rubble as things come toppling down, because someone has to stay there; someone has to be committed to picking up the shards, discarding those that are completely shattered and reclaiming those that aren't. Someone has to be responsible for burying—and then rebuilding. For this man, the evidence of history is that the church has always known dying within itself. More particularly, the church has seen forms die and then given birth to new forms, notably in the Re-formation and the Counter Re-formation that followed it. Actually, this dying is at the core of the phrase, "ecclesia semper reformanda," which means that the church must always be in the process of reformation.

One of my students offered me another example of dying structures. I showed a slide of a Korean Pieta in class one day that pictured a woman holding the body of her dead adult son, while a figure in the background screamed and cried. I then asked people to comment on where this Pieta mirrored their lives. A director of religious education in the group said that the Pieta revealed herself to herself in that *she* was the figure holding the dead body. Then she added, "That's me and I'm holding my parish. My parish is dead and I know it and everyone else knows it but we're still holding on to it. But I'm also in the background, screaming and crying that we've got to admit that death, let go, and bury what no longer lives."

Any of us who cite the dying of structures in response to this question are not necessarily naming parishes, congregations, or wider church communities. Nevertheless, our times indicate that certain patterns of leadership or forms of office in the church are no longer viable. This may not mean, as in my tradition, that papacy-episcopate-presbyterate-diaconate (pope, bishops, priests, deacons) is a set of dying forms or that in other churches, the board of deacons or the elders must go. But it is a comment on the way these forms are related to one another and to the church worldwide. It is also a comment on the *shapes* these forms take: pyramids instead of concentric circles or top-down directives emanating from a pinnacle instead of a mutual relation between center and periphery—something that occurs even in churches that are congregational in polity. Actually, in Catholic Christianity, papacy, episcopate, presbyterate, and diaconate are each vital realities. But in today's churches, many recognize morbidity in the *shape* of these offices, the *limitations* on those they include, and the large number of women and men they *exclude.* The shapes, limitations, and exclusions erode a bit more every time the whole church challenges them by speaking of and claiming itself as a "priestly" people or as "a royal priesthood"—the language used in the New Testament. The forms also change shape every time someone claims the call to ministry and to service—to diaconal life—on the basis of baptism and confirmation; they change every time women and male laity exercise pastoral office, even unofficially; they change every time gay men and lesbians who were previously excluded are commissioned or anointed to ministry.

A revelatory image is pertinent here, one that illustrates the death of forms of church organization. This is the image of a solid brick wall where a tiny plant has started to grow at the base. The wall may look impenetrable, but the plant is digging its roots into the earth tenaciously. At the same time, new shoots are eating at and weakening the cement between the bricks. The wall doesn't have a chance.

A second dying in the church today (one I return to in subsequent chapters, especially those on justice and on jubilee) is a dying particularly evident in North America, western Europe, and Australia, and even more evident in parts of the United States. This is the death of assumed privilege. More accurately, it is the death of the acceptance of privilege without accepting the responsibility that accompanies it.

Obviously, such dying does not apply to the church throughout the world in the same way it does to those of us in the richest 20 percent of humanity who use 83 percent of the world's resources while the poorest 60 percent subsist on 6 percent of its wealth. Privilege refers not only to economic wealth, however. Privilege—receiving special advantage because of birth or class or caste—is educational and political and technical too, with 10 percent of humanity controlling 90 percent of all research and development resources. Catechists need to remember there is such a reality as Christian privilege as well, such a thing as white privilege, such a condition as male privilege. We cannot get rid of automatic privilege such as white skin or male gender, but we can strive to refashion the moral landscape the acknowledgment of such privilege demands.

One of these demands is the religious commitment to return—a theme I develop in a later chapter. In connection with the death of privilege, however, I want to mention the return of resources. The call of justice is to the redistribution of capital: economic, educational, political, religious, racial, and gendered capital. Many adults today, answering this call, find return a kind of dying, even as they say, "I've been given so much; now it is my turn to give something back." In other words, they face and accept the death of assumed privilege, even as they face and accept the work of justice and relinquishment such death demands.

Along with structures of leadership and of privilege, there is one other dying to remember. This is real dying, dying that is more than metaphoric. *We* are dying; the people among whom we minister are dying, and even if the moment of death has not yet arrived, 100 percent of us carry in our selves the fatal element in all living—it ends in dying. We carry suffering and loss and movement toward death with us always. In the United States catechists today carry the loss of those who have been in the center of their work throughout the twentieth century, and the litany of the saints toward whom we pray for guidance in catechesis now includes Christiane Brusselmans, Kendig Brubaker Cully, Thea Bowman, Mary Perkins Ryan, David Ng, Fred Schaefer, Mary Reed Newland. At a Baptist religious educators' meeting I attended recently, dying and loss were honored on the first evening. During our introductions we were asked to reflect on a loss, a sorrow, or a dying we had brought to the meeting. We were asked, "How did you come?" Then we took time, if we wished, to name some of our responses in conversation with one another. Those interchanges shaped the entire catechesis of the meeting.

I cite our dying in response to the question, "What is dying in the churches?" because dying is a sobering corrective in catechesis, a reminder that we cannot do everything. I cite it because it sharpens the ways in which we teach our beliefs, symbols, and actions. I cite it too because dying is always part of the texture of our work, and living-toward-death colors the lives of everyone with whom and toward whom we catechize, in the guise of poverty and job loss and AIDS and domestic violence and cancer and Alzheimer's and SIDS, as well as in the whole sorry array of addictions that gnaw at our lives together, reminding us to walk gently among one another.

And finally, I cite it because it is a reminder of a second role demanded of those catechetical exemplars who would gospel Jesus. In addition to the role of midwife, we must take on the role of *mourner.*

If today's catechists and Christian educators are compelled to ask,

"What is dying in the Body of the Christ?" Christian conviction also compels us to be instruments of the sacrament of mourning, taking time in our communities to grieve the passing of structures and privilege and especially of sisters and brothers. We must address the grieving going on in the churches. Perhaps we will even be moved regularly to declare an hour, a day, or a week of mourning in our religious education settings, using this language of teaching in ways Gabriel has already noted. Mourning provides opportunities for ritualizing our responses to what has been lost or gone or has died naturally, even as it allows us to rage against the dying of the light. The role of mourner means that in the face of loss we must do what hospice workers are taught to do: show up, pay attention, tell the truth, and learn to ignore worry about results.

What Is Rising?

In the context of a new era, this final question becomes a catechetical opportunity to ask what is burgeoning, soaring, and new in our midst. What is the source of our Alleluias? As we mark the conclusion of a century and a millennium and explore teaching the way in a new era, what prompts catechists and religious educators to say of the Body of the Christ today, "Look! Here is resurrection. And here. And here."

We will have diverse responses, of course, but I suggest that the clues to how we respond to this final question come from resurrection tradition itself. A first clue comes from the phrase in the creed that says of Jesus, he descended into hell. The Canon of St. John Damascene in Orthodox tradition probes this teaching with the prayer in its Easter liturgy: "O Christ! You pierced the world *beneath* and snapped infernal chains that bind forever." Although the resurrection anthem is "And God shall raise them *up,*" and although many Christians sing that anthem regularly, it is important to remember that "up" doesn't come first in resurrection tradition. "Down" does. Resurrection—welling up, rising, soaring—is initially heralded by a descent, a going down, into the depths. Resurrection is initiated by a gathering of all that has gone before, including all those people who have preceded us. In the Apostles' Creed we pray, "He was crucified, died, and was buried," and then, "he descended into hell." That is to say, he made the journey *down* to the center. Jesus, who has become the first fruits of the whole Christ, went down into the depths. He went down not to "pretend" death, but to real death, and then brought forth what had been dead into the light, brought *everything* forth new and "shining like shook foil" (G. M. Hopkins).

In that movement down, under, to where the resurrection corn is green, catechesis meets the resurrection of tradition, which is not so much a body of truths as it is a communion of people. Tradition is those people who have made us *us*—the Shiphrahs and Puahs and Peters and Pauls and contemporaries like Sophia Fahs and Nelle Morton. But in the descent we also find the teachings that have made us us. Today, in catechizing toward a new millennium, we discover the rising of one teaching in particular: the "sense of the faithful."

In models and structures that are dying and in many places dead, the interpretation of teachings is generally left to senior or "expert" people. And although experts and seniors may be aware to some extent that they are interpreting data by choosing some aspects of it and ignoring others—as I am doing in this chapter—interpreters are less aware of how much potential we lose, even though if only a few people interpret, only a relatively few potential teachings emerge.

In contrast, if a community goes down into the tradition and retrieves—and here resurrection is the model—the community brings the entire "sense of the faithful" to new life. "The sense of the faithful is the intuitive grasp on the truth of God that is possessed by the church as a whole, as a consensus. It is active discernment, a power that belongs to the body of the faithful in response to God as Spirit."[13] Commenting on this theme in Catholic tradition, Vatican II taught that this sense of the faithful is infallible, saying that "The body of the faithful as a whole, anointed as they are by the Holy One, cannot err in matters of belief."[14] That means that the experience of the people is a source for theology. In language John Henry Newman used in the nineteenth century, the sense of the faithful should be consulted in the teaching of the church. My point here is that in response to the question, "Where is Resurrection?" one response is, "It is in the sense of the faithful that is rising today."

A further resurrection tradition can guide catechesis as Christians continue teaching the way. This is the recollection that Jesus did not rise alone. Gerard Sloyan, a U.S. catechetical mentor of the twentieth century, has reminded Christians that resurrection was first taught in Jewish tradition; it did not start with the Christian church. Sloyan makes the point that if, as a Jew, you had the faith in the resurrection that a Pharisaic Jew had, the appearance of the risen Jesus would not have surprised you. But what would have stunned you was that he rose *alone.*[15]

Put more simply, the first Christians believed that Jesus had risen, or more accurately, was raised, as the first fruits or down payment for the resurrection of the whole Christ. Today churches routinely teach people to fill up what is wanting in the Christ within our own communion and communities. But because he didn't—and doesn't—rise alone, Christians fill up what is wanting in the Christ even as they acknowledge there are other religious communions. We are at best *a* people of God, and not in possession of the fullness of all truth.

One corollary of this realization is that resurrection by its nature impels catechetical religious educators to realize that the resurrection of Jesus does not exhaust the reality of resurrection. Heirs to today's ecumenical insights, we are increasingly aware that God emerges in Buddhist, in Sikh, in Hindu, in Muslim, and especially in Jewish tradition, even as we who are Christians claim as the first fruits of resurrection the Jesus whom God has raised up. Resurrection is our most profound truth. But in a new world that honors many religious traditions, Christian catechists must admit that the opposite of a profound truth is not a superficial truth. The opposite of a profound truth is another profound truth.

Finally, there is the resurrection tradition that heralds a new millennium and a new world. That is the tradition of the *cosmic* Christ. Herbert McCabe, the great Dominican scholar, taught, "There are Christians who hold that the resurrection of the Christ means that, although he died, he still lives on in the churches in the faith of his followers, a faith expressed by word and sacrament in the church." So far, so good. But the Christians McCabe alludes to teach that the Christ lives on only in the church or is risen only in a "religious" world. This is not so. The fundamental objection to going this far and no further is that it conveys the attitude that the resurrection is a religious event that makes a difference primarily in the churches or for Christian people.

In contrast, the entirety of Christian tradition takes the resurrection to be a *cosmic* event. This means that what Christians call the Christ—that reality—is present to the whole world. The Christ is a *cosmic* Christ, whether persons are "believers" in our formulation of it or not; whether people are "religious" or not. The point is that the resurrection meant not just that a church was founded. Resurrection meant and continues to mean that the world is different.[16]

If that is true, today's catechesis demands evidence, and evidence assumes a third role in addition to midwife and mourner. This is the role of *witness* that may even spill over into the role of martyr since that is one meaning of the word "witness." But certainly catechetics summons all Christian people to witness.

It summons them to go about the world planting the seeds and being the voices of justice that attest to resurrection as this people in this age go out to gospel Jesus.

It summons them to witness a risen world to all the laity—young and old, yes, but also straight and gay and Latino and Anglo and black and white and red and yellow and women and men.

It summons them to a relational, sacramental spirituality that includes not only other people and other religions, but the nonhuman animals too, as well as the air, the water, the mountains, and the trees.

It summons them to mourn the death of structures and privilege honestly, even as they witness to the Easter and Pentecost messages so clearly that those messages are impossible to deny.

And what *is* the message? What *is* the catechesis? It is the amazingly simple one with which teaching this way began and continues to this day: The Christ has died. The Christ is risen. The Christ, the universal and cosmic Christ, will come again.

FOR REFLECTION AND RESPONSE

1. What is an original text, or story, or starting point that prompts your educating "in the way" in the same sense that Peter's original words do in the book of Acts?
2. In your tradition, what would you cite as *living* in the present era?
3. In your tradition, what would you cite as *dying* in the present era?
4. In your tradition, what would you cite as *rising* in the present era?

part two

DEVELOPMENT

Chapter 4

THE ROOTS OF MODERN DEVELOPMENT

GABRIEL: Until the 1980s I was not particularly interested in developmental theories. I had read works by Jean Piaget, Erik Erikson, Lawrence Kohlberg and their followers, but the theories and the experimental findings in this area seemed to me of limited significance for religious education. At a 1981 conference on "adult development," I was asked by a publisher if I would consider writing a book on development. My first response was that I lacked interest in the topic and had no inclination to argue about how to classify people in stages. On second thought, however, I decided that there might be some value in trying to lay out the larger context of developmental theories and that religious education might have something to say on the matter. The title of my book *Religious Education Development* has a double meaning: the development of the field of religious education and development as seen from within religious education. In that book I tried to give a fair but critical summary of developmentalists, including Fowler. I also offered a description of both religious development and educational development as an alternative framework for relating human to nonhuman life, and life to death.

If I were to write that book today I would expand the first chapter on the idea of development, emphasizing the economic roots of the term and the challenge of contemporary ecology. I wrote in that first chapter that what was needed was a book that might be called *The Development of Development.* No one has yet written such a book. Perhaps it would be too complex an undertaking because "development" is almost coextensive with modernity. In any case, we are all faced with the task of stitching together separate strands of history to provide an intellectual grasp of this idea.

Twentieth-Century Meaning

Development is a central idea in the educational literature of the twentieth century. Indeed, one could plausibly argue that it is *the* central idea in this literature and is the underlying assumption in all educational projects. In the moral area, development surfaced as the central idea of education to the extent that "moral development" and "moral education" were often used interchangeably. The recent reaction in the area of moral education implicitly challenges the idea of moral development. So far it remains unclear whether the critics of moral education/moral development are trying to undermine the idea of development itself.

In the early twentieth century, education was largely equated with development. John Dewey in his major work, *Democracy and Education,* wrote: "When it is said that education is development, everything depends upon *how* development is conceived. Our net conclusion is that life is development, and that developing, growing, is life."[1] Dewey was concerned here not with whether education is development but only with clarifying what development means. By identifying development with "life" he attempted to embrace the fullest meaning of the term. Any opponent of the position that education is development is seemingly cast into the position of preferring death.

Several decades before Dewey wrote that passage, development had taken center stage in educational discussions. Dewey's identification of development and life was in resistance to a narrow psychologism, exemplified in the work of Edward Thorndike.[2] Dewey had been an early advocate of the "new psychology," which offered great promise for educational reform. With better insight into the child's mind and more systematic research into classroom behavior, educationalists had hoped to revolutionize school practice. Dewey's broad philosophical outlook made him suspicious of education's control by psychologists. But his plea that "developing, growing, is life" was perhaps too vague an alternative. The psychologists by this time thought themselves in charge of growing and life.

By the second half of the twentieth century, educational psychology was indeed in control. Growth, life, and development were taken to be psychological terms; any college course called "human development" was located in the psychology department. The main educational conflicts were between differing schools of psychology. The language of education became almost totally absorbed into psychology. Although psychology continues to make helpful contributions to our understanding of learning, it is not healthy for education to have no other language to speak.

One of the most famous experiments in U.S. education occurred in the late 1950s and early 1960s. Because of the Soviet success with the earth-orbiting satellite Sputnik, the U.S. public had its full attention on the educational system. The rush was on to improve the teaching of math and science. The "new math" was wedded to Piagetian psychology. It looked very logical on paper; the logic of math corresponded to the logical development that Piaget had described in children. But for the most part, the heralded reform was a disaster, delaying much-needed educational reform. The mathematicians and Piagetians were not wrong; but there were other considerations than logical-mathematical ones at work, such as the backgrounds of the people teaching math in school, the experiences of schoolchildren and their parents, and the ability of politicians and school boards to comprehend what was going on.

In Christian educational circles, development made its most prominent entrance through the work of James Fowler, who coined the term "faith development." While dependent in part on Piaget's psychology, Fowler broadened the basis of his work, using the work of the more socially oriented Erik Erikson, among others. Fowler's synthesis provided flexibility but did not clarify how religion and psychology fit together. A 1987 conference in Tübingen placed Fowler's work in relation to that of Fritz Oser. This Swiss psychologist offered a purer rendition of Piaget as an instrument for understanding religious judgment, while Fowler provided a broader meaning of faith.[3]

Why has the psychological notion of development been so attractive to people in education? The answer, I think, is fairly obvious. Development offers a comprehensive explanation together with a guarantee of success if the whole system is put in place. Human teachers become less important because the possibilities for development already lie within the individual. Those who administer the system can modestly step back and watch success emerge. Endless studies can be done on refining the system or explaining why it does not work for some individuals under some circumstances.

Christianity and Development

Some people see development as incompatible with a Christian approach to education. Especially in evangelical circles, the alternative to development is said to be "conversion." Whereas development is thought to be an expression of human autonomy and self-possession, conversion is the acknowledgment of sinfulness and the need for redemption. Much of Protestant education remains in a bind that goes back a century or more: a liberal position that is reliant on psychology for the understanding of progress over against a conservative position that is suspicious of human claims to progress. Fowler tried to avoid this conflict by saying that "the Christian approach to the transformation from self-groundedness to vocational existence involves, then, the affirmation of *both* development and conversion."[4] That appeal is not likely to change the minds of conservative critics who believe that the Christian gospel is still being held hostage by modern psychology.

I sympathize with Fowler's attempt to transcend the split between conservative and liberal approaches to education. But whatever is proposed as an alternative is likely to be already marked by conservative rejection or liberal acquiescence. And trying simply to combine competing languages restates the question without solving the problem. If we are to examine the use of development in religious education, it is important to place the idea in a wider context than that of twentieth-century psychology.

The modern idea of development began to emerge at the end of the Middle Ages as a protest against a closed world, against the assumption that there is a fixed set of resources and goods. Previously it had been believed that people should be satisfied with their lives because there are only so many goods for distribution. The individual's vocation was to stay on the path that an all-seeing God had mapped out as the right one. In Christian terms, one was to follow the commandments of God and church. Heaven was the reward for a life rightly lived; hell was at the end of failure. Christianity was a more complex set of ideas and practices than this view conveys, but there was some truth to this description being the way that millions of people understood their Christian religion.

Over a period of several centuries this picture gradually changed. Genuine novelty came to be seen as a practical possibility. Scientifically based technology, discoveries of new lands, and political upheavals opened up human imagination to radical changes. "Development" came into the language as modern economics was being born in the eighteenth century. A new hope was generated, namely that life can be better right here on earth if human and technological resources are put together in an efficient way. Development was the theme of what came to be known as "capitalism," the creating of wealth by the wise investment in individual liberty, competition, and scientific know-how. In the nineteenth century, the young Karl Marx rejected this outlook or, more exactly, sought to go beyond it to community, cooperation, and a humanization of technology. Communism, like its capitalist competitor, had a theory of development that explained the past and guaranteed good times in the future.

If we were to dig further down into the roots of Western concern with progress and the future, Jewish and Christian belief in the goodness of time had a big part in the rise of modern science and technology. But Christianity had kept in tension a sense of end and a patience with what moves toward that end. In contrast, the founders of modernity liked the idea of history having purpose and meaning, but they rejected the idea of a final cause. Whatever meaning life has would have to be found in its origin and not in its conclusion.

The Image of Development

The word "development" means what "pops out of" the envelope. It affirms that what is to be studied is there from the beginning, waiting to be realized. The surroundings are important for development; organisms obviously interact with an environment. But there is no end point toward which a living being moves; it does not receive its meaning from an end to which it is drawn.

Development is the alternative to providence, predestination, and heaven. People who dismiss the idea of heaven as a childish myth still have a need to believe that their lives are going somewhere. Theories of development are a fervent belief, backed by some scientific data, that human life will get better if we do our part by clearing away obstacles to continuous improvement. Economics had a ready answer to how life could have a definite direction but no end point: development is in the direction of "growth."

Development, with its associated image of growth, is unavoidably a moral claim. Theories of development presume that the movement is from good to better, or at least from bad to less bad. Sometimes theorists try to avoid this claim, wishing to project an air of nonjudgmental objectivity. But the great interest in developmental theories is due to the belief that the theory describes a desirable movement and a way to recognize progress. William Perry, in his classic study *Forms of Intellectual and Moral Development,* is candid in admitting that "in any sphere of human development, perceptual, intellectual, social, emotional, and so forth, the word 'growth' suggests that it is *better* to grow than to arrest growth or to regress."[5]

Perry's reference to various kinds of development and their common hope of growth indicates the appropriation by the psychologist of what was originally the language of the economist. Just as human history was now imagined to have stages of development with undeveloped, developing, and developed nations, so too the individual was thought to develop in stages. It is easy to trace a physical "growth and development" of the child's organism early in life. Parallel to this physical development, Freud and then Piaget tracked what they took to be a separate world of children's thinking. They and other psychologists traced stages of development in thinking as the child progressed to a rational, objective, adult way of thinking.

The image of growth seems to fit for the first dozen years of life, both in relation to physical growth and the growth of the child's mental capacities. But can this metaphor be extended to human life as a whole? Or more particularly, if the term "development" is used for other than the biological and mental faculties of children, is it accurate to say that it is in the direction of "growth"? What may seem to be the right image in economics may be misleading when applied to personal life. And even within economics, is growth the adequate metaphor for the direction of the world's economies? Growth is an advantage for some nations, but is it at the expense of other nations? Similarly, growth in the cells of a human organism has to be in the proper proportion; the cells should eventually age and stop growing, otherwise the body develops the problem of cancer.

One way to approach a connection between economics and psychology is through religion. Religion does not simply add one more dimension to theories of development. There is a place for theories of religious judgment, such as that articulated by Fritz Oser. They are theories of the development of *judgment;* in this case, judgments about religion. But if one wished to find a theory of "religious development," the most likely place to look would be in the great spiritual traditions that describe a lifelong journey. The major theme of these journeys is not growth, but instead its near opposite: the letting go of our prized possessions by a disciplining of thought as well as emotion. Religion is mostly a process of de-idolization: "this isn't heaven; that's not God; the journey continues."

This tradition of religious development may seem worlds apart from Piaget or Kohlberg. Nonetheless, it may hold the key to what the modern world is searching for. The terms ancient/medieval/modern constitute a developmental scheme, embodying the firm belief that we are superior to our ancestors. But today there is a growing crisis in this belief system. The inventing of the term "postmodern" has done little but add to the confusion. By definition, "modern" means up to date, and points to what cannot be surpassed, the last stage of progress. Postmodern is an unintelligible term, except as it signifies the need to rethink the entire scheme of ancient/medieval/modern.

The arrogant presumption that the world moves from religion to metaphysics to science has to be rescinded. While the mathematical-empirical sciences have made invaluable contributions to human life, they cannot discern the purpose of life. We still need to circle back to simple questions of life and death, of human persons in an unimaginably immense universe. The funded wisdom for addressing these issues is not located in the latest experiments but in the religious and spiritual traditions of the race.

In human history, each new era must circle back to the wisdom of its predecessors if any bettering of human life is to be hoped for. The next "stage" is not a movement upward to a superior vantage point but a step toward an integration of previous stages. If we are wise, we can learn to stop making the same mistakes as our ancestors did. That would mean learning as a people to relinquish hatred of other people and attachments to things we really do not own.

The journey of an individual within a nation, tribe, or race has a similar pattern. We are born with nothing and we die with nothing. In between we get attached to things that we mistakenly believe are ours alone. Given that every individual is aware of his or her coming death as a developmental stage, it should not be difficult to be detached from possessions. But a culture intent on denying death erects some great idol or idols to distract people from the obvious. Developmental theories that profess to retain an openness to novelty either have to accept death as a stage of development or else close down development for the sake of illusory attachments. This is why religious development is not one more theory of development but is rather the *precondition* of development in economics, social science, morality, or psychology. Religion as de-idolizer keeps open the journey of development.

MARIA: When I was beginning my professional life as a religious educator, I assumed that the term "development" referred to personal human life. Like many of my colleagues and peers, I equated development with psychosocial/cognitive/moral/faith issues as these gave insight into human being and human life. But Gabriel's thought influenced me increasingly as the years progressed, and by the time his *Religious Education Development* was published in 1983, I had begun to suspect that the major aspect of development calling out to religious educators and pastoral ministers was not only or even fundamentally in the realm of psychology. It was in the arena of economics. It had become clear to me, as I think it will be to the reader from Gabriel's allusions to economics in the first half of this chapter, that in our world development and economic reality are inevitably intertwined.

I had also become persuaded that justice was an essential element in our work. The documents stemming from Vatican II, notably *Gaudium et Spes;* the 1971 Synod document, *Justitia in Mundo* ("Justice in the World"), which described social ministry as a constitutive dimension of the gospel; and the 1986 pastoral letter of the U.S. Catholic bishops, "Economic Justice for All," which linked justice and the economy, also contributed to my conclusion that when development was at issue, pride of place in our teaching had to be given to the economic realm. The last document, especially, was and is a powerful argument that the churches must practice what they preach about justice. Notably, they must practice economic justice as part of the kerygma at the core of catechesis.[6]

As I began to pursue this conviction, I realized that economic development could be distinguished as operative in three areas. The first area was in relation to the *oikoumene*—the whole, round, inhabited earth, or what we refer to today as ecology. Not only was there a close connection between the words *oikonomia*—economy—and ecology, there was a long tradition in Christian teaching that spoke of the *divine economy* as God's management of the household of creation, as well as of the households of redemption and fulfillment.

Second, I learned that before we immediately equate economic development with *the* economy—wealth and capital as these affect the development of communities and nations—we need to attend to economy itself, that is, to the ways of human householding and human housekeeping—the care of house and especially of home—and to the ways that the human household is situated within the household of nature. Educationally, the emphasis on both ecology and home economy help anchor our involvement in those economic issues that are both more obvious and more complicated.

These issues are, of course, those that arise from the third economic arena: economics understood as the production, management, and *development* of material wealth and the distribution and consumption of that wealth. As religious people we need to educate concerning the most commonly assumed aspects of economic development—capital, money, land, and goods—as well as concerning other less obvious but equally important economic subjects. For upon reflection I suspect most of us realize that in actual practice economics refers not only to monetary capital, but to the translatable "capital" value of schooling, education, skills, health, and social opportunities. Economics also includes the translatable capital value of the privilege about which I have already written—white privilege, male privilege, Christian privilege, U.S. privilege, political privilege—that makes the many forms of capital available to some but not to all. These three areas: ecology, home economy, and economics have implications for the way we educate about development.

Ecology. In the last thirty years, ecology has become a major issue in religious education. It comes late to its rightful place as an aspect of development, at least in part because advocates of the poor have been understandably suspicious that attention to the natural world might deflect attention from the urgency of economically impoverished peoples in our own country and abroad. Some Christians have even voiced the fear that too much attention to ecological problems could distract the churches from the tasks of promoting liberation and justice toward those who are most disadvantaged.[7] In recent years, however, more and more Christians have recognized the connection between economic development as it affects the human condition, and the overuse of the earth's natural resources in ways that do violence to all creation, human and nonhuman. Educators have recognized that ecology and ecological development deserve inclusion in the curriculum.

Thus in recent years we have rediscovered and begun to build on Christian tradition's long-standing concern with the earth as a whole and human beings' relation to it, a concern found in the biblical affirmations of creation, in Wisdom literature, and in the incarnational emphasis of John's writings in the New Testament. Over the centuries these teachings became associated with persons such as Francis of Assisi, Hildegard of Bingen, Benedict of Nursia, and their followers.

I once had a conversation with a seventy-five-year-old Benedictine sister about the ecological consciousness taking root around the planet today, and the proposal by many environmentalists that Francis of Assisi be declared the patron saint of the ecological movement. At that point, Sister reminded me passionately that reverence is not enough, especially today. "Wherever we go," she said with intensity, "we interact with the earth and its creatures, through technology and lifestyles and the ways we practice agriculture." Then, referring to her own tradition, she added, "Centuries ago, you may know, Benedictines, women and men, realized we were part of an ecosystem, and as farmers, builders, and scholars we transformed soil, water, plants, and animals by listening to them carefully and then responding to what they were telling us. We didn't use destructive chemicals or burn forests or exhaust the soil by overuse. We have to do that today, too, and exercise care for all creation."[8]

In a more extended reference to the relation between ecology and economic development, Thomas Berry, who has led the way in this discussion for religious people, has said that when we deal with economics as a religious issue, we can deal with it in different ways. One is to start with the capitalist market economy's neglect of its social responsibilities to ensure that the weak and less gifted are not exploited by the strong and the powerful. The other is to start with an even more basic difficulty that underlies all social issues: the industrial economy itself, which in its present form is not sustainable. Though we need to attend to budget deficits, a religious sense of economic development turns our attention to the *earth* deficit lying beneath them. About this deficit, Berry writes:

> Seldom does anyone speak of the deficit involved in the closing down of the basic life system of the planet through abuse of the air, the soil, the water, and the vegetation. [But] the earth deficit is the real deficit, the ultimate deficit, the deficit in some of its major consequences so absolute as to be beyond adjustment from any source in heaven or on earth. . . . This deficit in its extreme expression is not only a resource deficit, but the death of a living process, not simply the death of *a* living process but of *the* living process.[9]

Berry concludes that today our problem in facing this earth deficit is vastly different from previous centuries, because we human beings are now directly influencing the destiny of the earth. In a strong and pivotal censure of thoughtless development, Berry points out that the immediate danger we face is not *possible* nuclear war but *actual* industrial plundering. Thus as initial aspects of economic development, religious educators need to affirm the teaching that the soil and the water and the air must be guarded from misuse and overuse. We also need to relearn, if we have neglected them, the sacramental and biblical practices that accompany these teachings—such as periodically letting the land lie fallow.

Home Economy. When we move from the vocation of caring for the planet to focusing on our development as human beings, a second aspect of economic development becomes clear. This is the consideration of the ways we exercise human housekeeping and human householding—our care for our homes—and of the ways that the human household is maintained not only within the household of nature, but in relation to other human households.

Issues of economy as the development of human householding are closely associated with the exercise of the artistic imagination, especially as we use our imaginations to shape and fashion the world each of us inhabits. Poet-farmer Wendell Berry describes this artistic vocation by asking us to consider all the different ways we make the things we need: "How we work, what work we do, how well we use the materials we use, and what we do with them after we have used them—all these questions are of the gravest religious significance."[10]

Wendell Berry probes this significance by elaborating on the spirituality of dust and breath, saying that if we believe we are God's dust and God's breath, then each of our acts has a supreme significance. "If it is true that we are living souls, then all of us are artists. All of us are makers, within mortal terms and limits, of our lives, of one another's lives, of things we need and use."[11] Those who work with words as schoolteachers and writers do; those who work with brush and easel as painters do; those who work with wrenches and hammers and machines as mechanics do; those who feed and clothe children as parents do—all their works have an economic import, because we who do them are makers, artists, creators of human householding.

This notion of economy—making a household—usually centers life for human beings, and no metaphor of place has more powerful reverberations in the human psyche than the word "home": at its most basic, as Robert Frost reminded us, home is the place where, when you have to go there, they have to take you in. Home is the place where we learn care, responsibility, and the thickness of life. Home is the place where we are most likely to be ourselves, which is to say, "at home." But today, increasingly, especially if we are attuned to the teachings of our religious traditions, we are becoming aware that whatever we do in our homes, however we use their resources, and whichever ways we budget the spending of the capital they represent—each of these has an impact on the households surrounding us.

For example, because for them water is often rationed, Californians are regularly reminded of something the rest of us in the United States know but don't always allude to: we share the water with one another, wherever we may live. We share *everything* with one another. This ever-more-obvious truth should send us back to deeper reflection on the ways we develop economy personally, how we practice simplicity, and how we might rid ourselves of too much "stuff." In contrast to the overuse to which the consumer society impels us, we need to reflect and then act on the implications of *our* economy for the wider economy surrounding us.

Sharon Daloz Parks, who has written eloquently on household economics, offers a powerful example of such reflection. She quotes a young Quaker woman at college writing the following e-mail letter to her family at home, just before Christmas:

> I've been meaning to write about Christmas (and there is nothing like a smidgen of e-mail procrastination before biting into Beowulf). I still don't know exactly what I want for Christmas, but the main thing is I DON'T WANT JUNK. This is really important. I've been feeling lately like I have way too much STUFF. An idea might be blank tapes or good pens or nice colored paper or something really useful. I'm working to break the chains of consumerism—starting with myself.[12]

That is not all there is to the letter, however, for the young woman goes on to comment that her realization she does not need junk is not a wish to forgo gifts; she knows that the exchange of gifts is one of the most distinctive marks of human community. But she also knows that gifts and consumerism are not the end point of gift giving. Instead, giving gifts is a ritual designed to create a disposition of gratitude followed by a passing on of another gift in an ever-widening circle of recipients.

Commenting on the young woman's letter, Parks compares it to a related incident that occurred in Massachusetts at exactly the same time. In the latter incident, a Jewish businessman in Malden, Massachusetts, suffered a major factory fire and attracted national attention because, despite the devastation, he still chose to give his employees their year-end bonuses, two months of salary, and six months of health insurance. In addition, he promised that the factory would be rebuilt. Parks remarks on the confluence of the two incidents and suggests that in differing ways, the college student and the businessman both exemplified religious economic attitudes in their words and actions. She cites Quaker Thomas Kelly as a proponent of such attitudes: "Prune and trim we must, but not with ruthless haste and ready pruning knife, until we have reflected upon the tree we trim, the environment it lives in, and the sap of life which feeds it."[13]

Economics. Although ecology and the economy of human householding are part of economic development, they receive relatively slight attention as aspects of that development. In fact, they are often relegated to the realm of spirituality, where the meaning of that word is assumed to be a synonym for "otherworldly." In *this* world, however, especially in the United States, "economics" and "the economy" are central; in this world, we live and die in the context of commerce and consumption, buying and selling, having and getting.

As a way of educating religiously in this economic world, I have posited a number of guidelines that can help the ordinary person in responding to economic reality.[14] Among these guidelines are the following: First, there are limits to growth. Gabriel commented above on the metaphor of growth; I want to add to that here by noting that environmentally concerned scientists throughout the world have given widespread publicity to this guideline via the "limits to growth" theory, concerning what is and what is not sustainable life on this planet. Further education is necessary, however, on the image of growth itself. On one hand is the image of growth embodied in all living creatures: we are born; we achieve a certain height, weight, maturity; we decline; we die. On the other hand is the image of the unhealthy proliferation of diseased cells that issue in growth without limit, which, though resulting in death, is neither a fitting nor a healthy image of development.

In place of a pattern where some cells proliferate while other cells wither and die, the economic necessity today is for a pattern that works toward equal or balanced sharing of the goods of life. In economic terms this requires some redistribution of capital. Growth in the accumulation of capital where the capital of some exponentially exceeds the capital of others needs to be stopped so that the entire organism of the earth's people can be made healthy. Such healthy redistribution of capital can be fostered as other forms of capital besides money are redistributed. For example, the redistribution of the capital of *land* from colonial powers to indigenous people during the twentieth century—in South Africa, in India, in the Philippines—is a reminder that the growth of empire needs to be limited for the sake of those who dwell on planet earth.

Second, there are limits to earning. Herman Daly, a Methodist layman and economist with years of service at the World Bank, talks as many others do of ratios in earning—what is sometimes called limited inequality. Just as the business section of the press will occasionally note a company—Ben and Jerry's, for example—that pays its chief executive officers only a few times more than its just-hired trainees, Daly points out that those in both military and civil service in this country earn a ratio of around ten to one: the highest paid member of the military earns no more than ten times the lowest paid member. In colleges and universities, the ratio is around seven to one, with distinguished professors earning no more than seven times the salary of the lecturers who have not yet finished their dissertations. These ratios are in sharp contrast to the CEOs' salaries—the chair of General Motors versus the assembly-line auto worker—or to entertainers' salaries—where "stars" earn many more than ten times the salaries of bit players. In the United States, salary imbalances became a national issue during the baseball strike of the mid-1990s, not only when it became clear that the player with the contract for $7 million a year earned sixty times more than the large number of players making $120,000 but when it became impossible to find out the salaries that owners paid to themselves.

Third, there are limits to accumulation. The Jubilee traditions that I write of in chapter 9 are pertinent here. To the question, "How much can I acquire?" they teach that the answer is "Only what you can accumulate in fifty years." This means that a will can be a document of economic justice, or it can create further division between rich and poor, especially in the case of inherited but unearned wealth. The experience of limiting accumulation can guide businesses and corporations too. In the mid-nineties, for example, a consortium of semiconductor companies volunteered to give up a $90-million-a-year federal subsidy. The consortium, Sematech, had been created several years earlier to encourage U.S. production of semiconductors. As a result it began to produce them, and by 1994 the future of the industry was assured. So Sematech decided to stop the subsidy on the principle that they didn't need it anymore.[15]

Fourth, there are no limits to all people having the right to certain benefits: literacy; education in basic skills, including basic economic skills; life, liberty, pursuit of happiness. One of these rights is health care. I do not understand how congressional lawmakers in the U.S. avoid affirming this as a right of every citizen, especially since their own health care and that of their families is so extensive, as is my own.

Still another basic right is food. A new federal law that went into effect in the United States on October 1, 1996, shows one way that this has been addressed. Nicknamed "Good Sam," the Federal Good Samaritan Law is designed to counter the situation in which our throwaway society discards 14 billion pounds of food each year according to the EPA, a good portion of which is still fresh and edible. However, until the new law was passed, many companies throughout the U.S. had refused to give their leftovers to programs that provide food to the poor, fearing to be sued if something they donated were to make someone ill. The new law exempts nonprofit organizations and, to use the biblical term, "gleaners" from being sued. These gleaners are volunteers who collect what is left in the field after harvesting, and they and the organizations donating the food are now exempt from liabilities that arise over food contributed in good faith.[16] This means that now, giant corporations such as Pizza Hut and 7-Eleven are making millions of pounds of food available to those who need it most. The Agriculture Department has even prepared "A Citizens Guide to Food Recovery" to help individuals as well as corporations to participate in food recovery.[17]

Fifth, there are also no limits to two other things. The first is, apparently, human resistance when faced with the theology of relinquishment where the demand in our lives is to simplify and to work to redress massive economic inequality. Too many of us are frightened by the call to divest ourselves and to move toward the detachment that characterizes genuine holiness in all religious traditions. But the other unlimited factor is the human imagination, especially the North American human imagination, with its "can do" assumptions and its willingness to take on the care and feeding of those who need it most.

Some of the people I have met in religious education circles exemplify this commitment to economic development: the woman who told me that she and her husband had sold their second house because two homes in this needy world seemed to them an obscenity; the couple who decided to forget about stocks and bonds in order to invest in the schooling of a child not their own, because that child was poor; the lawyers in local soup kitchens throughout the country who make their pro bono services available every week to those who need them; the widows in hundreds of parishes and congregations who, although without the economic security of monetary capital, nevertheless give their time and their ministry as a way of acknowledging their gratitude for what they do possess; the struggling communities of congregations of nuns who nevertheless sink whatever capital they have into the economic development of others less fortunate than themselves. These are some of those who are living the great calling of economic justice for all today—those for whom economic issues rest at development's center.

FOR REFLECTION AND RESPONSE

1. Imagine that you are asked to teach a class on the meaning of development. What do you say?
2. Gabriel suggests that it is not healthy for educators to speak only the language of psychology. What are some of the alternative languages that religious educators might speak?
3. Why are the great spiritual traditions the most likely places to look for a theory of religious development? How is religious development the *precondition* of all other kinds of development?
4. As part of your religious educational life and work, what is one way you can incorporate the ecological dimension of development?
5. As part of your religious educational life and work, what is one way you can incorporate the economy of home and household?
6. As part of your religious educational life and work, what is one way you can incorporate economics?

Chapter 5

DEVELOPMENT AND GENDER

MARIA: In the early 1990s, I participated in a conference on the relation between the psychology of women and the development of adolescent girls. During the years preceding that conference, I had been in regular contact with Judith Dorney, one of the Harvard educators designing the conference, and had thereby kept abreast of the research that was the focus of the meeting. As a religious educator, I had also been involved in the lives of adult women, especially with women's spirituality, and by that time my own research had broadened so that it included, in addition to these first two interests, the religious education of women in middle and later life. The intersection of these three issues: the development of girls, the spirituality of women, and the religious education of jubilarians—women who are either approaching fifty or have already reached their jubilee years—are my concerns in this chapter. I will write about each of these themes first; Gabriel will follow with commentary on the relation between development and the lives of men and boys; and we will conclude with some joint recommendations.

The Development of Girls

The Harvard conference (actually held in Cleveland) that I note above reported on work that had been done by a team of Harvard researchers at Cleveland's Laurel School for Girls (a K–12 setting).[1] This work furthered previous educational attention that had been given to young women at the Emma Willard School for girls in Troy, New York; to urban students in the Boston and Cambridge areas; and to the seminal work of Carol Gilligan that is reported on in *In a Different Voice.*[2] It is striking to recall just how recent such work is. For in the early years of my own involvement in religious education, concentration on gender simply did not exist; most of us used "he" and "him" to refer to humanity or "man," and rarely did we seek to probe the implications of social location. Developmental studies, in contrast, were at the core of the preparation of religious educators, and from graduate school to diocesan, synodal, and judicatory teacher training programs, students were expected to learn Piaget's schema on cognitive development, Erikson's on psychosocial development, Kohlberg's on the development of moral reasoning, and, by the mid-seventies, Fowler's on faith development.

With the work of Gilligan and her colleagues, however, those enterprises began to be viewed through new lenses. Questions were raised about the possible biases of developmental researchers, and about the use of male-only populations to provide the basis of theories that were then applied to all human beings, the last concern especially pertinent to the Kohlberg framework. The irony surrounding that framework was that an enormous amount of data existed about the development of moral reasoning in males, but the conclusions drawn from it were not offered about *males* but about human beings in general.[3] In contrast, the new attention to female gender did not assume that research findings would have the same implications for boys as they did for girls or for men as they did for women.

The initial finding I want to single out from this newer research was the educated hunch that a genuine developmental danger occurs for girls at the end of childhood. This danger was posited as an apparent dilemma in the lives of girls, who, as they were preparing to enter their teenage years, were caught between two choices, neither of them positive. In contrast to the self-esteem, strength, and commonly practiced self-assertion they'd known as girls of 6 and 7 and 8, it now appeared that they had to choose either (a) to mute their voices and stop saying what they knew—especially what they knew about human relationships—in order to be thought of as "nice" girls or "good" girls or "perfect" girls, or (b) to continue the outspokenness of their childhood and be labeled aggressive or bossy—or worse, be placed on the margins of life socially just when the approval of peers was becoming increasingly important for them. Not all girls made one or the other of these choices. Nevertheless, the presence of the very real *possibility* of the dilemma had been uncovered. The shorthand way of naming the dilemma was the danger of a loss of voice. Girls did not stop talking; they simply hedged about saying what they knew. And this possibility raised a further one: how much of the loss of voice in girls was due to behavior they saw modeled in adult women?

Subsequent research by the American Association of University Women corroborated and actually strengthened the earlier work by studying boys as well as girls, even as girls were looked at through the lenses of racial and ethnic diversity. That is, the AAUW studies looked at African-American and Latina girls as well as white girls,[4] and discovered that from elementary to high school, white girls' self-esteem moved from a 65 percent positive to a

22 percent positive level; Latina girls' from 68 percent positive to 30 percent positive; and black girls' from 65 percent positive to 58 percent positive.[5] In Canada, similar findings were noted, this time in a report entitled *A Capella,* a name the Canadian Teachers' Federation chose for their study of almost a thousand girls. In their report, they wrote: "To sing 'a capella' is to carry a tune without instrumental accompaniment. It's a high-risk musical style; it's much easier to lose pitch when the orchestra isn't providing a familiar melody. You can lose your way without a strong rhythm section to keep you on track. Young women in Canada today are living 'a capella,' and for the most part their song is not being heard."[6]

Concern for girls was not only over the loss of voice in young women of the developed Western world, however. By the '90s, the global situation of girl children became a major issue at the United Nations. In 1990, for example, UNICEF issued a report called "The Girl Child. An Investment in the Future"[7] because awareness had grown concerning girls in poorer, less economically developed countries in the world. In such countries it was clear that girls receive less health care, less schooling, and poorer nutrition than boys—which limited not only the girls. It limited their countries' social fabric too, since most of these girls would one day become mothers and, without proper food, schooling, and health care, would be likely to repeat cycles of poverty. UNICEF argued that such results could be counteracted if concentrated attention was given to female children and the adult roles for which they are destined.

In addition, and in concert with other agencies, such as the Children's Defense Fund, the World Council of Churches, and the International Catholic Child Bureau, the United Nations has—in the '90s—been at the forefront of publicizing and urging an end to both the slave trade of children (for example, in Sudan) and the sexual exploitation of children—boys as well as girls—in the brothels of Southeast Asia. Supported by a multi-billion-dollar sex tourist industry, where the "tourists" are businessmen from North America, Asia, and Europe, the practice throughout the world of using children sexually cries for redress and for the help of committed adults such as religious educators. From the loss of voice, to the loss of health, to the loss of bodily integrity, to loss of life itself—the last loss in countries where female fetuses are routinely aborted and girl children routinely left to die—these young people provide riveting examples of the need to make gender a priority issue in religious education.

We will suggest several forms of response to these situations in the last part of this chapter. Here, however, one of the most obvious responses presents itself. Educators, armed as we are with microphones and community positions and moral power, need to break the silence that surrounds the terrible, terrible risks to the spirits and bodies of too many girl children in our world. Voices must be raised in shouting a prophetic "No" to the evil that routinely condemns them to suffering and death.

The Spirituality of Women

The second issue influencing gender and educational development is spirituality. In today's world, both within and outside the churches, spirituality is a major interest, and the perennial presence on the best-seller lists of books on spiritual life continues to confirm spirituality's importance. Influenced by feminism, the women's movement, and a genuine sense of female life throughout the entire world, however, we have discovered that spirituality is not always and everywhere the same. In other words, our spirituality—which can be understood as our way of being in the world in the light of the Mystery of God or the Sacred—takes on different meanings depending on our *temporal* location: for example, living at the dawn of a new millennium; our *geographical* location: for example, being city folks or rural people; our *ethnic* location: growing up Italian, South African, Mexican, or Belgian; and our *gender* location: growing up as boys or girls and becoming either women or men.

With reference to the last of these, we have discovered that our gender identity shapes our spirituality. Reflecting on that identity, many of today's most articulate women have discovered that our way of being in the world is influenced and fashioned by being in the world as female. Routinely, women's spirituality is characterized as rooted in our bodies, attentive to ritual, inclusive of the nonhuman universe, reliant on women's experience (not only on men's), and insistent that the political cannot be separated from the personal.

One way of imagining the breadth and fullness of women's spirituality is as a series of steps. Unlike the pattern of steps in most developmental theories, however, where movement proceeds up a series of steps akin to those on a staircase or a ladder, leaving the earth and ascending higher and higher to a pristine "heaven," the steps in women's spirituality are better construed as steps in a dance.[8] Throughout our lives, women have discovered, we move backward *and* forward; we are alone *and* partnered; we are slow *and* swift; we are solitary *and* we are celebratory. The steps we take in our spiritual lives follow a choreography that moves from Awakening (said Meister Eckhart, "This is spirituality: waking up!") to Discovering (our power, our gifts, the communities that support us) to Creating (our lives, our world) to Dwelling (finding and making—and sometimes leaving—our "place") to Nourishing (attending to the feeding and care of our ways of being in the world).[9]

So far so good, except that in our times and in our world, the dance does not stop at Nourishing, which is the development of practices and disciplines that nurture spirituality. Often in previous centuries spirituality has ended there. However, in today's world and, more pertinently, out of the experience of women's lives, two additional steps have become necessary. The first of these is *traditioning.* The second is *transforming.*

I highlight the importance of traditioning here because it is the step in spirituality that accepts and acts upon adult women's responsibility to the development of succeeding generations, and more specifically to our concern for the next generation of women. Closely related to Erik Erikson's developmental passage of generativity, which is the concern for establishing and guiding the generations yet to come,[10] traditioning is the step where we recognize our vocation to hand on and hand over the richest and fullest aspects of life to those who will come after us.

Mistakenly, tradition is often thought of as words, rules, or doctrines handed on and handed over. But, in a strange paradox, this is not actually its meaning. For no such thing as "tradition" exists to be handed over. Rather, it is the action of handing on and handing over that is the tradition. Tradition is the process by which humans communicate ways of knowing, ways of being, and ways of doing from one generation to the next. Tradition is the handing on of *life* and of *living.* Tradition brings together past, present, and future. When we consider spirituality as a way of life and living in the world, the step of traditioning becomes the movements of handing on this life.

Four overlapping roles exist as part of adult women's acts of traditioning. The first is *parenting:* performing the daily tasks of ensuring the nurture of life; ferrying back and forth; feeding body and spirit; keeping harm at bay. The second is *teaching:* the actual work of instruction that is performed by schoolteachers with the next generations, as well as the many ways that all adults show children and teenagers and younger adults how to live in the world.[11] The third is *mentoring:* where circumstances set up a one-to-one relation between the adult woman and the younger person, with the mentor standing alongside and not in front of, overseeing the other, who is in the role of apprentice. The fourth is *modeling:* a paradoxical role that is both powerful and largely unintended. For whether we assume we are role models or not, the next generations are still always asking us, "In what way does your life tell me about my life?" automatically observing the more seasoned person in order to see how things are done and whether they want to follow suit. Taken together, these four roles are ones we live out toward our daughters—and our sons—as we become adult women.

At its best, living out these roles gathers toward a closing step in this particular choreography: transforming. This is the culminating step in the dance of women's spiritual lives, the hoped-for outcome. Out of the earlier experiences of Awakening and Dis-covering, Creating, Dwelling, and Nourishing, awareness finally dawns that in claiming a spirituality unique to ourselves, we are giving birth to something new. It is not only a new self, however, or a new person—that would be too small. Instead, it is the awareness that in renewing ourselves and our own lives, we are renewing the face of the earth, transforming it so that it is an earth and a world hospitable to the young, the fragile, and the needy. It is a world where justice prevails.

This will mean—and here again is a tentative connection to the next generations—that we are all necessary partners to one another, listening to each other as carefully as we can with the poignant recognition that even today too many women have been taught, even as young girls continue to be taught, "Don't speak." For adult women and men, it will also mean that in order to transform our broken world, we will confront our own silences as well, raising our voices against faulty systems, structures, and customs and working to change the present world into a new Jerusalem where there is neither mourning, nor crying, nor pain.

The Religious Education of Jubilarians

In continuing these studies, I have found in recent years that a third developmental issue is central to gender education: the realization of the particular and pertinent traits that become central to religious life when women have entered the years after fifty and become "jubilarians." The term jubilarian is derived, of course, from the biblical jubilee, with its counsels to count up seven "years" of seven years so that the total is forty-nine years, and then to hallow—to make holy—the fiftieth year. Biblically, as well as in ordinary life, the fiftieth year symbolizes passage to wisdom, to wholeness, to mature moral agency, and to detachment.

Over the past ten years, I have had the opportunity to be in contact with several hundred women who have entered this Jubilee time,[12] and in conversation and collaboration with 140 of them, to corroborate this view. The interviews I have done and the questionnaires to which many have responded indicate that a set of shifts occur between the mid-forties and the nineties that are amenable to further development and further education. The first shift is toward the acquisition of wisdom. That is, later life is a time when modes of knowing develop that are deeper and broader than they were previously because, in large part, the experience of life is deeper and broader too. The development of "understanding, discerning, or having insight into what is true, right, or lasting" (one definition of wisdom) is not only at the rational level or learned from books—although these are critical and important sources. Still, physically as well as mentally, "wise blood" now begins to shape life, and intuition and the capacity to read situations is based on evidence accumulated throughout six, seven, eight, and more decades of living.

Jubilee time also offers an invitation to wholeness, and to the claiming of parts of life that have been waiting for attention. One woman I interviewed, for example, told me that as a young bride, and throughout the years that she was raising eight children, she had consciously put parts of her life "on hold." Then she continued her account by saying, "But now my children are adults and on their own, and I have discovered new work I must do as I integrate the parts of myself waiting in the wings." In her case, she was referring particularly to pastoral, ministerial work beyond her own home, although other women will be involved in quite different calls. The move to wholeness, however, seems to be a constant: those who feel they are too busy signal their need for calming down and claiming contemplative quiet; the unschooled seek to satisfy their hunger for learning; and the solitary honor social needs. One seventy-six-year-old woman told me that some years after her retirement she suddenly had to have major surgery, and the decline in her physical energy precipitated the new behavior of drawing on the strengths of others. "I came to accept the fact," she concluded, "that we're all tied up together in the 'bundle of life' and our *interdependence* fills existence with much more meaning."

Mature moral agency is a third direction of the jubilee years. Although it manifests itself in a range of different ways, one result arises in the situation where an older woman has lost a treasured sibling, an intimate friend, a lifelong spouse. Suddenly, the person who—in the family or the friendship or the marriage—has been responsible for the finances or the storytelling or the creativity in the network of friends and family is gone. Responsibilities that person shouldered now rest on the one who is left, one who is "in charge" in ways she has not practiced for years, or perhaps has never known at all. Until quite recently, for example, many women who were suddenly widowed had to learn the art of balancing the checkbook—a metaphor for the many balances that are now in the portfolio of their mature moral agency.

At another level, however, it is not just the circumstances of age but age itself that heightens mature moral agency. The "elder" is precisely that: senior, superior, in a governing role, more experienced, and therefore a more profound source of understanding what actions need to be taken in a particular situation. With its cult of youth, U.S. culture as a whole has been slow in acknowledging the power of significant elders, except in the traditions preserved by Native Americans. However, as life expectancy has grown throughout the twentieth century from fifty years in 1900 to seventy-five and eighty at present, respect for age—especially in the family—has come to carry with it a healthy respect for the thought-through decisions offered by those who know how to back up their decisions and choices with the fullness of long life and experience. For the jubilarian, mature moral action comes from the convictions grown throughout a lifetime that *here* is the way I must go and *this* is what I must do. There is no other "I" to show me the way.

Education during elderhood is also needed, finally, in the ways and forms of detachment. As life approaches fullness, completeness, and the death that symbolizes this fullness, persons begin the work of divesting: letting go of things and possessions at one end of the spectrum, and relinquishing life itself at the other. By the late seventies, for example, "things" are held lightly and tend to have less importance—with the exception of family photos or treasures that have belonged to beloved persons—than do the gifts of the sun and the moon, the earth itself, life, and health. Life is coming to an end, and the full picture of the journey from birth to death is etching its every detail into experience. With the knowledge that we leave the planet as we entered it—that is to say, with nothing—the wise, whole, responsible elder begins letting go and moves into the state of detachment: holding on lightly to whatever is at hand, even as she expresses profound gratitude for the gifts that have been hers, and thanks to the Giver who now summons her home.

GABRIEL: I will add some comments on each of Maria's three points before we draw some conclusions about gender and education. My comments are made from a man's perspective on the question of gender today. I will be briefer than Maria, and what I say is based more on personal impression than scientific studies.

My brevity and style are due to the fact that the area of gender study is dominated by women writers and by the study of women. We lack studies of boys' development and of men considered as a gender. The present situation is illogical, and the imbalance could worsen existing problems. In the school where I teach, "gender issues" is one choice in a short list of required courses. I hear resistance and anger among many men (and some women) students because they object to a course on gender that they experience as a course on feminism.

This imbalance is unfortunate because the term "gender" was invented (or refashioned) just a few decades ago to open a better dialogue between the sexes. It provides a new instrument to examine the complex relation between women and men. It allow us to differentiate between biological and social components in discussing what should be changed and how it can be changed. Whatever problems of gender there are can only be solved if both men and women change.

Development. Maria has pointed out the irony that almost all studies of development up to twenty years ago were in fact studies of male development. And given the nature of longitudinal studies, the use of samples from the 1920s, 1930s, and 1940s means that longitudinal studies remain almost exclusively male.[13] These studies are now being complemented by many studies of girls' development. However, studies of boys—with explicit attention to gender—remain very few; eventually such studies might provide a new angle on human development.

The studies that find a loss of voice in girls at adolescence are of interest to men as well as to women. One immediate question that follows from these findings is whether the girls' loss is the boys' gain. Do boys find what girls lose? In studies of classroom behavior, such as *Failing at Fairness,* the answer seems to be yes.[14] The "unfairness" implied in the title refers to boys' receiving more than their equal share of attention and rewards. However, if the main issue is that girls no longer speak the truth as they experience it, then it would not be illogical to suspect that boys have a similar problem.

I do not teach thirteen- or fourteen-year-olds, so I have no personal data on the beginning of adolescence. I do teach many eighteen- and nineteen-year-olds. For the past decade at least, I have been very aware of a possible bias against women in the classroom. Do I recognize the woman's hand as readily as I do the man's? Do I engage in dialogue differently with men and women? Do women and men differ in the candor of their comments? While none of us is the best judge of our own biases, I have not detected a loss of voice among the women I teach. I find that there are many students who seem to lack a voice, but I find that factors other than gender are more prominent. Ethnicity is probably the best indicator, especially when linked to a different kind of educational system in the student's past experience.

Numbers can be important when the question is outspokenness. If a class is 80 percent Korean, a Korean student is more likely to speak up than when the class is 10 percent Korean. Some classes I teach are fairly equally divided into men and women; in others there is a majority of women. That may seem to be an unusual situation, but it is in fact the common one in U.S. colleges today. While women may have a long way to go in influencing public life as senators, CEOs, or generals, they have made extraordinary gains in school achievement and in entrance into universities and professional schools. Today 67 percent of female high school graduates go to college, compared to 58 percent of males. In 1970, women were 41 percent of college students; today they are 55 percent. Among students for masters' degrees, 60 percent are women; women are now the majority in medical schools. Almost two-thirds of African-American students who earn college degrees are women. Women still trail men in mathematics and some of the sciences, but the real problem here is that the United States compares miserably with most advanced countries in international tests of math and science.

I do not disparage the findings on girls' losing voice. However, these data need to be put in the perspective of longitudinal studies of women. They also need to be seen in relation to men with an acknowledgment of where women already surpass men. Race, ethnicity, and class should not be completely bracketed out in comparisons of boys and girls.

From my own experience I have the impression that young men are more fragile and unsure of themselves than are young women. They are confused about what they are supposed to become as adult men, both in regard to their work and to their family role. In contrast, many of the young women seem to think, whether or not they are right, that the world is now going in their direction and that they have choices. If young men are having these problems, some women may be tempted to say, "it's about time" or "let them find out what we have always known." I do not think the human race can afford that. Boys and young men today need sympathetic understanding, which in the long run will be a plus and not a minus for women too.

Spirituality. "Spirituality," like gender, is also a newly refashioned term related to the emergence of women's concerns. Until recently, "spirituality" was a term that was largely confined to a private devotional region in traditional religions. Today, almost the reverse is true. Many people speak of spirituality as ecumenical, future-oriented, and more relevant to their lives than religion.

Similar to the way in which the term gender has given us a new tool to examine past and present, "spirituality" reveals the complexity of "religion," a term whose current meaning goes back only a few centuries.[15] Until modern times, religion was an element in the virtue of justice. Although there were clear distinctions between, say, Christians, Jews, and Muslims, the difference was not one's religion but what people one belonged to and one's way of life. The mystical strand of these different groups was always more similar than the exterior and institutionalized elements. Especially in Christian history, women dominated this mystical side. Women today who speak of "spirituality" are recovering this mystical side, which includes the personal, the communal, the symbolic, the compassionate.

By finding their spirituality, women have taken the reformer's lead away from theologians, administrators, and legal scholars whose control in the past was solid. Women have traditionally had numbers on their side but have been willing to take the direction of male leaders. We are probably only in the first stage of rebellion against this tradition. But the rebellion is in favor of an older and richer tradition of personal and communal transformation. In this century, the now mostly middle-aged women who were born into religious institutions ruled by men are discovering an alternate way to self-discovery, communal sharing, and encounter with the divine. What this will mean for Judaism, Christianity, and Islam is beyond anyone's guess at present, but some currently hot topics may turn out to be minor irrelevancies when the full revolution becomes evident.

What about middle-aged men in this upheaval? During the 1970s a literature on "male midlife crisis" flourished and then seemed to recede. Although this male experience was not directly tied to the feminist movement, it was probably reacting to the same phenomena as feminism was, but from another perspective. The institutions that men had put their trust in, including church, were shown to be built on shaky foundations. What constitutes a "successful career" for a man was thrown into doubt. Men in their forties and fifties started finding that their lives lacked meaning and purpose. The problem might be labeled psychological, but the capacity of psychologists to treat this problem has led to challenges and crises within psychology itself. In today's terms, men were in search of a spirituality.[16]

The end of the 1980s saw an effort to start a "men's movement" that would consciously imitate some of the strategies of the women's movement. That is, men would gather in retreats or communal settings; they would share their hopes and anxieties in verbal and nonverbal expressions. Robert Bly's book *Iron John* caught the public eye and sat atop the best-seller list for over a year.[17] Bly interprets ancient myths with special attention to the relation of sons and fathers. In traditional cultures, according to Bly, boys were initiated into manhood by a brotherhood of elders. In modern times, fathers are expected to perform this role, but it is beyond them. So, middle-aged men, both gay and straight, may still be in search of a father.

I worried at the time of the publication of Bly's book that the movement would be too closely identified with him and with his exclusive focus on absent fathers. In a short time the news media moved on to other topics and a "men's movement" seemed to dissolve. Phenomena such as the Million Man March on Washington or fundamentalist Christian gatherings of Promise Keepers are treated as disconnected curiosities instead of symptoms about the life of men in the United States today. I suspect that the changes that have been occurring in men's lives since the 1950s are continuing to cause a spiritual crisis. Some of the sources of spirituality for men might be the same as for women. Although a male spirituality would have to discover a truly masculine way to relate to other men, to women, to children, to God, men would be helped in their search by conversations with women. Unfortunately, men and women in middle age often find it difficult to talk to each other

Jubilarians. One optimistic note in studies of human development is called the sexual diamond theory. It contends that at the age of twenty, men and women are not far apart in their aspirations; at age forty they are at opposite ends of the spectrum; at age sixty they are back close together again. Part of this theory is that after age forty men start recovering a suppressed "feminine" side, while women are recovering a suppressed "masculine" side. By the time they reach old age, men and women are complete beings.[18]

The biggest problem between men and women in the later years is the absence of men. The men are not running off in search of a better life; they are dying. If there is to be gender mutuality in retirement villages or nursing homes, men will have to improve their physical health. Some improvements have been taking hold: better diet, less tobacco, more exercise. But by almost every standard of health and longevity, men remain the weaker sex. Much more dramatic change will be needed before the statistics get back to anywhere near equal numbers of men and women in old age.

For those men who do live long enough to retire from their jobs, old age can be a time of great refreshment and peace. They are allowed just to be, to be a self. When middle-aged men are asked on airplanes, "who are you with?" the expected answer is not the name of one's wife and children but the name of the corporation paying for the plane ticket. Many men become almost totally identified with their jobs. Although suppression of the personality is different for men than for the women that Maria interviewed, it is a tragic parallel. Public man and private woman do not make a healthy unity; men and women need to find the other half of themselves if they are to relate well to the other gender. The retrieval of a "feminine" sensitivity in men and the retrieval of a "masculine" aggressiveness by women might be a passing phenomenon of our turbulent times. But there may also be something inherent in the constitution of men and women that makes such a circuitous route to elderhood necessary.

We may never be able to sort out sex from gender, the elements given by genetic makeup in contrast to social formation. The good news is that by old age it does not much matter. Old age is a time for mature men and mature women who peacefully embody the multiplicity of every tradition. Men still have their quirks and women theirs, but the emphasis is on a common humanity. Rabbi Abraham Heschel, a wise elder, said: "When I was young I admired clever people; now that I am old I admire kind people." Kindness is a skill that has to be learned, but it is within the ability of all. The world still needs clever and energetic administrators of the world's complex systems, but the old have to embody an image of humanity that does not cause the young to flee from every sign of aging.

Educational Demands of Gender Issues

MARIA AND GABRIEL: Each of these three issues is a distinct and important one under the heading, "Gender and Development." Clearly, however, the issues are not separable. For although they can be distinguished from one another (as we have just tried to do) they are necessarily related. Having made this point, we now ask: what specifically educational demands do the issues we are considering make on all of us?

First, attend to omissions in religious education curricula. The three issues we have named are not often part of curricula, or if they are, are not given due attention. Therefore, as a work of advocacy we and our students need to do more than monitor the many forms of curriculum to see if the language and examples used include the actual, lived experiences of girls and women in concert with boys and men. We must also attend to the curriculum the world itself offers in the situations of children worldwide: the dangers of violation they face, the ways spirituality is presented to them, and the wisdom of age that is present as capital for them to draw on in every community.

Second, enlist the support of men and boys in attending to girls and women, and of women and girls in attending to boys and men. Analogous to those white people who do not reflect on racial issues as "their" issues, men often do not realize that gender is their concern too. This is a complicated issue, since many times girls and women need to meet in exclusively female groups in order to address the concerns important to them. In other words, there are times when men are not wanted. But the converse is true with respect to men and boys as well. In addition, we are only at the beginning of research into *male* gender and education, and the energy of men and boys must be directed not only to women and girls, but to themes that are gender-specific to them. On this point, Richard Rohr, who has been in the forefront of religious people dealing with masculinity, has been an important voice. His recent warning that "toxic masculinity is so feared and hated [today] that the healthy and necessary form [of masculinity] is denied existence, voice, and face" is an important caveat.[19] Over the long haul, gender and voice are issues for all of us. Still, because of the power that men continue to wield in religious and other institutions, their actions as well as their support is crucial on issues of concern to women.

Third, encourage opportunities for girls and teenage young women to express and confront their resistances. Young women are generally aware that if they are in danger of some kind of loss—of voice, of self-esteem, of physical integrity—they will feel resistance to such loss. They will suspect they are being asked to give away parts of themselves that they wish to keep. When this happens, they need to have older women as advocates who will assure them they are joined in their resistance to losing part of themselves, even as the culture seduces them to be less than they are. Young women also need the advocacy of men. Thus adult women and men must let it be known they are there for the next generation—as listeners, as mentors and models, and as partners.

Similar attention needs to be given to the resistance of boys and men. We are far less attuned to the resistances they feel and experience. They themselves may also be unaware of their own resistances, since boys are far more likely to be deprived by societal forces of a sensitive and direct access to their feelings. As men search for a genuine masculine spirituality, one of the components of that search needs to be their partnership with the next generation of boys.

Fourth, arrange for intergenerational meetings between girls and women and boys and men to consider issues of spirituality together. In the case of girls, the hunger that women manifest today in the search to learn about foremothers—from Vashti and Esther to Rebecca and Rachel to Julian of Norwich and Hildegard of Bingen—symbolizes the great search to understand aspects of the past that have been denied not only to females but to males. Thus, conversations and presentations by women of every age about those who served as foremothers can instruct women among themselves; they can also recognize that this broad heritage has been denied as well to boys and men.

Fifth, as a way of shaping and deepening spirituality for men as well as women, and for boys as well as girls, seek to design prayer services that use women in every pastoral role. Choose readings where women are central figures. In speaking of the divine, use images such as Mother and Holy Wisdom—Sancta Sophia—and address the Holy not only as lamb of God but as hen of God. Refuse to limit God to male attributes, and make available music that features female performers singing the gospel as well as singing gospel music itself.

Sixth, in teacher preparation, be sure that gender issues are included. In some churches throughout the United States, recent sexual abuse scandals have precipitated a new aspect of preparation where basic guidelines are laid down for those adults who will be working with children and teenagers. Equally important here is education in gender issues of the kind that we have stressed in this chapter, education that includes specific attention to the differences and similarities in the next generations as they grow into adulthood. These are some of the ways that the girls and boys we love can become the complete, whole persons their Creator destines them to be.

FOR REFLECTION AND RESPONSE

1. What are some significant curricular omissions concerning gender that you would like to see addressed?
2. What are some ways that you can enlist the support of women concerning gender issues for boys and men, and support of men concerning gender issues for girls and women?
3. How can you help to surface resistances to losses that both girls and boys may face in their own gender development?
4. What intergenerational opportunities can you imagine for girls and women, and men and boys, to meet across age boundaries?
5. In designing a prayer service, worship, or liturgy that addresses the roles of women and girls in the history of religious and spiritual life, what are some key elements you want to be sure to include—for both genders?
6. What are at least three aspects of teacher education you will advocate so that gender issues are not left aside in the preparation of schoolteachers and/or catechists?

Chapter 6

DEVELOPMENT AND DEATH

GABRIEL: I have often said to religious educators that religious education has two great moments: being born and dying. If we could do a good job with both of those teachable moments, then what is in between would mostly take care of itself. Those two moments of birth and dying are revelatory of life as a whole and transitional to a life as yet unimagined. The person undergoing these revelatory moments of transition has very little control of what is happening, although the dying person has implied an attitude toward death throughout life. Educational help has to come from the surrounding community; thus, some of our most important religious educators are health care providers: nurses, midwives, physicians, counselors, and their helpers.

The great religions of the world have usually been aware of the supreme importance of the moments of birth and death, as well as the interconnection of the two. Christianity has been resistant to speaking of death as a rebirth because the doctrine of resurrection differs from the reincarnation cycle of birth and rebirth common in Asian religions. Perhaps Christianity prematurely excluded reincarnation without allowing for its possibility in lives cut short before their time. And in all cases, death/resurrection might be helpfully put in the context of a kind of birth. I concentrate here on dying and mourning as religious acts that invite educational discussion.

For the past fifteen years I have team-taught a course called "The Meaning of Death." The course is very popular, which never ceases both to surprise and worry me. Why are so many young people so interested in death? Each year registration for the fall course opens and closes on one weekend in March. Someday I would like to teach the course with a dozen students, but I limit enrollment to fifty and end up by taking a few dozen more. I would not teach the course alone. I first fell into the course as its manager with two teachers whose full-time work is counseling the dying, eventually taking over for one of them. I cannot claim to be an expert on the subject, but after the death of both my parents and several close friends I am not completely lacking in experience of death.

I discovered in the early years of teaching the course that most of the students are looking for a form of therapy. They have had a parent or grandparent die, they have a friend with AIDS, or they may have contemplated suicide. My colleague provides a wealth of therapeutic material, especially in the marvelous stories she can tell from experiences she has had with the dying and the bereaved. My part in the course is to deal with historical, philosophical, and religious material, which is not the primary concern of many of the students. While most of them profess a skepticism about religion (they are nominally of all religions with Catholicism usually ranking first), most of them are looking for something "spiritual."

I have mixed feelings about the existence of such a course. Its academic standing is questionable. The study of death does not fit easily into being a classroom subject, although death, as an inevitable part of life, could show up in almost every course. I often think that students come to the course simply to hear two adults speak candidly about one of the few taboo topics in the students' experience. At least for now, I see some value in a college course on death. In elementary and secondary schools I would prefer to see death introduced more casually into several curriculum areas.

As noted in previous chapters, classroom instruction is only one part of education. In the first meeting of the course I always reflect on the limitations of the classroom. I emphasize to the students that I cannot teach them how to die. Everyone does have to learn how to die from parents, friends, and other people, but a classroom is not designed to teach that. I also would not require students as part of a course to confront death in a morgue or funeral home. I might suggest attending an art exhibit or a movie in conjunction with the course. But I restrict the course requirements to reading, discussion, and occasional viewing of video clips. I have discovered that some students who never speak in class still get much out of the course.

Stages of Dying?

The attempt to develop an academic discipline called "thanatology" has not succeeded, at least not yet. The book by Elisabeth Kübler-Ross, *On Death and Dying,* remains the one undisputed classic.[1] Although there are occasional dissertations inspired by that book, no one has steadfastly followed up *On Death and Dying* to establish a more scientific basis for work with the dying. That includes Kübler-Ross herself who, almost immediately after the success of her book, proceeded in a very different direction. She became convinced not only of a life beyond death but of the presence of spirits communing with her. Many people who were enthusiastic about her early work were horrified at her casually referring to conversations with dead people. Her insistence in recent years that "death does not exist" seems to be a direct contradiction of the work for which she is most famous.[2] It is also contrary to both Christian and Jewish traditions, which have never denied the existence of death.

The best-seller list in recent years has regularly carried books claiming knowledge of the moment of death and what lies beyond death. I find it difficult to become engaged with these books. Perhaps there is some truth in them, but how can one judge? At least with Kübler-Ross one knows that she is drawing on an extraordinary fund of experience. Many other people have simply discovered that death can be a fashionable and profitable topic to write about.

The one recent book that is a worthy follow-up to Kübler-Ross's early work is *How We Die* by Sherwin Nuland.[3] Equal parts personal memoir, medical history, and philosophical rumination, the book is written in spare and powerful prose by a surgeon with forty years' experience. Kübler-Ross's name does not appear often in Nuland's book, but she and the movement that she inspired are the background of Nuland's attempt to face the issue of death realistically. Opposing what he takes to be sentimental and romantic talk about death, Nuland immerses the reader in the harrowing details of disease and death. Like many writers today, he professes no religion but wishes to leave the door open to some "spiritual" significance of death.

Kübler-Ross is famous for elaborating five stages of dying—denial, anger, bargaining, depression, acceptance. She did not provide a scientific argument for this pattern, despite the fact of using the language of developmental stage theory. Each chapter simply recounts conversations with the dying that she interprets and classifies. At the least, one would have expected a few cases discussed longitudinally, that is, one person exemplifying all five stages, but the book reports no such cases. The names of the five stages are borrowed from ordinary speech, each of the terms having a wide range of ambiguity. When the theory has been challenged by critics, Kübler-Ross and her defenders have been quick to admit that variations in the scheme are possible. The defenders grant that one or more stages can be omitted, or that the stages may overlap, or that the order of stages may be different, or that a patient may regress. But when one has enunciated a pattern and then admits innumerable qualifications, at some point there simply is no pattern.

Over the years I have come to understand Kübler-Ross's pattern in a way that not only saves some of its meaning but can suggest a greater significance than it is usually thought to have. Her stages may seem to be a case of "developmental theory" with pretensions to scientific objectivity. But parallel to what I said in chapter 4 about "religious development," Kübler-Ross's stages are not just one more dimension of development. Instead, they challenge the modern idea of development itself. Not surprisingly, what Kübler-Ross found in listening to the dying bears a much closer relation to medieval mystical journeys than to social science theories in the modern age.

Modern developmental theory, as noted earlier, began as a protest against a closed world; it claims to maintain openness and to let loose creativity. As a theory of human history or economic progress, development may be sustainable in the face of ambiguous data. But what about the individual person? Does the certainty of a wonderful economy in the distant future keep the life of today's individual "open"? Most works in psychology talk glowingly about the future and the need to grow, to be creative, to be open to new experiences. Not far below the surface, however, every person knows that the future holds only one certainty: I die. Ernst Bloch put it bluntly: "The axe of annihilation is the most stringent of non-utopias." William James put it more imaginatively: "The skull will grin at the banquet."

The simple fact of dying is what Kübler-Ross placed on the table before psychology, which seldom speaks candidly of death. Freud's attempt to introduce a "death drive" into his psychology was largely unsuccessful. I think that theories of development are like instructions on how to get to the roof of a high-rise building; what they fail to note is that when you get there you get pushed off the roof. With all the wizardry of modern medicine, the death rate is still one hundred percent.

Kübler-Ross's stages make sense both as stages of dying and stages of living, or better, as stages of living that include dying. What she found from interviewing a few hundred people in a modern hospital is that people keep struggling near the end of life to find some sense in their lives. She also found that most people, given some help, do come to a peaceful resolution about their imminent deaths, that is, about a life that now includes dying. Religions have always been concerned about what is in a person's mind at the moment of death.[4] And even a secular audience can respond to the efforts of a Helen Prejean trying to get a condemned prisoner to die with an attitude of love and repentance.[5]

The "five stages" of dying do admit of great variation, but there is nonetheless a definite pattern proposed. Practically every dying person begins by denying that death is imminent. This is a healthy reaction which sustains a person's resistance. The alternative is to collapse on the spot and give up all fight. In her chapter on denial, Kübler-Ross says that denial is usually replaced by "partial acceptance."[6] What happened to the in-between stages? And is not acceptance something you either have or do not have? What I think her words suggest is that the whole of life is a dialectic of denial/acceptance. Total denial of death would exclude acceptance of life as well as death; total acceptance of death means that the person is leaving the land of the living. Thus, in the ordinary course of life, there is partial denial/partial acceptance.

Strong denial at the diagnosis that one is terminally ill is followed by a series of "stages" in which emphasis on denial or acceptance varies. The direction is not necessarily in a straight line; it would be surprising if it were. Rather, there is a circling movement that includes not only present possibilities but past actualities. Eventually this circling back through the past reaches the beginning of life. In this way, birth and death (rebirth) tend to converge. Each stage of this movement can be given a name, such as anger, bargaining, and depression; or hope, submission, resistance, resentment, rebellion, resignation, and so forth.

There can be an indefinite number of such stages but I think that (as in most mystical writing) there is always an odd number of stages. A series that splits evenly between yes and no is followed by a conclusion that is a yes inclusive of no. What can be called a last stage is actually an attitude underlying all the stages and eventually embracing all of them. The first no to death (which is a yes to life) is followed by a yes to death (which is a no to life). It is in this way that anger follows denial or that depression follows bargaining. A similar pattern of yes and no can be repeated any number of times until a crucial degree of acceptance of one's entire life has been reached.

Reaching the final condition of acceptance is clearly what Kübler-Ross advocates. She wants patients to reach this stage and says that a majority of her patients do.[7] In calling this stage "acceptance," I think she chooses the right term; it is a word connoting an attitude of receptiveness to reality. Freedom is present in acceptance—not as a choice among alternatives but in the deeper freedom to say yes or no to what life offers. Acceptance is what human beings practice every day until the moment when death is near and they must accept that "this is the whole of my life, this is who I am and have been." If the fact of death were the only thing at issue, we would speak of acknowledgment or recognition of a fact rather than acceptance; we do not accept the fact of death, we accept our life—including the fact of our own dying.

Kübler-Ross chose the right word, but I think she failed to provide an adequate description. More important, her description carries a bias that makes her vulnerable to criticism. While her intention was to humanize death, to insist on the need for a caring community that would surround the dying person, her description of acceptance as the need to be left alone can be read as inviting isolation, of leaving the dying person to his or her solitariness. I think she was unwittingly led into this description because of an assumed choice between the mechanizing and medicalizing of death over against its biological naturalness. A community context gets lost in that contrast. The assumed choice between a natural death and a dehumanized death is unfortunately becoming the common way to look at death.

Natural Death?

Although Sherwin Nuland is critical of Kübler-Ross, he agrees with her that death should be natural. Neither author argues the point; that death should be natural has become the starting point in today's discussions. Since California passed the Natural Death Act in 1976, the naturalness of death has been taken as an unquestioned good, and the basis for ethical discussion of euthanasia and suicide. I think this assumption needs questioning. True, it is natural for a living being to die; this statement is practically a definition of terms. But the relation between *human* nature and death is more complicated. An individual human being's death is not comprehended by the claim that it should be experienced as natural.

The most consistent meaning of "nature" throughout the last 2,500 years has been what is born, grows, declines, dies. The humans cannot step outside nature; they cannot remove themselves from the cycle of living and dying. Human death is not unnatural; it is not opposed to nature, because human beings are not opposed to nature. But to say that human death is natural is not to say enough. Bertolt Brecht's "they die like all the animals" is not in fact true. They (the humans) die as do all animals, but they can foresee their deaths in ways that not only change human life but can change all life on earth. They ritualize death in puzzling ways so that "the gorilla, the chimpanzee, and the orangutan must look upon the human as the weak and infirm animal that stores up its dead."[8]

The humans' nature is to transcend nature. In doing so, they can mess up the cycles of nature unless they understand and work with the rhythms of nature (both within and outside themselves). Humans are in the food chain, but their presence changes the food chain. What is not natural about humans is expressed in such terms as history, art, culture, reason, intelligence, freedom, and science. In Edmund Burke's succinct phrase, "man's nature is art." Even if they were to try, humans could not abandon their art, science, politics, and religion. Placed in the middle of the world's garden, they are the responsible ones. They are not one species equal to all the others but the species receptive to all meaning within nature.

All the major religions of the world would object to reducing human death to the merely natural. Primitive religion saw death as a punishment for angering the gods; the founders of the modern age rejected that idea as superstitious, but they still placed death outside "man." Jewish, Buddhist, Christian, and Muslim religions accepted the naturalness of dying and yet insisted that human beings experience their own dying as something more than natural. Even during the last two centuries while "man" was conquering nature, individuals found their life's meaning outside this battle, usually in religion. An individual today who does not subscribe to one of these religions is still likely to have a more than natural view of his or her own dying. Writing a book, painting a picture, or singing a song can be an attempt to find meaning beyond death. So can caring for the next generation and the generations beyond that.

All of the major religions understand that the human being is natural but not entirely so. The natural drive toward death is paired with the will to live; a human life from its inception involves resistance to nature and its accompanying death. These days one often hears the statement that "we should not prolong life artificially." But the whole of history is the story of prolonging life artificially, that is, the use of artifice to protect humans against heat, cold, infection, starvation. The person who resists death to the last moment is not necessarily denying that death is natural. But human beings try to exercise some control over the manner and timing of their dying.

Sherwin Nuland constantly repeats the phrase "death is not the enemy, disease is."[9] That statement may be a helpful caution to physicians and researchers. But while death is not the enemy of life, it is the enemy of *my* life; it is my mortal enemy. Throughout my life, death as well as disease is the enemy. There may eventually come a time in life when that enemy is seen as less hostile and even in some ways like a friend. Kübler-Ross's "moment of acceptance" is the recognition that there is no longer an enemy to fight.

At the press conference when Cardinal Joseph Bernardin announced that he had a terminal illness, some eyebrows were raised at his statement: "We can look at death as an enemy or a friend. . . . As a person of faith, I see death as a friend, as the transition from earthly life to life eternal."[10] Is this a statement of denial or acceptance? No stranger can say for sure. But given the person making the statement and the circumstances of the announcement, it most likely represents the end of a process by which the feared enemy of death has become transformed into something like a friend. In contrast to Bernardin's statement, Cardinal Lustiger of Paris raised other eyebrows when he said of Pope John Paul II: "There is no fear in the face of the void."[11] A description of death as "the void" does not make death sound like a friend. But Cardinal Lustiger was expressing the realism that has been part of the Christian view of death: it is real; it involves anguish, suffering, and incomprehensibility. One has to grant all this without despairing in the face of death. One has to live every moment to the last with a hope that goes beyond imagination.

Dietrich Bonhoeffer put death in proper perspective: "Wherever it is recognized that the power of death has been broken, wherever the world of death is illumined by the miracle of the resurrection and of the new life, there no eternities are demanded of life but one takes of life what it offers, not all or nothing but good and evil, the important and the unimportant, joy and sorrow; one neither clings convulsively to life nor casts it frivolously away. One is content with the allotted span and one does not invest earthly things with the title of eternity; one allows to death the limited rights which it still possesses."[12]

Mourning

Just as there are "stages" that a person goes through in dying, there are parallel or analogous stages that a mourner goes through. Actually, stages of mourning are the better documented of the two processes. What the dying person experiences will forever have a mysterious aspect. The caregiver can only with limited success get inside the dying person's experience. In contrast, we know from millennia of human experience what mourning is. Almost all human beings by the time they reach adulthood have some experience of mourning. And religious traditions embody a wisdom regarding in what ways and for how long we should mourn.

People's attitude to dying and to what follows dying is heavily dependent on their experience of mourning. In some ways that is obvious, but I think it is not usually reflected upon in relation to religious belief. A person's hope in resurrection (or some other formulation of afterlife) is sometimes dismissed as egocentric and selfish. But such hope more often reflects the experience of mourning the death of a loved one. Although it is difficult to imagine the person living on in some bodiless existence, it is more difficult to believe that the person has simply ceased to be.

Modern secular thought usually dismisses such beliefs as superstitious projections. Modern science has brought welcome enlightenment on many matters, but on what lies beyond death science can neither prove nor disprove anything. We are essentially in the same position as people were centuries or millennia ago. All beliefs come back to experience in the widest and deepest meaning of that term: the "funded experience of the human race" is the best guide we have. The process of bereavement, practiced the world over, is a solid part of that experience.

In my book *Showing How: The Act of Teaching* I include the languages of mourning and comforting as two of the therapeutic languages used in teaching. Unless we learn both to mourn for someone we love and to comfort someone who is in mourning, we are likely to be blocked from learning how to deal with other important things in life.

Mourning and other therapeutic languages require ritual forms. If there are no rituals, emotions are either repressed or else emerge in disorderly and dangerous ways. The modern era has not dealt kindly with any rituals, but this is especially the case with those rituals that surround death. We still have funerals that are carried out with attention to ritual detail. But a process of bereavement lasting days, weeks, and months afterwards has been more difficult to sustain. It is widely assumed that within a very short time after the funeral "you should get over it," "put that behind you," and "pull yourself together."

Each of the religious traditions recognizes the need to take time; "every cell of the body has to be informed of what has been lost." Such time needs markers that gradually become less frequent from the first day to the first year's anniversary. The conventional wisdom in today's textbooks and popular psychology is that each person is different so that to have any stipulations about a bereavement process is to limit individual freedom. Rituals do need some flexibility of application, but the solution to mechanical rigidity is not to abandon the ritual. An abandonment of ritual does nothing to enhance personal freedom.

Each culture has its own distinctive patterns of mourning, but some themes cut across most cultures. For example, weeping and crying aloud are the common reaction to being grief-stricken. Most religions caution against *excessive* manifestations of grief. The Talmud says "do not mourn overmuch," even while Jewish tradition lays out a detailed pattern for mourning. *The Tibetan Book of the Dead* condemns wailing as excessive; it is especially concerned with the practice of sacrificing an animal as part of mourning. The instruction warns against taking out your sorrow due to a human death by putting an animal to death.[13] The noted anthropologist Ruth Benedict cites a more extreme example of this tendency: the chief of the Kwakiutl tribe mourned the death of his sister by killing several warriors in a neighboring tribe.[14] We moderns do not react in such direct fashion, but surely much of the violence in the world comes from unrelieved grief. We lack religious rituals that allow expressions of grief without an embarrassing loss of control and without violence toward oneself or others.

I said above that the stages of mourning are better established than are stages of dying. People often die suddenly and, whatever may flash before their minds in a split second, it is difficult to imagine their experiencing the stages of dying that Kübler-Ross described. In contrast, people do not have sudden bereavement, even though the process of bereavement can begin with a sudden and almost unbearable shock. That initial shock is inevitably followed by months of grief. Those who think that they have avoided grief are likely to discover a few years later the need to do "grief work"; otherwise they come down with bodily diseases, whose connection to grief has been documented in the last half century.[15]

The stages of grief, like stages of dying, are threefold: a no to death which is a yes to life, followed by a yes to death which is a no to life, followed by a yes to life which encompasses death. As with the dying person, the mourner can go back and forth several times in the first two stages before finding a resolution in the third. Thus, there can be five, seven, or nine stages.

The first stage—a no to death—is a denial which is to be expected even when the loved person is very old or has been sick for a long time. The shock caused by a death can be much greater in situations when the death was completely unexpected. Probably the worst case is the sudden death of one's child. In his autobiography, Mark Twain described the death of his twenty-four-year-old daughter Sally: "The intellect is stunned by the shock and but gropingly gathers the meaning of the words. The power to realize their full import is mercifully wanting. The mind has a dumb sense of vast loss—that is all. It will take mind and memory months and possibly years to gather the details and thus learn and know the whole extent of the loss."[16]

The bereavement period following the funeral is intended to allow the words slowly to sink into the mind and heart. During this time one says no to life, withdrawing from much of one's usual involvements. But while it is important to be left alone when one wishes, a community should remain on the periphery to provide a listening ear or a conversational partner when they are wanted. Being *wanted* and being asked for do not always correspond here; the mourner may not voice the need for company. The offering of companionship to the mourner has to be made in an unobtrusive way. When the deceased is a child, communication between the parents is crucial; nothing strains a marriage like the death of a son or a daughter. Time does not heal all wounds unless it is accompanied by reflection, communication, and understanding.

Harold Kushner, commenting on the book of Job, says that Job's friends did two things right: they showed up and they listened—for several days. They went wrong only when Job asked "why," which they took to mean that they should supply an explanation.[17] There are many right things that one can say to a grieving person, but there are a few things that are wrong (for example, "God took your mommy because he loves her"). Trying to explain to someone why the death of a beloved person is really for the best is not usually a good idea.

Finally, the mourner comes to a place where life gradually wins out over depression and despair. One does not return to the same old things; instead, one finds a new life with a dimension that had been missing. One becomes capable of giving comfort to other mourners. Sometimes it is the memorial service after a year that helps to draw a line ending the period of no to life, yes to death.

If the person was very close, then life will continue to carry an element of sorrow that may never be assuaged. With the old, the death of one spouse is sometimes quickly followed by the death of the other, suggesting that the bond to the dead is stronger than that with the living. But even then the yes may be to a new life that includes reunion through death with the loved one. Love is stronger than death, and despite death's seeming victories, the process of bereavement is the reminder that death is followed by life.

Response

MARIA: Several years ago, I was teaching a course on parents' involvement in the religious education of their children. One of the class members was awaiting the birth of his first child. The four months of our course coincided with the final four months of that pregnancy, and Frank's deepening involvement in issues of birth and childhood often made those issues more real for all of us. The joy and community we experienced together was shattered, however, when the baby was stillborn, and joyful anticipation of the future changed overnight to grief and then to mourning. I date my conviction of the importance of mourning in religious education to that tragic occurrence. Mourning educates us not only about the death of children, but about the entirety of life.

As Gabriel has already pointed out, death is a developmental certainty in human life, and dying is one of the two greatest moments in religious education. The deep mental and physical anguish we feel on the occasion of death leaves us with feelings of desolation and loneliness that must be expressed. My contribution to this essay is a reflection on this expression, mourning, which is a response to the experience of bereavement and the inevitable presence of the grief that accompanies loss. I want to explore mourning not only as a subject in education, but as a process of education too.

What Mourning Is

The poet John Keats described mourning as

> Most like the struggle at the gate of death
> Or liker still to one who should take leave of pale, immortal death
> And with a pang as hot as death is chill
> With fierce convulse, die into life.[18]

Mourning begins with the recognition that a struggle has begun that may, indeed, cause fierce convulsions in our souls and in our bodies that provide entry into another realm of life.

In 1942, a tragic fire swept a Boston night club called the Cocoanut Grove. Within thirty minutes, 492 people were dead. After the occurrence, Erich Lindemann interviewed survivors and bereaved, and gave us one of the first extended descriptions of what is involved in grieving and mourning. Six characteristics were especially evident: (1) somatic distress—pains in the body; (2) intense preoccupation with the image of who and what was lost; (3) guilt; (4) a disconcerting lack of warmth; (5) disorganized patterns of conduct; and (6) the feeling you no longer fit.[19]

I find a remarkable degree of correspondence in the presence of these characteristics not only in the bereaved of that tragedy, but in many educational situations today. In this brief response, I will comment on this presence as a part of learning; as a needed prelude to action; and as an aspect of developmental theory.

Mourning is a part of learning. Whether our major role as educators is as schoolteachers, as parents, or in the daily exchanges of friendship, it is generally not too long before life teaches us that genuine learning includes genuine mourning. St. Paul reminds us that when we were children we thought as children, but in the adult years, we put away the things of childhood and replaced simple, uncomplicated knowledge with a world of complexity, ambiguity, and paradox. Over the last fifty years, in all religious communions, this putting away has become evident. In Catholic Christianity, for example, the easy and unquestioned truths of childhood have been a catalyst for mourning as these truths have given way to newer expressions, often leaving the religious believer in a state of genuine loss. The reforms and renewal following Vatican II, although mandated and accepted in most places, have proved painful for many in the church. In Protestant Christianity, biblical study has caused not only enlightenment but pain, as different schools of criticism (e.g., form criticism, literary criticism) have removed the surety and security that once accompanied the *un*-critical acceptance of many biblical texts.

Religious educators need to be aware that resistance to new learning is often a manifestation of grief. However, we also need to be aware that when new learning occurs, the grief may have other causes. It may be due to the immensity of the effort required to seek justice, love kindness, and walk humbly with God. As the world of the twenty-first century arrives, for example, the disparity between the lives of the rich and the poor, the imbalance of resources between the strong and the weak, may cause reactions that are not only akin to mourning but actually are manifestations of mourning itself: stuckness, anger, the feeling of being overwhelmed. Ironically, in a world tempted to go mad with acquisition, mourning may be a very healthy response. But it may also be a necessary first step in further education.

Mourning is often a necessary prelude to action. A famous, but to my mind incorrect, proverb is often cited when people are claimed by mourning. This is the adage, "It is better to light one candle than to curse the darkness." In contrast, many of us discover that we cannot act, we cannot light candles, unless expressions of mourning are legitimized and noted; and unless we do take time to curse the darkness surrounding us. These expressions can be as simple as a go-around in an adult education setting where participants are asked to complete the sentence, "One thing I miss today that was present in the church of my youth is ______." They can also be as lengthy and as complicated as preparing for and carrying out a service of remembrance at the one-year or five-year anniversary of a church bombing or a church closing—a service that is a necessary preliminary to dying into new life.

I once heard Elie Wiesel, the writer and Nobel Laureate, note a variation on this theme. Speaking about the Holocaust to a group of graduate students, he counseled them to have an attitude of sensitivity, adding that wherever we walk, people who are in our immediate company carry immense burdens of grief that are not always noticed by the naked eye. "And therefore," he said to the students, "you must walk gently. You must be sensitive." Our too quick need to *do* something is sometimes too abrupt. It needs always to be tempered by reverence, sensitivity and periods of simple being with one another in daily life.

Mourning is an aspect of developmental theory. Gabriel writes above that much of the violence in the world comes from unrelieved grief. Relative to this topic, Carol Gilligan, in a review of a book on depression in men,[20] highlights the necessity for mourning by men who are overcome by depression. Gilligan notes that depression is a sign of the inability to mourn and actually is a response to loss. But because from their boyhood men are taught not to cry, to forgo closeness and tenderness, and to allow privilege to fill them instead, they are often impelled to deal with their grieving by terrible and damaging violence. Gilligan's comment that the author takes the men's movement into a dialogue about gender that can vastly benefit both men and women is a reminder to listen—and to mourn—from one of the most significant developmental theorists of our time.

I want to add to this the hunch that much of the failure to become our best and deepest selves developmentally is also the result of unrelieved grief. In my own adult life, for example, I have become aware that my childhood loss of my father to abrupt, sudden death would have been even more traumatic without the profound and healing Catholic rituals of mourning that sustained my mother, my brother, and me. At one time or another, everyone is marked by similar wounds. Ignoring their sources in the deaths of our own lives as well as in the experiences of those we educate is an ignorance stage in educational development that we cannot afford.

FOR REFLECTION AND RESPONSE

1. Choose one experience of death that has had an impact on your life. What did you learn from it?
2. Gabriel describes a university course on death. What are some ways you would consider introducing death in elementary and/or high school?
3. In transcending what is natural, how can we human beings understand and work with the rhythms of nature and other-than-nature (e.g., art, religion) concerning death?
4. What does it mean to you to "see death as a friend"?
5. Reread the passage from Dietrich Bonhoeffer on page 96. What do you want to remember from this passage? What does it lead you to hope?
6. Describe an experience of mourning—from your own or others' experience—that for you was healing and affirming of both living and dying.

part three
SPIRITUALITY

Chapter 7

SPIRITUALITY AND ITS ROOTS

The Spiritual and Today's Spirituality

GABRIEL: Our title for this chapter is intended to suggest a parallel with chapter 4 on the historical roots of development. Spirituality, like development, can be one of the main allies of religious education, but a misconceived spirituality can be a chief competitor. The spiritual has a much longer history than does development, while it is also having an expansive renaissance. A *new* spirituality wishes to address the novel situation of the present, but it necessarily carries with it meanings from the past. It is important to be aware of that history and to recall how recent is today's widespread interest in spirituality.

In this chapter I lead off with a historical and philosophical reflection on the spiritual as a backdrop to today's spirituality. In the second section of the chapter, Maria focuses on some of the essential components of this spirituality. In the third section, I describe a meaning of spirituality in Christian history and use the environmental movement as a test case of spirituality. In section four, Maria attends to specific exercises and practices that nourish Christian spirituality.

In 1963, Paul Tillich published the third volume of his *Systematic Theology,* a book that dealt with God as spirit. In the opening pages of the book, Tillich offered this caution: "It seems that, while it may be possible to rescue the term 'spirit,' the adjective 'spiritual' is lost beyond hope. This book will not even attempt to re-establish its original meaning."[1] Anyone who was inclined at that moment to disagree with Tillich's judgment would most likely have been skeptical of his optimism about saving "spirit." Spirit, spiritual, and the narrower cognate "spirituality" seemed to be relics of centuries past.

At the time that Tillich's book was published, I was a doctoral student interested in historical curiosities. I took a course that year entitled "Advanced Spirituality." The course was mainly a study of the sixteenth-century Spanish mystics, Teresa of Avila and John of the Cross. Even within a school of theology, the half dozen of us who elected to study spirituality were thought to have a peculiar taste. Consider the contrast today. In the 1990s one could hardly avoid discussions of spirituality on television and in popular magazines. Every large bookstore has a wall that is stacked full of the most recent books on spirituality. What has caused this eruption? Is this interest in spirituality good or bad? Is the interest just a passing fad?

I think that the driving force behind the emergence or reemergence of the spiritual is the desire for a unifying idea. There is a deeply felt need for something that would overcome the fragmentary character of contemporary life. The spiritual holds out the promise of healing our world's splits. The human world has become physically smaller with the invention of the jet plane, television, and the Internet. Economically, the world is, to the benefit of the rich, united. In most other ways, however, we confront puzzling differences and dangerous conflicts.

One of the few terms that runs throughout the histories of both East and West (as well as indigenous cultures that may not be included in this division of the world) is "spiritual." In recent centuries, however, it has been the East that kept alive the spiritual. The recent rediscovery of the spiritual in our culture, starting in the 1960s, came mainly from the East, from explorations of Eastern thought by young people in North America and Europe, as well as from meetings of religious scholars where Hindus, Buddhists, and Muslims often took the lead.[2]

Related to this East-West spiritual bridge is the promise that the spiritual can overcome the dualism of religious and secular worlds. About two decades ago, when I started teaching a course on mysticism, I was struck by how many students would say that they were interested in the spiritual, although they did not consider themselves religious. They were using "spiritual" to transcend the Western dichotomy of religious and secular. This preference for spiritual over religious has now become commonplace, not only in college classrooms but in assemblies with people of any age and any background.

It has become socially acceptable to be interested in the spiritual, while religion has at best held its ground as a stabilizer of the social order. But very often religion as the unifier of one group is thought to breed political intolerance in the wider world. Religion's association with conflict, throughout human history and continuing to the present, cannot be denied. Thus it is understandable why many of the young, and some not so young, place their hope in the spiritual to provide the benefits but not the narrowness of religion.

The attempt to overcome the religious-secular dichotomy suggests several other variations on the theme of cultural division. One division in the modern West has been between philosophy and religion. "Spiritual" has a history in both philosophy and religion that now allows for a better conversation between these disciplines than has been possible for several centuries. On another flank, science and philosophy have also opened up a new avenue of discourse in this century, aided by talk about spiritual reality. Who could have imagined at the beginning of this century that at century's end physicists would be writing books on spirituality?[3]

I think that the term "spiritual" is functioning today as "natural" did in the eighteenth century. Almost everyone can subscribe to some meaning of the term, and it is thought best not to push for any clear definition. Throughout most of the seventeenth and eighteenth centuries science and religion were not in conflict; they were joined by their common affirmation of nature and the natural. (Their common enemy was magic.)[4] Today the vague, generalized meaning of "spiritual" is seen to be an advantage, the reason why there is not likely to be a "spiritual war" (while dozens of religious wars still rage). Nevertheless, a premature unity based on a high level of generality can breed its own illusions.

Although the spiritual lays claim to being the great unifier, every term carries a historical baggage of excluding its opposite. For a word to mean *x,* it has to deny *not-x.* There is nothing wrong with this negation so long as one is aware of the exclusion, particularly when the term is being used with pretensions to an all-inclusiveness. Whatever people may *intend* the term spiritual to mean today, its history situates it in two main oppositions: the inner as opposed to the outer, and the non-material as opposed to the material or bodily. One can try to recast these oppositions, and words do indeed change their meanings over time. But one has to move from the strength of a term and find allies to overcome its weakness, which is why spirituality needs religion. The divorce of spirituality from religion leads to a disastrous escapism. Religion, with its historical emphasis upon external acts, is a necessary restraint upon the spiritual drive to unity.

Do we need another term that would join the spiritual and religious? It might be desirable, but history supplies no heir apparent, and the attempt to invent a term will only result in the kind of jargon that threatens to overwhelm books on spirituality. Instead of looking higher for a more abstract unifier, I am proposing that we dig down in the earth for a rooted spirituality, one nourished by centuries of religious practice. The result will not be a grand system that transcends all divisions. The more modest aim is to find a way of living in today's world that draws upon dimensions of reality that are easily obscured by the "busy-ness" of the ordinary. While the lifeblood of religious education is spirituality, the converse should not be forgotten: spirituality's expression has to be guided by a lifelong and lifewide education in religious living.

The Greek and Hebrew roots of the spiritual are different but not incompatible. The main image in biblical history is the breath of life; spirit is quite literally the air we breathe. Spirit is the within of things, it is what animates a living body. The origin of the Greek philosophical idea of spirit was probably similar; spirit has an affinity with soul and nature, all three arising from the experience of a living being. The Greeks, however, moved in the direction of philosophical-scientific concepts. In the realm of abstract ideas, matter and spirit were separable and often opposed. The radical opposition of matter and spirit has been a tendency not only in Greek philosophy but in Eastern thought and in many modern forms of idealism.

Along with an impulse toward dualism, philosophy and religion have also sought ways to overcome the division. One of the most impressive attempts at unity was the neoplatonism of Plotinus. Inspired by elements of Plato's thought and absorbing ideas from India, Plotinus created a grand design in which matter existed only as a limit of spirit. Plotinus's thought, especially as mediated by Pseudo-Dionysius and Thomas Aquinas, provided the philosophical unity of Christian theology throughout the Middle Ages. The mystical tradition of the West, which is still very much alive today, is traceable to Plotinus's philosophy of a One beyond being. The human quest within this design is to return to the One from which all things have emanated.[5]

Many young people who are interested in spirituality may have to travel around the world before they can discover their own history. But they ought to be given the chance to encounter the great mystical teachers of the Middle Ages and the Reformation. They ought to know that the quest for a unity beyond all divisions of nation, gender, and species is not a creation of the twentieth century. Many people do respond to challenging works in the history of Christian spirituality. The extraordinary interest in Meister Eckhart, perhaps the greatest mystical teacher of medieval Christianity, is evidence that many people respond to a religiously deep spirituality.[6] One of Eckhart's twentieth-century successors, Thomas Merton, was building a bridge between Buddhism and Christianity before his untimely death in 1968; his books continue to inspire a new generation of readers. So too do many of Merton's successors who, while deeply rooted in their own Christian, Jewish, or Buddhist traditions, carry on a dialogue that is now worldwide. Thomas Moore's *Care of the Soul* has been notable among several best sellers on spirituality in drawing heavily upon fourteenth- and fifteenth-century spiritual masters.[7]

Components of Today's Spirituality

MARIA: Over the past two decades, as I have introduced courses, seminars, or workshops on spirituality to a wide range of audiences, I have found it helpful to present a working description of spirituality. Today, since people use many definitions and many meanings to delineate spirituality, this has not always been easy. Still, I have found it not inappropriate to refer to spirituality as "our way of being in the world" and then to add to that the phrase, "in the light of the Mystery at the core of the universe." I am trying to do several things in the choice of that language: emphasize the this-worldliness of today's spirituality; note that spirituality is generally connected to a "way" or a set of ways (or disciplines); broaden existence in the world beyond doing to being; and stress the sacred character of existence by referring to Mystery—the cloud of unknowing or not-knowing[8]—that suggests to us we are always in the company of something "more." At the same time, I try to make it clear that the search for a language true to spirituality is never complete, never finished. As the Buddhist teaching puts it:

> However hard you search for it
> You will never be able to grasp it.
> You can only become it.[9]

Working from this meaning, I have discovered that being in the world in the light of Mystery has several essential components. First, spirituality is both *personal* and *communal,* or better, it is *personal/communal.* The personal/communal character of spirituality is illuminated by the teaching that although the impulse in mysticism is to pray to the Sacred Other, "Thou all, I nothing," it is more true to the human condition to amend that and to say, "Thou all, I *not quite* nothing." For we human beings are persons, with all the greatness and responsibility that personhood suggests. An ancient rendering of this same conviction is found in the psalms that bear the question, "What are human beings that you are mindful of them?" (Ps. 8:4) and respond with the answer, "You have made them a little lower than God and crowned them with glory and honor" (Ps. 8:5). A contemporary rendering reminds us that the greatness of being persons lies in our capacity to be brothers and sisters to one another since *to be is to be with.* In other words, the rootedness of our spirituality derives from being creatures bonded with the rest of creation—persons in community.

The next two components of spirituality flow from this personal/communal dimension. Essential to contemporary spirituality is its concern with *justice* and its concern with *the non-human universe.* Justice is so important to spirituality that we spend all of chapter 8 on its centrality. Therefore I will not comment on justice here, except to point to it as part of the inscape of each dimension that follows. On the other hand, concern for the nonhuman universe has made a stunning recovery in our time after centuries of neglect as a component in the western world's spiritual life. The consideration of religious traditions beyond our own has made those of us in the "developed" world aware that both personally and communally, we are responsible to the land, the air, and the other animals since our destinies are irrevocably intertwined.

At one time the sacramental imagination flourished in Christian spirituality, acting as the "persistently central assumption that certain objects or actions or words or places belonging to the ordinary spheres of life may convey to us a unique illumination of the whole mystery of our existence, because in these . . . something numinous is resident, something holy and gracious."[10] Earth, water, fire, wind: these were ordinary realities that impelled us to awe. With modern industrial practice, however, many of these ordinary spheres of life have been injured and, along with the pollution of water and the dissolution of part of the ozone layer, we have lost the wisdom that directed us to look for holiness in our environment.

Our own times are recapturing that wisdom; it is no longer unusual to come across prayers to the wind or to the waves. A spiritual director will counsel a directee to go out and "pray a tree." Indigenous peoples have been crucial as our teachers in this reclaiming, whether they are North American natives or aboriginal inhabitants of Australia. The Balgo ancestors of some of the latter went in search of living water and kept stopping along the way to dance and sing. But when they found the living water they named it, and their song finished: " . . . and they went underground / and they are there today / they found the Living Water."[11] Today, indigenous peoples are helping the rest of us to rediscover the living water in our own lives and communities through a renewed spirituality.

Another component of contemporary spirituality is *age*—and *Age.* The first refers to the different ages of life: childhood, adolescence, young, middle, and older adulthood, elderhood. As I have worked in spirituality education, I have discovered that different developmental circumstances—adolescence or new parenthood or promotion to a managerial job or an empty nest or retirement—contribute to different emphases in spirituality throughout the life cycle. Although each of us carries our complete selves within us, from inner child to inner elder, our "way of being in the world" and our relation to Mystery are inevitably altered by the changing circumstances of our lives. Some facets that we have overlooked come to the forefront, taking center stage, even as other aspects lie dormant for a while only to reemerge. A new marriage or a new baby is the center of our spirituality at one time in our life; a bout with cancer claims our attention at another. Going forth to make our fortune demands a different form of prayer from the returning home of later life. The depths of our souls respond uniquely to the loss of a spouse or beloved companion who has journeyed with us through the years. So *age* is a central component throughout our lives in shaping and reshaping our spirituality.[12]

But so too is *the Age:* the time in which we live. Because our spirituality is not only personal but communal, the historical emphases of the religious traditions that nourish us (Christianity, Buddhism, Judaism) have a spiritual impact on our lives. The church of the first centuries, for example, was a community of martyrs and outlaws until Constantine made Christianity legal; the impact of monasticism brought about withdrawal from society through the vocations of monk or nun; scholasticism made sure spirituality was in the mind as well as the heart; the discovery of a "new world" made exploration central even as it spelled tragedy for many native peoples; the Reformation shook the entire system to its foundations. Our own time, with its stress on liberation and connectedness, has influenced the ways we exist in the world and has reshaped many of our spiritual "ways." At the same time, as Gabriel has already pointed out, historical study of other Ages from today's vantage point has brought us in touch with ancestors in the faith and surfaced the stories of women and men we did not know, or knew only slightly. In this context, Gabriel has mentioned Meister Eckhart, Teresa of Avila, and John of the Cross. Added to them today are representatives of still other Ages such as the Beguines, Hildegard of Bingen, and Julian of Norwich.[13]

A fifth component of contemporary spirituality is its reliance on *experience,* notably on those aspects of human experience that have been neglected in the past: the experiences of women, of children, of the poor; the experiences of caring for persons with disabilities or for those whose voices have been silenced for political or economic reasons. Experience as essential to spirituality is clarified by a related component, the emphasis on communal and corporate *rituals* that are either being created anew from the fabric of today's experience or re-created from the shards of shattered or discarded practices now seen as relevant. Today men and women routinely design rituals that are nonsexist, inclusive, participatory, and attentive to fire, water, earth, and land. At the same time, they also design rituals that are largely bodily and/or nonverbal, relying on dance, movement, sitting, chanting and song, and incorporating long periods of silence. The power and influence of Creation Spirituality signifies the hunger for such ritual;[14] those filled shelves of modern bookstores describing such rituals, to which

Gabriel has already alluded, signify the fact that these hungers are being addressed.

Finally, *new or redefined understandings of the Sacred* pervade spirituality today. At the same time that the Sacred One or the Holy or Thou continues to be addressed in the prayer arena of spiritual life, awareness also exists that in the end, no words are possible or fitting to address the Holy. Persons live comfortably in this awareness, content to be silent before the great Mystery at the core of the universe. Paradoxically, however, powerful attention is being given to celebration of and address to the Divine or the Sacred under a range of titles. The Goddess is invoked and addressed in contemporary spirituality by drawing on images such as virgin, mother, and crone; by probing the mythologies of Greece and Rome; by attending to Hindu reverence for Kali and her incarnations as Devi, Mali, Shakti. ("We all come from the Goddess; and unto Her we shall return:" I have sung—and led—that chant many times.)

The female face of the Sacred is recalled, especially, in biblical evocations of Wisdom and of Spirit/Sophia, even as, in Christianity, the Holy Spirit is coming to the fore as the Spirit often does in millennial times. Spirit comes not only as a feminine presence, but as a reminder to Christians of the God Who arrives at Pentecost.[15] As such, a spirituality of the Holy Spirit is developing as church people remember the Person of the Trinity associated with breath, wind, fire, and water; the One who is actively present in human life in the charisms (or gifts), roles, and ministries of persons; the One who is evoked (in the Sequence for Pentecost) as washing the stained soul, watering the parched, and healing the wounded.

These seven components, then, act as clues to a new or renewed spirituality. The personal/communal; justice; the nonhuman universe; age/Age; experience; ritual; and new understandings of the Sacred are interpretive keys not only to the spirituality we have received from the past; but to the ones we are creating in the present and to those that will constitute our ways of being in the world in the light of the Mystery that is not only here, but is still coming.

Spirituality in Christian History

GABRIEL: I do not disagree with Maria's description of spirituality as "our way of being in the world." The question that this description raises for me is why this word rather than others—for example, religion, philosophy, manners, style, outlook? What does the term spirituality offer that is distinctive?

I suggested earlier in this chapter that spirit and spiritual have long and varied histories in both Eastern and Western thought. The common root for spirit/spiritual is the breath of life or the inner principle of living beings. In this section, I wish to focus more narrowly on "spirituality," a term obviously derived from spirit/spiritual but also having its own history.

The term spirituality has always been linked with human interiority, the sense of a space within that sets off the human being from its closest kin. That inner self is always linked to outward expressions, but in quite divergent ways. The outward activities can be understood as merely the means to protect the inner life from external intrusions, or the outward activities can link the depth of human reflection to a wide realm of political and environmental concerns. I will use the contemporary environmental movement as a test case for a spirituality. A Christian spirituality is my main concern, but spirituality of its nature opens out to a conversation with other religious traditions.

"Spirituality," with its distinctive reference to interiority, had to emerge slowly in history. Although it is now difficult for us to imagine the experience, human beings did not at first sharply distinguish an inner life and an outer world. It is a relatively recent experience for a human being to look inside at a separate space where thinking and choice are imagined to transpire. Socrates in Greek philosophy and the prophets in the Bible probably represent the breakthrough stage in Western history to an inner life of unique individuals. Even then, centuries passed before human beings in general grasped an inner life as an inheritance of human birth. We misunderstand Plato, for example, if we assume that his "ideas" were mental as opposed to physical, located inside the mind rather than outside.

The transformation of Plato's ideas into an inner world was left to one of Plato's greatest followers, Augustine of Hippo.[16] I said above that Plotinus provided the philosophical unity for the Middle Ages. Augustine, a near contemporary of Plotinus, provided related meanings of religion and spirituality to the thousand years of Western history that followed him. To a large extent, Protestant and Catholic Christians are linked today through their common Augustinian heritage.

Augustine's life, one of searching for the true home of the human heart, is reflected in his writings. In the 1960s, Augustine was sometimes called the first "existentialist." That title seems a long stretch; calling him the "first modern" seems a fairer assessment. Hannah Arendt credits him with the first clear concept of "free will," even if under the bondage of sin.[17] Augustine was a psychologist, journalist, and philosopher of history. In his

Confessions, he used the techniques of the novel and autobiography many centuries before these genres became common.

There is a famous moment in the *Confessions* that is especially relevant to my concern here. Augustine comes across his teacher Ambrose who is reading a book. Augustine remarks that people are astounded by the fact that Ambrose reads without moving his lips.[18] This tiny detail is revelatory of a new era in human history: reading silently to oneself was a development tied to a new interiority. Spirituality in the full sense of the word was now possible. Not surprisingly, all uses of "spirituality" in Western history go back to Augustine. His name was always invoked by the founders of schools of spirituality. These spiritualities were usually tied to monastic orders, such as the Benedictines and Franciscans.

Augustine has taken a lot of criticism in recent times, especially from women writers. Some of his peculiar quirks concerning sin and sex unfortunately found their way into Western theology. But in Augustine's writings, an emphasis on interiority never disconnected him from the world about him. In the hands of lesser figures, the spiritual life—the practice of spirituality—could come to mean an escape from politics, bodiliness, and ordinary life. With too close an identification of spirituality and the monastic orders, spirituality was considered outside the life of the ordinary Christian. In the first uses of "spirituality" in the English language, the term is contrasted to "temporality."[19] The very idea of interiority ran this risk: the danger that in affirming the interior, one was negating the exterior ("the world").

Augustine does share some blame for a peculiar choice of imagery. Although he seeks God in the interior of his soul, he equates the inner with the higher.[20] On any logical basis, this makes no sense to me. But Augustine had absorbed what was a common image: God is higher. That God is greater, that God is more powerful, loving or wise, no Christian, Jew, or Muslim can deny. But is higher better? From shortly after Augustine straight on to Kohlberg, "higher is better" has meant going up a ladder above the pettiness of the everyday physical world to a rational, disengaged, and "spiritual" outlook.

Contrary to a widespread assumption in today's ecological literature, Christianity did not install "man" over "nature." This seventeenth-century language is anachronistically read into the Bible and the literature of the Middle Ages. But Christianity did assume that higher is better, that God must be above. When Enlightenment thinkers tried to replace Christianity with a secular philosophy, they installed "man," the rational individual, in the place of God; thus "man" was now thought to be higher, placed outside and above an object called "nature." Contemporary writing, while castigating Christianity, has absorbed its unfortunate image that higher is better. So long as "man and nature" are the terms of discussion there is no way to rethink the relation of human and nonhuman. It is ironic that Francis of Assisi, today's patron saint of nature, never used the word "nature" in his writings. As G. K. Chesterton writes of Francis: "He did not call nature his mother; he called this donkey his brother and this bird his sister."[21]

Francis's sentiment is a key to a rich Christian spirituality in which God is not above man and spirit is not above body. In a religion that believes in a God who creates all things and is present to all creation, God can be imagined as above and below, inside and outside, East and West. None of these directions is a geometric fact but each of them can express a metaphorical truth. Furthermore, what are opposites in geometric terms are religiously a paradoxical pair. Only the paradox of seeming opposites keeps us aware that God is greater than all of our words. For example, nineteenth-century theologians coined the double term transcendent/immanent to describe the relation of human to the divine: presence and distance increase together. The twentieth century's use of "the transcendent" as a name for God misses the point and cannot express the Jewish, Christian, or Muslim belief in the One who is beyond all names and at the same time is closer to us than we are to ourselves (Augustine) or closer to you than the great vein in your neck (the Qur'an).

Any spirituality today has to be aware of past pitfalls, deficiencies not easily avoided. Interiority has to be linked to a historical tradition, to a disciplined community life, and to a concern for all creatures both human and nonhuman. That kind of spirituality is present throughout the history of Christianity, although it is sometimes obscured or relegated to the fringe. Protestant Christianity for a long time had a bias against spirituality because of its close association with the corruption of the medieval monastery. That has changed now as Protestants and Catholics have tried to recover the best of the whole Christian tradition.[22] A serious dialogue with the distinctive spirituality of the Eastern church is still in the future. The recovery of the richest strand of Christian spirituality is aided as Christians learn from others. In their struggle to hold together inner and outer, Christians can be helped by Buddhists to develop contemplative practice, while Christians can learn from Jews about external struggles against injustice.

We cannot simply take over the practices of another religious group. The time and manner of Muslim prayer would not mean the same thing if they were imitated by Christians. A Christian nevertheless can appreciate the disciplined prayer life of a Muslim or a Jew and consider doing something comparable in Christian terms. The danger in the current craze for spirituality is that some people try to invent their own spirituality with a cafeteria-style choosing. The result has no historical roots, but it allows the individual to proclaim a concern for the whole world, not just one religious tradition. What could be better than embracing the whole world?

The answer in the Bible is that one can only embrace the universe by helping the neighbor who is in need. (I think a similar sentiment can be found in Islam and Buddhism.) The neighbor can be one's kinsman; it can also be a total stranger or even a wounded animal. There is no imposed limit on a vision of the universe, but vision has to be tied to concrete acts in the present.

The people today who wish to save the whole world—not just humanity—should be encouraged. But they need to be reminded regularly that an interior life is needed (to undercut one's egotism) as well as acts of daily kindness to this friend, that stranger, this cat, or that tree. Not everything exists at the same level. Humans are the greatest creatures we know of; they are so not in age or size but in responsibility, a conviction that, far from showing a lack of respect for nonhumans, is the basis of all respect.

A "new spirituality" today, often aligned with concern for the environment, is one of the hopeful signs of our age. The tragedy would be that this movement rejects the Jewish and Christian roots that any spirituality in the West has to draw upon. The real opponent of today's spiritual revival is the deism that arose between 1680 and 1780, a desiccated religion and spirituality that strongly influenced both secular thought and Christian practice. A God who is outside the world, who is known only by inference, and who rules the world by arbitrary laws is now under attack from all sides. The question for the immediate future is whether Christians can engage in a way of life—a spirituality—that manifests a care for all creation, thereby providing an alternative to a well-meaning but rootless spirituality. Without education in Christian sources and living testimony of Christian communities, the emergence of a spirituality equal to the task is unlikely.

Nourishing Spirituality

MARIA: Whenever I teach a course on spirituality, I ask the participants to make a commitment to engage regularly in some definite practice. "Decide on a weekly set of disciplines," I suggest as I ask them to pick from a list that includes such options as spending twenty minutes a day in prayer, contemplation, meditation, silent stillness, or sitting; choosing to travel for one day a week without the use of a car; fasting from solid food at one meal or for one day weekly; offering several hours of service to others; journal writing; Sabbath keeping.[23] In that assignment, which assumes they take the practice of spirituality seriously, I am drawing on what I take to be two of its essential elements. The first is that in every religious tradition, spirituality has always been associated with some kind of regular practice or discipline. The second is that such practice must incorporate both attentiveness to human interiority and attentiveness to outward expression—the link Gabriel describes as bringing together the depth of humanity with the realms of social, political, and environmental concerns.

Three Sets of Practices

One way to distinguish between practices or disciplines is to point out that they include at least three sets. One set of practices emphasizes individual interiority; a second emphasizes group ritual; a third emphasizes the integration of these. Among the individual disciplines are prayer, contemplation, and fasting; among the group disciplines are worship, service, and prophetic protest; among the integrating ones are embodiment, memory, and justice. Obviously, there are many more and this list is not exhaustive. In addition, even in this listing the disciplines overlap. Prayer, for example, can be practiced alone, with others, or as a means of integrating body and spirit. Prophetic protest can be by one person or by a group of people, and it can be a powerful source of ending divisions or integrating. Attending to memory can be a solitary activity between a person and the Source of Wisdom or a group activity where a great number of people bring together past and present. So there are no hard and fast boundaries. Still, it remains true that the point of departure for each discipline is slightly different, as is its emphasis or focus.

Among the *individual disciplines,* the primary one is prayer, so fundamental that it is often made synonymous with spirituality. We probably pray more than we think we do: an informal "God help us" is, for all its informality, still a prayer. But prayer is generally understood to encompass those actions we take when we pause to *praise* the Holy, acknowledging we did not create the world; to offer *thanks,* acknowledging that all, including our own lives, is gift; to *ask divine help,* acknowledging we are needy creatures; and to ask *forgiveness,* expressing repentance for our lack of love, our lack of responsibility, our refusal to be whole.

As I have already indicated, prayer is not the only individual discipline: this first set also comprehends contemplation, meditation, centering, sitting, fasting. Centering, nonetheless, has a close relation to prayer. It is a process that begins with quiet, relaxed sitting as a person attempts to become aware of his or her inner calm. The process demands that persons wait on the Sacred Presence within and around them, discovering that after a time a single word may emerge: "yes," "no," "peace," "hope." Centering requires that we repeat the word slowly and effortlessly, a practice that helps us to move into a deeper serenity and mindfulness.

Group disciplines come to the fore when we engage in particular practices and rituals with others. When we participate in worship or liturgy, this is an intensely corporate act, a gathering of the people—for example, to tell the story, break the bread, share the cup, and then go forth in spirit and in truth. The going forth, especially to do the works of feeding the hungry, sheltering the homeless, clothing the naked, and visiting the sick and imprisoned is another form of group discipline. Our own times have seen a reclaiming of these works of mercy as central to spirituality and part of its core. In ordinary, daily life, moreover, people need to remember that much of their lives is devoted to doing exactly these works: feeding, clothing, visiting, and caring for one another. Such works, instead of being thought of as apart from spirituality, are actually a part of it. Similarly, going forth to a job away from home, either because doing that job earns the resources that help to feed and clothe others, or because the work itself contributes to the world in some way, is part of the practice of spirituality too. So is the going forth of children and young people to school in order to learn and to study, since schooling and studying are that person's way of being in the world in the light of the Mystery at the universe's core.

Integrating disciplines are the third set of practices, especially those that bring individual and group together. Some are integrating because they wed body and spirit—the practice of art and the practice of play, including sports. The loving and mutual practice of sex is an integrating discipline too, serving both as a great art and as a great form of play. Still other disciplines are integrating because they unite past and present, often healing the past by reflecting on it in the present: through healing memories, through family reunions and reconciliations, through simple requests for and reception of forgiveness on the part of community members toward one another.

But the present can be healed by the past as well. This happens when understanding emerges from the discipline of storytelling that is so essential in Christian and Jewish traditions. The discipline of storytelling is focused on stories of foremothers and forefathers, particularly in the communities of our families. When we know our family's stories, we often discover why the present is as it is, and why we are as we are.

One discipline that does not fit easily into the category of individual or group or integrating discipline is adoration. Perhaps this is because, like the Sacred Itself, adoration acts as a beginning and an end, a top and a bottom, a within and a without for our spiritual lives. Adoration is the discipline through which we acknowledge that we did not create ourselves and we are not in control of the universe. Instead, a Center of everything exists, a Center in which we live and move and have our being. We may name this Center differently: Wisdom, Mother, Goddess, Father, Thou—or we may not name it at all. We may find it very difficult to believe in while raging against its power, even though we recognize a hunger and a need for it within ourselves. During the Holocaust, we are told, the Jews of the camps put the Holy One on trial and found the Holy One guilty. Then they went off to pray.

But the point with reference to spirituality is that without a Center things will fall apart; they will not hold. Without a center, we cannot find our place and we cannot find our peace. And adoration is the discipline that says the Mystery at the core of the universe is our center. Adoration is the discipline that nourishes us by teaching us we are great and beloved creatures, we human beings. But we are not God. Instead, we are here to kneel before Mystery, and that action will help us become fully human.

FOR REFLECTION AND RESPONSE

1. What characteristics of spirituality do you most associate with your own practice of spirituality?
2. What changes or additions would you hope to make in your practice of spirituality in the future?
3. As you have aged, what about your spirituality differs from the spirituality of your childhood or younger adulthood?
4. What have you learned about spirituality from the ancestors in your tradition?
5. What have you learned about spirituality from religious traditions other than your own?
6. What is one thing you would cite as important to tell others about spirituality?

Chapter 8

DOING JUSTICE

MARIA: Some time ago, I was worshiping at a small parish in the South Bronx section of New York City. The quiet meditation time that follows Holy Communion was coming to an end. As it did, the pastor stood and summoned by name a number of men and women in the congregation. They rose and came forward, eventually standing in a semicircle at the front of the church. Then, as the rest of us extended our hands in support and blessing, the pastor moved from one person to the next, anointing and commissioning them to work they had already agreed to. The work was advocacy within the local school district. They had pledged to hold the district administration accountable in developing several long overdue programs for their children. That morning, the congregation ratified that work with many vocal "Amens." As the liturgy ended, the anointed were sent forth to take part in action for justice designed to have an impact on the next generation.

Justice and works that serve justice are the center of this chapter. We first explore the meanings of justice; I reflect on biblical meanings and Gabriel on classical philosophical meanings. Then, I draw some implications for education, and Gabriel concludes the chapter by considering the essential relation between justice and responsibility.

The Bible and Justice

The ritual of commissioning to ministry by the assembled community that I described above is not a new one in Christian tradition; the sacraments of baptism and confirmation have always held pride of place in reminding the anointed and gathered community that it is always and everywhere called to live the gospel and to follow Jesus in doing works that serve justice. This is essential to Christian vocation. But in the second half of this century, in the United States and in the rest of the world, this tradition has been given new force and new energy. The civil rights movements of the sixties and seventies; the end of apartheid in South Africa; the collapse of the Berlin wall; the end of colonialism; the rekindling of feminism; and other rebirths of justice around the globe have forced churches to return to their scriptural roots and to take seriously the teachings and traditions surrounding justice that lie at the core of Christian identity.

For Catholic religious educators, the 1971 Synod of (the world's Catholic) Bishops lifted justice to prominence with the striking reminder that the work of justice is a constituent element of the gospel. For them and other Christian educators, sustained study of the Hebrew Bible over the past hundred years had already recovered the realization that the scriptures were not a series of *texts* about justice so much as they are an entire *treatise* on justice. In contrast to assuming that the meaning of justice arose from the image of a blindfolded woman holding a scale that balances the goods of this world equally, all of us began to realize that this image actually limits the religious meaning of justice. For the justice of God is neither cold nor calculating. Instead it is tempestuous, passionate, and hotheaded. In recent decades, we have been reminded that justice was preached by prophets who were scandalized by the sufferings of widows and orphans forced to live in slums.[1] We have learned that God is "a lover of Justice" (Ps. 99:4); that Jeremiah speaks of God bringing justice to the world and finding it a delight (Jer. 9:23); that Isaiah, asking in what sense God is holy, answers his own question by asserting that God's holiness is *shown* as God's justice (Isa. 5:16). We are told that Amos reports God thundering:

> Even though you offer me your burnt offerings and grain offerings,
> I will not accept them;
> and the offerings of well-being of your fatted animals
> I will not look upon.
> Take away from me the noise of your songs;
> I will not listen to the melody of your harps.
> But let justice roll down like waters,
> and righteousness like an ever flowing stream.
>
> (Amos 5:22–24)

In the New Testament, Jesus aligns himself with these great traditions, citing Isaiah 58 and 61, when he speaks in the synagogue at Nazareth and announces that the Spirit is upon him in proclaiming good news to the poor, release to the captives, freedom to the oppressed, and sight to the blind. Indeed, the summation of his ministry comes in the passage found in Matthew 25, as he reveals himself in the hungry, the naked, the stranger, and the prisoner to whom justice is due: "Even as you did it to one of the least of these, you did it to me" (v. 40).[2]

In the Bible, many words are associated with justice. The Hebrew word for justice is *mishpat,* which has a variety of meanings such as justice, judgment, rights, vindication, deliverance, and custom. Strong evidence exists, however, that originally *mishpat* referred to the restoration of a situation or an environment that promoted equity and harmony—shalom—in a community. It referred not only to awareness of the brokenness in the world, but to the human vocation to repair that brokenness and to recreate a world where justice and peace would embrace.[3] Or, to use more contemporary language, justice meant a world where compassion would be wedded to power, and then everywhere could be called Eden once again.[4]

Education for Justice

In seeking to give flesh to such meanings and such dreams, local religious communities have many forms at their disposal. Each of these forms is essentially *social,* which is to say that justice is always relational, and neither individualistic nor isolated. The forms mirror the range of curricular forms that we wrote about in part 1 of this book, and taken together lead to the fullness that is a just education. These forms are social care, social ritual, social empowerment, and social legislation.[5]

Social Care. Care is a virtue, a power, and a strength that has received considerable attention in recent years. Carol Gilligan, writing on distinctions in moral reasoning between men and women, has alerted educators to an entire ethic of care.[6] Nel Noddings has illuminated the social dimension of care by noting that the exercise of care always involves the one caring as well as the one cared for.[7] And the churches, in individual congregations and parishes, are almost always involved in *pastoral* care, responding to every social need imaginable, from domestic violence to families coping with Alzheimer's to bereavement and grief over the deaths of family members, intimates, and friends.

In connecting care with justice, it needs to be said that all acts of care have an impact on the wider society. Care is rooted in attitudes of relation, receptivity, and response, and these attitudes contribute positively to the social order and the social fabric. We can exercise care toward ourselves and toward our neighbors; we can exercise it in our local communities, as did the parishioners cited above; we can exercise it on a global level. Its most familiar forms are feeding the hungry and ministering to those who are sick or dying. At its best, however, it moves in the direction of helping others help themselves, although it is basically inseparable from the gospel and the ethic of love for God and neighbor.

Social Ritual. Besides the direct forms of ministering exhibited in social care, we educate for and through justice when as groups and communities we come together in prayerfully fashioned ways to insist on services that are missing: holding prayer vigils to petition for police presence, demonstrating in favor of fair housing, fasting for freedom. These rituals of petition and protest as well as others of gratitude and thanksgiving draw on the religious awareness that the whole self, body and spirit, must be involved in the works of justice. Walking in silence or holding a vigil at a prison or courthouse to protest an execution is an act of justice; so too are patterned activities (one meaning of ritual) through which we align ourselves with the victims of violence and suffering.

Helen Prejean, known for her involvement in rituals of both protest against the death penalty and solidarity with crime victims, describes her involvement in one such ritual. She is visiting a victims' assistance organization called Survive, made up of mostly indigent black women trying to cope with the death of sons, daughters, spouses, parents: "Mostly sons—almost all of them killed with guns," says Prejean. As each of the women speaks, "a litany punctuates the testimonies—'Oh Lord . . . Yes, Lord . . . Jesus . . . Say it . . . God makes a way out of no way'—and then the mothers tell of the death of children: of guns; pills; alcohol. Mostly they talk of carrying on."

Recounting her participation in this ritual of prayer, Prejean says that although the sorrow and loss are overwhelming, she doesn't feel devastated. She thinks that may be because for these women, the prayer "God makes a way out of no way" is not an empty, pious sentiment but the bread they eat and the path they walk. It is also the piece most closely related to Prejean's other work for justice—her full-time involvement with an abolitionist group that seeks to eliminate the death penalty.[8]

Social Empowerment. Education for justice can sometimes be limited solely to work for and toward others: direct service that, although alleviating suffering, does not move toward enabling those who are suffering to claim their own power to change social systems and social policies that perpetuate injustice. So a third form of justice education is designed to help others claim their own power. This issue recalls the proverb "give people a fish and they eat today; teach people to fish and they feed themselves in the future."

In the contemporary United States climate of negative response toward recipients of welfare, empowerment as a work of justice must receive priority. At the same time they protest against cuts in aid to the homeless, the unschooled, the poor, or children, local communities need to gather the skills of their more fortunate members and transfer those skills—of literacy, health care (especially prenatal care), and homebuilding—to others so that power is shared, abilities are developed, know-how is enlarged, and injustice is alleviated.

Social Legislation. Education toward justice is prophetic in its attention to care, priestly in its participation in ritual. Still it is incomplete unless it is also political, meaning that it should attend to empowerment. For permanent social change—the redistribution of the goods of God's great earth (which is another meaning of justice)—ultimately occurs only when the imaginations and the energies of people are touched in ways that enable them to refashion existing institutions whenever these institutions prevent people from living complete human lives. Our society does this refashioning through the kind of political action that lobbies to enact just laws and overturn unjust ones.

The mark of a just community is that its members are obviously working in ways that serve justice: this is where the word of justice becomes flesh. It is also the destination of the journeys of care, ritual, and empowerment. Still, even the most just communities are always in danger of succumbing to the infection of inaction that blocks involvement in political life, and in the worst case refuses to take part in it. Such inaction in the face of injustice is a demon that needs to be cast out so that public action may take its place. In turn, that action must be directed to enacting legislation through citizens' lobbies, through monitoring social legislation, through political action committees, and through focusing on pending laws as the subject of prayer. Such action must go on even as others in the community take on the necessary tasks of study, teaching, and instruction that will inform understanding of the desired legislation.

Secular Justice

GABRIEL: My response to Maria's description of biblical justice will parallel the response I made in our chapter on curriculum. That is, I will present the way the modern secular world tends to approach justice. The reason for presenting this view is that it is inevitably part of our experience, especially for those of us who live in the United States. I do not propose that this view is superior to the biblical idea of justice. On the contrary, I think that the biblical idea is a necessary context for the modern view. But the relation of biblical tradition to the rest of our experience raises an issue of method that is crucial for an approach to religious education.

The issue can be illustrated with this quotation from the excellent essay by Daniel Maguire, "Doing Justice to Justice":

> But what then precisely is this justice upon which God puts so high a stake? For one thing, it is utterly un-American in its concept. The United States' concept of justice is that of a blindfolded lady holding a scale which is perfectly balanced. The Bible would have none of that. Biblical justice would rip off that blindfold and check to see who is dickering with the scale. And sure enough it would be discovered that the scales do not balance.[9]

The main problem here seems to be that the scale is not balanced, which in turn is hidden by the existence of a blindfold. Is the problem a tampered-with scale or is it the scale itself? If the image of the scale is the problem, do we reject that image or do we incorporate it within another image?

My starting premise is that the biblical idea of justice is not "un-American." The "American idea" has always been a strange combination of the evangelical and the secular. For the meaning of justice the latter source—a Greco-Roman ideal filtered through eighteenth-century rationalism—has tended to dominate our legal structure. But biblical ideas have never disappeared, and in some eras, including the present one, they have a prominent place in the culture. If the biblical idea itself were "un-American," then it could only be preached in order to denounce the existence of the United States rather than be taught as a way to improve the nation.

Affirmative action programs seem to me an example of the biblical idea of justice that Maria has described. While such programs have recently been out of favor, their existence over a period of three decades has been a remarkable recognition that justice requires something more than a color-blind and gender-blind activity. There has always been opposition to these programs because they go counter to the professed ideal of individual equality. People in the United States are not going to vote against equality, but most people at some level of consciousness grasp that equality alone is insufficient as an answer to injustices in our history.

Equality has been a powerful cry in the modern world and continues to be heard as a protest against governmental oppression. The United States did not invent the idea of equality, but it has been a chief exporter of the ideal. The theoretical elaboration of the ideal of equality came mostly from British and French political writers: Locke, Hume, Rousseau, Mill. Against class privilege, the cry was raised, "one man, one vote." The tragic flaw in U.S. practice was that, according to the Constitution, the black man counted for only three-fifths of a person. What was also missed was that the declaration "all men are created equal" did not ensure justice to women.

The secular philosophical ideal of equality is traceable back to Greek philosophy. In many areas the Bible and Greek philosophy could be blended together by Christian thinkers. On the idea of justice, the two sources do not contradict each other, but they stand in considerable tension. The classic statement of justice is found in Plato's *Republic*, where Plato sets forth the doctrine of four moral virtues: prudence, justice, fortitude, and temperance. Medieval theology took over this description, submerging justice into a philosophical system that was not entirely consonant with the Bible. With our contemporary understanding of biblical justice, we need to consider at what points Plato may need resisting.

The first book of the *Republic* asks, "What is justice?" One of the interlocutors answers that "Justice is the rule of the stronger." The answer is outrageous, but said with irony it may be a helpful reminder of what is often called "justice." Socrates counters this cynical attitude with the principle that justice means "each man according to his due." For describing what that principle entails, the remainder of the *Republic* sets out the description of a perfect state where people know their place and each individual contributes to the peace and harmony of the whole.

One striking feature of Plato's *Republic* is the equality of men and women. At least, the only difference between the sexes is that "one bears, the other begets," a difference that Plato sees as irrelevant to membership in his guardian class.[10] The U.S. military in the 1990s, with the elimination of all gender discrimination, is probably the first attempt in history to follow Plato all the way on this point. Plato's republic depends on virtuous leadership by the best men and women. Justice in the state takes precedence over the happiness of individuals, including the guardians themselves.

The *Republic* still exercises a great influence over modern reformers. The most systematic application is to be found in Marxist Communism, where all men and women are to be comrades and the leaders are to serve the good of the state. Several brutal features of the *Republic* also surfaced in Marxist and other modern experiments. The equality of men and women as envisioned by Plato required the abolition of the family and the extinction of unwanted and defective infants. The most frightening line in the *Republic* is the reply to the question of how to put into practice the plan for a perfect society: "Send everyone out of town who is over ten years old."[11] The leaders in Cambodia during the 1970s may never have read the *Republic,* but they followed its logic when they sent millions of people "out of town," that is, out to the countryside to die.

Equality unrestrained by other considerations can turn ugly and brutal. Australians have a striking image in referring to the "tall poppy syndrome." When someone starts rising above the rest of the crowd, he or she needs to be cut down to the same height as everyone else. In Australia, the United States, and numerous other places today an "egalitarian" society is thought to be highly desirable. Pretensions to superiority based on class are mocked.

With respect to the protection of individual rights, equal treatment before the law is indeed to be treasured. But human life as a whole requires "discrimination," judgments based on quality, not quantity. To help the poor and the dispossessed, we have to recover the positive meaning of "discriminate," which refers to the ability to see color, gender, age, and other factors before deciding whether or not they are relevant to the issue at hand. A biblical justice discriminates about whether equality is the proper measure in particular situations or whether a transforming of the situation is needed.

Implications for Education

MARIA: What we have already written demonstrates that there are many ways to speak of justice. Nevertheless, in this section I want to lift up two additional meanings of justice as particularly important for educators. The first understands justice as fidelity to the demands of all our relationships.[12] The second recognizes that justice means we find out what belongs to whom and give it back.[13] Although these two meanings cannot be separated from one another, they can be distinguished in ways that shed light on justice from complementary and somewhat different perspectives.

Fidelity to Our Relationships. Because justice is essentially social, its practice is a necessary component in our relations. For human beings, the set of relations that justice encompasses is as broad as our lives themselves. Nevertheless, our realization of the range our relations encompass is sometimes kept purely in the realm of *human* relations. Therefore, I want here to single out the relation human beings have to the nonhuman universe: to the trees, the rivers, and the soil, and to the nonhuman animals who share the earth with us.

As this set of relations has become real for many U.S. Americans, we have recognized the indigenous peoples of this country as models and mentors for practicing this aspect of justice, and have turned to the North American natives whose awareness of and reverence for the nonhuman universe was unknown to too many of those who first came to this land during the Age of Discovery. Sometimes the insights of those who loved this land during hundreds of years before Europeans knew of its existence are limited to the poetic realm. We remember those who prayed to the grass, saying that although they knew it would have to bend as their feet trod upon it, it would know by the reverence of those steps that they meant it no harm. Or we recall the native person who knelt by the animal it had killed for food and asked forgiveness before removing its hide. But we do not include our relations to the grass and the other animals as part of the purview of justice, nor do our actions manifest awareness of the moral demands our prayers place on us.

The growing awareness of interconnectedness among all earth's creatures in the past half-century, however, has begun to sharpen the realization that the nonhuman is not here only for our use, nor is our relation to it only one-way. Instead, the partnerships in which humanity is involved go beyond our connections with the other humans to include every flower, every insect, every dog and cat. The Dakota and Lakota peoples have framed their prayers in recognition of this insight over the centuries. At the end of their prayers to the Great Spirit, for example, they use a phrase that functions similarly to the word "Amen" among other religious peoples. In contrast to those who use "Amen" and translate it as "So be it" or "Let it be so," the Dakota use the phrase *Mitakuje Oyasin* at the closing of their prayers, with the unique meaning, "For all our relations." When they pray, it is never only for themselves. It is always in acknowledgment of the great web of connections that binds creation, the web that includes not only humans—the two-leggeds—but the four-leggeds and the wingeds and the gilleds as well. The blessing requested belongs to the earth, the water, and the mountains.

This prayer might also be rendered, "Let justice be done to all our relations." For implicitly it reminds those who pray it that nonhuman creation can be beaten and destroyed, raped and pillaged. The winged creatures can suffer from pesticides or contaminated air. The gilled can die in polluted water. Cattle can feed on the produce of damaged soil. Even when they are part of our prayers, the nonhumans can be left out of our acting for justice. In biblical terms, however, the work of justice includes the demand of these creatures for recognition as heirs to the great gifts of being and existence which belong to the nonhumans as well as the humans.

Justice means we find out what belongs to whom and we give it back. The most immediate meaning of this rendering of the work of justice is the redistribution of resources, notably capital; I highlight this rendering in the chapter on Jubilee that follows this one. Here, however, I want to focus on some of the ways this meaning of justice impacts human beings across generational life, especially in the family setting. Biblical justice is very concerned with the family: it is concerned with families in debt, for example, making it clear that family morality is without meaning if families are split up or dispossessed by economic forces that make them powerless. This situation recalls the "cruel jest" Martin Luther King Jr. once noted: urging people to pull themselves up by their bootstraps despite the fact that they have no boots.

Traditions of justice in the Bible are not directed only to the poorest families in our midst, although the poor must be granted preferential option. They are relevant traditions for all families. Finding out what belongs to whom and giving it back is a counsel that is also directed to the imbalances among the generations in families as well as to families in all economic circumstances.

The counsel belongs, first, to the generations coming after us. In Richard Ford's novel *Wildfire,* for example, a mother tries to teach this meaning of justice to her teenage son. "Your life doesn't mean what you have, sweetheart, or what you get," she tells him. "It's what you're willing to give up. That's an old saying, I know. But it's still true." When he says (understandably) that he doesn't really want to give up anything, she responds with sensitivity that she knows that, but goes on, "Oh well. Good luck." Then she elaborates. "That's really not one of the choices," she says. "You have to give things up. That's the rule. It's the major rule for everything."[14]

It is not only a rule for children, however. It is a rule throughout life. Necessary losses meet us at every juncture—beginning with the loss of the security of the womb for life in the world, continuing on with the loss of the safety of early childhood for the adventure of school, and extending to giving up the home of our parents for one we establish ourselves. Later, if we become parents, we learn to give up authority over our children as those children enter adult life.

But becoming adult also directs attention to finding out what belongs to the generations that have preceded us and giving back to them what is theirs, not ours, on the journey through life in acts of simple—but not easy—justice. This may include returning to our own parents the dreams and wishes they have had for the way we might live our adult lives, or the choice of a marriage partner who is different from the one they would prefer, or the return of their hopes for a career they wish we might choose because it is their wish, not ours. In later life, finding out/giving back has profound meaning as the generations before us begin to age and then to die before our eyes, and we discover that finding out what belongs to whom and giving it back refers to a work that most older adults must do: return the bodies or the ashes of our dead to the earth and the God from whom they've come, even as the next generations will one day do for us.

Finding out what belongs to whom and giving it back reveals interpersonal and intrapersonal dimensions as well. Counselors and others who work with persons abused by domestic and/or sexual violence must often help them to do the difficult work of giving back the guilt and burden and feelings of responsibility for the violence done to them as an aspect of their own healing. Even in the life that has been free of such trauma or violence, however, many men and women discover that there are parts of themselves they have never claimed, and they find out what they must return to themselves in the human search for wholeness. For example, men in our society who have shut down their feelings or "become" their job often stop in their middle years for an extended period when they redress the imbalance in their lives between work and personhood. And women appreciatively and wisely affirm the sentiment whenever someone repeats to them the first words of Jenny Joseph's great poem, "Warning." They too acknowledge that when they are old women they shall *also* "wear purple" because they recognize the justice they must direct to themselves. It is justice found as they restore lost or forgotten parts of themselves and "make up for the sobriety of their youth."[15]

Finally, justice demands that attention be paid to those families who are structurally or institutionally disadvantaged. This is a circumstance for many of us who are both *doers* of the word of justice and *receivers* of the word. For at some time or another, all of us are strangers, or orphans, or widowed, or refugees in a strange land—and in need of the ordinary justice that sees us through medical necessity, accidents, sorrow and loneliness. A marriage ends—through death or divorce; a child dies—through accident or disease; a church is ruined—through malicious arson or neglect; a home is lost—through flood or blizzard. But the human situation is constant. Loss arrives; the imbalance of having and not-having remains; the exchange of life for death and death for life goes on. In all of these events, the work of justice claims us daily as we seek to find out what belongs to whom and to give it back.

Justice and Responsibility

GABRIEL: In my previous section I pointed out a tension between the philosophical ideal of equality and the biblical view of a justice that discriminates. My task now is to propose a proper synthesis, one that encompasses a principle of equality but does not reduce justice to that principle. I propose to do that through the idea of responsibility.[16] At the end of his description of justice as a balance and integration of classes, Plato sums up the issue by saying that justice means "everyone should mind his own business."[17] That principle needs to be seen within a call to justice that makes us aware of what the human business is.

One immediate problem I have in using responsibility to bring together philosophical and biblical meanings of justice is a current way of speaking that opposes justice and responsibility. Such an opposition is not helpful for either justice or responsibility. It has become a common contrast, in part inspired by Carol Gilligan's criticism of Lawrence Kohlberg's gender-biased scheme of moral development. In her essay "Justice and Responsibility," Gilligan describes her task as "adding to Kohlberg's focus on justice a complementary ethic of care."[18] She often expands this formula by saying: "Whereas justice emphasizes the autonomy of the person, care underlies the primacy of relationships. Thus justice gives rise to an ethic of rights, and care engenders an ethic of responsibility."[19]

There is much in this contrast that is inviting. An emphasis on care, compassion, and responsibility is a healthy one. Much of that emphasis comes from women scholars. The unfortunate inference, however, could be that the men will take care of justice, while the women tend to responsibility and that, furthermore, justice is a simple principle of equality. Kohlberg's assumption that justice means "to treat each man impartially" stands in a long philosophical tradition. Although that tradition is firmly embedded in our history, it can and should be challenged. Rather than adding an "ethic of responsibility" to an "ethic of justice," the meaning of justice has to be altered. By bringing forward care, compassion, and responsibility, Gilligan has in fact drawn upon the biblical strand of the American ideal. But instead of juxtaposing responsibility and justice, we need a *responsible justice* as the context of equality and rights.

Responsibility is a term that arose out of Jewish and Christian traditions. (There is no equivalent term in Greek philosophy.)[20] In being an aural/oral metaphor, it has a clear affinity with the biblical idea of justice. Its etymological root means to give an answer to a call. Responsibility is not one of the virtues; there are no medieval treatises on the virtue of responsibility. Instead, it underlies all the virtues because it expresses the Jewish and Christian understanding of human nature. In that framework, each human being is born responsible (able to respond). Our vocation is to become more responsible. Each response makes greater response possible.

Greek philosophy was based on visual metaphors. The guardians in the *Republic* have a vision of the good that moves them to do the right thing for the state. Justice in this context is a viewpoint, a vision of how the pieces go together. When each man and woman minds his or her own business the state becomes a smoothly functioning and beautifully shaped system.

The aural/oral metaphors of the Bible do not reject the visual. Instead, they situate it. The humans are first of all listeners; their second characteristic is to be answerers. Not perspective but action is demanded, "the work of justice." The first thing created in Genesis is light; but it is created because God *says:* "Let there be light." So it goes throughout the whole Hebrew Bible and into the New Testament. God commands and humans "obey," a term that means to listen. Faith comes by hearing the word spoken and saying, "Amen." As the masterstroke of creation, God placed the humans in the middle of everything. From that spot they cannot see all creation but they can listen to all of it. The humans are the responsible animals, called to listen to a divine voice that sounds through every creature.

In the twentieth-century use of the term responsibility, emphasis is placed upon what people are responsible *for.* The more important question is often neglected, namely, the question of who and what human beings are responsible *to.* We cannot rightly decide what we are responsible for except by listening to our own bodies, to other people, to tradition. We cannot deal with our ecological problems if we do not listen to what other animal species have to say and what the universe of living beings is trying to tell us.

Within this context of listening to all creation, the platonic principle "mind your own business" might now be acceptable. It need not be an encouragement to complacency or passivity. Rather, it can be an encouragement to focus on what we can do in response to the troubles of the world while not stepping on the freedom of others.

We ought to be responsible for our own actions, nothing less and nothing more.[21] Those actions need to be directed toward overcoming destructive divisions in the world. Such action requires time to heal the splits within our own lives. And for helping others, skillful and indirect help is most often needed. Responsibility for other people is always limited by their responsibility for their own actions. An adult sometimes has to intervene in a child's taking responsibility, but this should only be to do what the child cannot do. When an adult is incapacitated, someone has to step in to assume responsibility; this intervention can range from offering assistance to a person in a moment of need all the way to taking over responsibility for someone who is permanently comatose.

The call for responsibility in the complicated structures of today needs careful examination. If there is one thing politicians seem to agree upon these days it is that people should be responsible. The centerpiece of the Republican program in 1995 was the "personal responsibility act," which was written into law by a Democratic president in 1996.[22] This code name referred to minimizing the federal government's role in welfare benefits. Although there was resistance to the radical nature of the proposed solution to the welfare question, the question itself had been successfully redefined. That question pitted individual responsibility against government support. The argument became less about the money the federal government was spending and mostly about the moral harm that welfare payments do. To accept welfare, it was said, is to reject "individual responsibility."

There seemed to be near consensus in Washington that the moral uplifting of the poor required cutting off welfare benefits. Except for some religious organizations, such as the United States Catholic Conference and the Children's Defense Fund, there were few voices of public protest. The principle of no more handouts to people who do not work neglects two important facts. First, several million of those welfare recipients are children, several hundred thousand of them with disabilities. Second, the government considers an unemployment rate under 4 percent to be unacceptable and would move to prevent that from happening; thus government policy would not allow everyone to work.

Giving people money can in some circumstances perpetuate unhealthy dependency. A responsible justice would discriminate among the needs of people and provide help to get people out of poverty. No one really knows how to do that, but the question cannot be addressed so long as individual responsibility is set against government help. Most people can become more responsibly in control of their lives if they are given help by private and public agencies.

A justice that responds to the needy among us is not "un-American" even if at times the country seems heartlessly intent on demanding that each individual should measure up to one standard of self-sufficiency. Those of us aware of the biblical meaning of justice have to make our voices heard in responding to the needs of the poor and the sick, children and mothers, the hopeless and the luckless. Anyone who demands that everyone pay his or her own way might reflect on the fact that a single genetic flaw or a split-second accident can reveal one's own dependency on the care, compassion, and responsibility of the community.

FOR REFLECTION AND RESPONSE

1. Recall a time in your life when you experienced injustice. Describe it in detail for at least one other person. In what ways did the experience help you understand justice?
2. From your own experience, choose and describe a time when you were involved in one of the following: social care, social ritual, social empowerment, social legislation. What were some of the circumstances that made these acts of justice possible?

3. Literacy, health care, and homebuilding are cited above as works of justice. In your congregation/parish/diocese, what is one example of each of these that is already going on? What would it take for everyone in your group to produce another example?

4. In what ways is the meaning of justice as equality to be treasured? In what ways is the meaning of justice as equality in need of completion by the biblical idea?

5. What are at least three occasions in family/community life where you need to find out what belongs to whom so that you can give it back? How will you do this?

6. What is the difference between a visual image for responsibility that sees what needs to be done in contrast to an oral/aural image where responsibility means to listen and answer?

7. *For whom* and *for what* are you—and your community—responsible? *To whom* and *to what* are you responsible? What do you understand as the difference between these two?

Chapter 9

PROCLAIMING JUBILEE

MARIA: Almost twenty years ago, I began to explore the intuition that Sabbath is the primary source of Western spirituality. During that exploration, I discovered that Sabbath could refer to varying lengths of time. It could mean the seventh-day Sabbath described in Genesis, when God finished the work of creation, rested, and hallowed the day itself. It could mean the Sabbath of the tenth day of the seventh month, the Day of Atonement, or the Sabbath of Pentecost, a Sabbath "day" so important it was forty-eight hours long. It could refer to the yearlong Sabbath of the seventh year, where everyone and everything rested, including the land, and during which no planting, no pruning, no harvesting, no gathering into barns was allowed. It could even mean the Sabbath of the exile, found in 2 Chronicles (36:21), a Sabbath of seventy years that—at least metaphorically—lasted an entire human lifetime. Finally, Sabbath's breadth included the Sabbath described in the twenty-fifth chapter of the book of Leviticus. Here was a Sabbath so great it was called "the Sabbath of Sabbaths" and lasted two full years. This final Sabbath is the Sabbath of the Jubilee.

In this chapter, I will write about the Jubilee, which I believe is a particularly appropriate spirituality for our time. I will cite several of the sources that have been important to me in coming to this conviction. Then I will reflect on the core Jubilee traditions and on some of their implications for religious and educational life. Gabriel will conclude the chapter with a response.

I begin by noting that Jubilee is a spirituality. As I wrote in chapter 7, I use the term spirituality to refer to our way of being in the world; spirituality includes the listening and responding we do to life—and death—in the light of the Mystery at the core of the universe. Human beings live in the world in many different "ways," and almost always the times shape those ways, which in turn eventually constitute an entire spirituality. This is the claim I make for the Jubilee. For religious people standing on the threshold of a new millennium, the year 2000 of the Common Era, the Jubilee is particularly appropriate as a spirituality. This is because it is attentive to the demands of the times in which we live, demands that encompass care for the earth, forgiveness of debts, freedom, justice, and jubilation.

Similarly, and equally pertinent to the themes of this book, Jubilee includes what are—or ought to be—essential components of religious education and pastoral ministry: contemplative quiet, liberation, redistribution of resources, and the festivity and gratitude commonly expressed through liturgy and worship. These elements can serve as a curriculum for classrooms and schools but are not limited to these settings. They also can serve the family as it educates. They can serve dioceses, parishes and congregations, and judicatories as sources of pastoral practice. They can serve businesses and nations. As we noted in the curriculum chapter, each of these settings is a form of education. In the case of the Jubilee, however, education is to a wider, deeper spirituality than we have heretofore known: one that is demanded by the arrival of the new millennium.

Sources

In providing an initial understanding of Jubilee, pride of place belongs to the biblical record. The Jubilee is the central focus of three major scriptural texts: one from the New Testament, the other two from the Hebrew Bible. The New Testament text is in the Gospel of Luke and describes what happened on the occasion of Jesus' return to Nazareth where he was brought up.[1] It is the Sabbath and Jesus goes to the synagogue, as was his custom. There the scroll from the prophet Isaiah is given to him and he finds the place (Isa. 61:1–2a) where it is written:

> The Spirit of the Lord is upon me,
> because he has anointed me
> to bring good news to the poor.
> He has sent me to proclaim release to the captives
> and recovery of sight to the blind,
> to let the oppressed go free,
> to proclaim the year of the Lord's favor.
> (Luke 4:18–19)

Then Jesus rolls up the scroll, gives it back to the attendant, sits down, and with the eyes of everyone fixed on him makes the stunning proclamation, "Today, this scripture has been fulfilled in your hearing."

Here I want to draw the reader's attention to the significance of the words, "to proclaim the year of the Lord's favor." Scripture scholars studying and writing about this text corroborate the conclusion that the "year of the Lord's favor" that Jesus was proclaiming was a Jubilee year. As far as we can judge historically, it was the year 26 of the Common Era, and in that year, on that day, in that Nazareth synagogue, Jesus did nothing less than announce a Jubilee.

Equally significant scripturally is the reading from Third Isaiah that Jesus chose on that Sabbath. Although he also included a citation from Isa. 58:6 ("to let the oppressed go free"), the central text he chose bears the critical phrase that Jesus repeated: "to proclaim the year of the LORD'S favor." Immediately after those words, as Jesus certainly knew, Isaiah's teaching then flowered into a powerful and poetic description of an approaching time that would be characterized by relief for all who were suffering:

> . . . to provide for those who mourn in Zion;
> . . . to give them a garland instead of ashes,
> the oil of gladness instead of mourning,
> the mantle of praise instead of a faint spirit.
> They will be called oaks of righteousness,
> the planting of the LORD, to display his glory.
> (Isa. 61:3)

But the third text is the centerpiece, and both Luke and Isaiah assume it. This is the Jubilee text itself, found in Leviticus 25 as part of the Holiness Code. The fifty-five verses of this chapter describe the Jubilee, "the year of the LORD's favor." From their own religious heritage, with its centuries of study of Torah, both Jesus and Isaiah knew of the continuing ideal of the Jubilee. They knew it too from the despised *prosboul* used by wealthy landowners to squirm their way out of Jubilee forgiveness of debt. They had learned that Jubilee was a heightened, holy time that began with the Lord speaking to Moses on Mount Sinai, and that Leviticus described it in extraordinary detail. Commentators such as André Trocmé, John Howard Yoder, J. Massyngbaerde Ford, and J. A. Sanders agree that by citing Isaiah in that humble Nazareth synagogue, Jesus was not only declaring a Jubilee; he was also repeating what the prophet Isaiah had done in an earlier era.[2] Both Jesus and Isaiah refer to Torah and to Leviticus 25.

Although they have pride of place, the scriptural texts are not the only sources of Jubilee for religious educators today. In addition to Trocmé, Yoder, Ford, and Sanders, internationally respected religious leaders such as Emilio Castro, Mortimer Arias, Dorothee Soelle, and Sharon H. Ringe have examined the Jubilee in their writings.[3] The Pope has issued a pastoral letter, *Tertio Adveniente Millennio,* on the coming of the third millennium.[4]

Pax Christi U.S.A. dedicated the year from August 1994 to August 1995 (the latter the fiftieth anniversary of the Hiroshima and Nagasaki bombings) as a Jubilee year, pledging "to use the time to grow in commitment to nonviolence through prayer, education, organizing, and witnessing to the God of life and resisting the forces of violence that threaten our communities, nation and world."[5]

In addition, in the summer of 1995, the Evangelical Lutheran Church in America (ELCA) chose Jubilee in a countrywide gathering as the basis for its educational efforts of "teaching to reach," linking five different Lutheran centers through teleconferencing to do so.[6] Herman Daly, formerly of the World Bank, and Alvin Schorr of Columbia University, both secular economists, have posed Jubilee as a model for programs that reduce income inequality.[7] Panamanian missionaries have called for a Jubilee year during which the World Bank and other creditors would forgive the crushing national debt of many Latin American countries.[8] Individual religious people such as Jewish thinker Arthur Waskow and farmer-theologian Richard Cartwright Austin are proposing jubilee spirituality as a resource for our times.[9] And parishes, local church staffs, and denominational boards are considering the act of declaring a Jubilee year in order to focus on the religious ways of being in the world that constitute Jubilee teaching.[10]

These ways encompass five core traditions to which I have already alluded. These are the traditions of fallow land, forgiveness of debts, the proclamation of freedom, the practice of justice, and finally, the sounding of the trumpet—the *yobel*—that ushers in a great feast. Taken together, these traditions constitute the fabric of Jubilee teaching. In what follows, I give a brief description of each.

The Core Traditions of Jubilee

Let the land lie fallow. The first of the traditions is commanded in the opening verses of Leviticus 25. When the people come into the land that God is giving them, the land is to be granted a Sabbath. It is to be rested every seven years. Then, when seven sabbatical cycles—seven years of seven years—are completed, so that the total is forty-nine years, it is time to hold a Jubilee, when

> you shall have the trumpet sounded loud; on the tenth day of the seventh month—on the day of atonement—you shall have the trumpet sounded

> throughout all your land. And you shall hallow the fiftieth year and you shall proclaim liberty throughout the land to all its inhabitants. It shall be a jubilee for you: you shall return, every one of you, to your property and every one of you to your family. . . . For it is a jubilee; it shall be holy to you. (Lev. 25:9–10, 12a)

This hallowing of the fiftieth year is done within the context of rest for the land. As the Jubilee begins, the attention of those keeping it must be given to the act of resting the earth. "That fiftieth year shall be a jubilee for you: you shall not sow, or reap the aftergrowth, or harvest the unpruned vines" (v. 11).

The implications of this initial command for spirituality and for education are many.[11] Here I will note only the twofold nature of this teaching. First, it refers to our relationship to the land, and by extension to the entire created universe. Human beings are *responsible* for the land (and the water and the air); we may not destroy or abuse it; we may not plow and plant it into nothingness. Instead we must care for it; we must rest it; we must grant it a Sabbath. Second, we must also let the "land" of ourselves lie fallow. We must let the listening and receptivity and acceptance and joy that Sabbath brings be part of our own lives too. We must take time to turn from the world of creating and business and activity so that we pause to acknowledge and celebrate the presence of the Creator of the world.

The word "fallow" is particularly instructive here—for both the earth and for us human beings. For land that lies fallow is not inert. Instead, it is land that has been prepared, not so much plowed as pre-plowed. It is land in which furrows have been created and the soil broken up loosely so that the earth is receptive, waiting, ready for whatever seeds will eventually be placed in those furrows as the start of new life. "Let the land lie fallow" is an essential command in a living spirituality.

Forgive debts. The time of Jubilee is an opportunity to *grant* forgiveness of any debts owed to us—and to *ask* for forgiveness too. We have evidence that the ancient Hebrews incorporated this element into their teaching by observing the practice of neighboring tribes, neo-Assyrians and Akkadians whose leaders regularly granted amnesty to people in debt.[12] In the ancient practice of the Jubilee, this had special meaning for all those who had sold themselves into bondage or had signed on as indentured servants in order to pay debts incurred by themselves or their families. Remarkably, this is not only a piece of the history of a people thousands of years ago. Instead, it remains a circumstance played out today by many people in the world's poorest countries—notably in Southeast Asia—who have sold themselves or their children or their labor into debt in order to pay for food and shelter. And even though Jubilee forgiveness eventually extends beyond the remission of such debt, every commentator on this aspect of Jubilee names the forgiveness of monetary debts first. Jubilee forgiveness starts not with remission of "sin" or "trespass" or "wrong" but with the removal of the very specific burden of financial debt. Significantly, Jesus himself placed this form of forgiveness at the center of the Lord's Prayer with words that translate as "Forgive us our debts as we forgive our debtors."[13]

That said, the Jubilee then directs attention to our need not only to grant forgiveness but to ask for it too. This touches personal spirituality deeply, reminding human beings that we are capable of inflicting great harm on one another, for which we must atone. This is especially true for those who have power over others, whether this is adult power over children, male power over women, professorial power over students, or the power of agribusiness over migrant workers. But seeking and granting forgiveness has implications on the historical level too. In Pope John Paul II's recent letter on the coming Jubilee—what he refers to as the "Grand Jubilee of the year 2000"—the Holy Father proposes a serious examination of conscience for the Catholic church directed toward confessing the sins, the errors, and even the crimes committed by our ancestors over the last two thousand years. As indicated on other occasions when the pope has spoken to this issue, these trespasses for which Catholic Christians must ask forgiveness include the excesses of the Crusades, the Inquisition, the burning at the stake and the martyrdom of Protestant Reformers. Similarly, in 1996 the United Methodist church asked forgiveness for the nineteenth-century massacre of Arapaho and Cheyenne led by a Methodist lay preacher. Such actions summon all Christians to repent and ask pardon for the involvement of their churches in the slave trade; for the churches' failure to act with justice toward the indigenous peoples of the Americas and other lands; and for the practices of anti-Semitism that contributed to the *Shoah*.

Proclaim freedom. Arguably, this third Jubilee command is the best known, especially in the United States. The words of Lev. 25:10, "Proclaim liberty throughout the land to all its inhabitants," are engraved on the Liberty Bell in Philadelphia, marking this tradition as especially important to the citizens of this country. These words are particularly cherished by citizens whose people, past and present, have known the absence of freedom in their own lives. For example, African Americans have a profound understanding of Jubilee as release from slavery, and such works as *The Fires of Jubilee: Nat Turner's Fierce Rebellion,*[14] *Frederick Douglass' Civil War: Keeping Faith with Jubilee,*[15] and novelist Margaret Walker's *Jubilee*[16] testify to this understanding.

A first set of freedoms that the Jubilee lifts up are the freedoms of prisoners and slaves—in the biblical record directed to Hebrew slaves, but in more recent interpretations of Jubilee understood to be a universal directive concerning all those in captivity. In our own time this means that Jubilee spirituality has a precise and explicit concern for prisoners, for prison conditions, and for the disproportionate exercise of judicial power in the lives of the indigent where, as one prison advocate notes, "A rich boy's prank is a poor boy's felony." But Jubilee also has a singular concern for children. In Jubilee teaching, when the release of captives is noted, the phrase concerning the liberation of captive people includes the words, "They and their children with them" shall be released (Lev. 25:41, 54).

Freedom and liberty are not only understood as freedom *from,* however, for Jubilee freedom is also freedom *to.* Here, the freedoms noted are as important for contemporary people as they were for our biblical ancestors. Among these are the freedom to go home ("You shall return, every one of you, to your property and every one of you to your family," vv. 10 and 13); to remember—especially the care of God ("I am the Lord your God who brought you out of the land of Egypt to give you the land of Canaan," v. 38); and the freedom to engage in re-creation (Lev. 25:1–7 and Luke 4:16–30). Not only does the Jubilee proclaim liberty throughout the land, it proclaims it to all its inhabitants. And that proclamation cannot become reality without recreating systems, structures, and institutions whose present forms oppress people or keep them from freedom. With this realization, the freedom to recreate becomes dangerous. For it is not popular work to attempt to change the world, especially when this includes efforts to redress inequities among human beings. This is something Jesus found out at Nazareth when the reception of his Jubilee proclamation, begun in the context of an admiring congregation, turned into harsh murmuring that eventually ended in his being thrown out of the synagogue (Luke 4:22–30). Nevertheless, this is the recreation that accompanies the liberation commanded by Jubilee.

Practice justice. Return is one of the central works of Jubilee; it takes several forms. I have already pointed out a first meaning of return: the return journey back to our family, our people, and our property. At other times, the Jubilee journey is to the places of our birth or to our religious traditions. However, return has two additional meanings, both related to justice. One has particular import for those of us who are older. As we move into our middle and later years, we often count up the blessings we have received and describe ourselves not only as grateful, but as impelled to "give back." We use phrases such as, "I've been given so much in life. Now it's my turn to give back, to return." The other meaning of return lies at the center of Jubilee justice. It is the redistribution of capital.

The biblical redistribution of capital that Jubilee proposed was associated almost entirely with land. For ancient peoples responding to the Jubilee, the fiftieth year was the time not only to make a journey back to their place and people. It was also the time to restore property to its original owners. The instruction found in Leviticus reads, "The land shall not be sold in perpetuity, for the land is mine; with me you are but aliens and tenants," says the Lord (v. 23). In addition it reads, "throughout the land that you hold, you shall provide for the redemption of the land" (v. 24).

In our contemporary world, capital initially refers either to land or to money or securities—stocks, bonds, CDs—that are redeemable as money. This *is* a very important understanding of capital. But it needs to be said here that although the contemporary situation is such that land cannot always be returned, many if not most of us are privileged people who have capital in innumerable other forms besides land and money—forms that can be shared with one another. Jubilee summons us to redistribute it among those who are poorer and less fortunate than we are. And what is the capital we possess as privileged people?

Many of us possess the capital of literacy and learning that can be shared in works such as teaching and instruction. Others of us possess the capital of health care and of dental care that we can redistribute in activities as extensive as working with Physicians Without Borders in needy countries or as simple as volunteering one day a month in a local hospital or nursing facility. Others of us carry the privileges associated with white skin, or male gender, or Christian faith, or U.S. citizenship, and need to be alert to the imbalance of favor associated with such privilege, even as we work to address the imbalances that prevent equal treatment under law. Still others of us are rich in "social capital," which refers to *relationships* among persons, groups, and communities that engender trust and/or mutual obligations—everyone in a neighborhood looking out for everyone else, for example.[17]

One form of social capital that we dare not forget is decision-making power. Carol Lakey Hess writes that "those who share the goods they themselves value while holding on to the right to determine what is good still exercise domination over those toward whom they are benevolent. . . . Sharing goods is benevolent, but sharing the power for making decisions, defining culture, and shaping procedures is much more important."[18]

The Jubilee command to practice justice is pertinent here because it calls us to recognize the links between privilege, giftedness, power, and our responsibilities to one another. Life is not fair. Neither is the incidence of poverty, disease, powerlessness, or homelessness as it falls disproportionately on some groups—women and men and children of color, for example—more than on others. Privilege and power remind us that works that serve justice are limited only by our imaginations. Without such works, every Jubilee is incomplete.

Hold a great feast. Only when each of these Jubilee traditions becomes a staple of our moral and religious lives can we take part completely in Jubilee's final command: gather together, sound the trumpet (the *yobel,* from which we take the word "Jubilee"), and prepare to hold a great feast. As the scripture continues, "For it is a Jubilee; it shall be holy to you." This scripture instructs us that our spirituality is also incomplete if it is only the listening of Sabbath, only the essential responses of forgiveness, freedom, and justice. To be whole, our spirituality must include festivity and song, joy and jubilation, ritual and liturgy, and most importantly, thanksgiving. This is the fifth and final Jubilee teaching.

The reasons we must celebrate a Jubilee today are many: the times demand it; it is a profound religious response to questions of poverty, homelessness, and hunger; it is an act of faith that puts faith into practice. But the most important reasons to celebrate a Jubilee today is the opportunity it offers to pause, to hold a Great Feast, and to render thanks to the Giver of all good gifts. We celebrate Jubilee as an act of gratitude. That song of gratitude is wanting, however, if it stops at *Jubilate,* whose translation is "Give thanks and glory and praise." It must go on to *Jubilate Deo*—give thanks and glory and praise to the Giver. Before the Mystery of Being itself, no matter how we name this Mystery, we must give thanks and we must *be* thanks, or perish from ingratitude.

As a people, Jews—ancient and modern—have never forgotten this. Even when captured by the conquering armies of Nebuchadnezzar who exiled them to Babylon, even in the ghettoes and in the camps, they praised and gave thanks to their God, Yahweh. They created the biblical book called Psalms, where characteristic opening verses are: "I thank you, Yahweh, with all my heart; I sing praise to you before the gods" (Ps. 138:1) and "I will praise you, Yahweh, with my whole heart; I will tell of all your marvelous works (Ps. 9:1).

As the centuries piled up, the Hebrews acted on the counsel of the Talmud that in every generation, at every Passover feast, at every weekly Sabbath, and during every seventh year, each would regard herself or himself as though she or he had just emerged from Egypt, and in remembering give thanks. Such is the tradition that reminds us why we celebrate Jubilee, and how, and why—to be complete—our song and our spirituality must begin and end with *Jubilate Deo.*

Response

GABRIEL: I have not been as avid a student of Jubilee as Maria has. But I have been impressed by the way that she has developed a whole outlook under the biblical ideal of Jubilee and by how well contemporary audiences respond to her teaching of a Jubilee spirituality. Maria's interest in this theme and in the related theme of Sabbath has led me to reflect on the sources of my own understanding of ethics. Her work has made my dependence on Sabbath and Jubilee more explicit for me.

One of the books that Maria draws on for an exposition of Jubilee is John Howard Yoder's *The Politics of Jesus.* When I read that book in the 1970s, it transformed my understanding of the New Testament's relation to contemporary ethics. The key to Yoder's reading of Luke's Gospel is the placing of the Jubilee year at the beginning of Jesus' preaching. By situating Jesus in his appropriate Jewish context, Yoder offers an alternative portrait to the liberal versus conservative opposition that has bedeviled Christian teaching since the mid-nineteenth century.

What is called the conservative view of Jesus' teaching is that he propounded an "other-worldly" ethic. The centerpiece of that ethic is supposedly found in the Sermon on the Mount. There Jesus demands that we be perfect as his Heavenly Father is perfect—an ideal that is obviously impossible to fulfill (Matt. 5:48). The entire sermon is understood to be a set of beautiful but impractical ideals designed to remind us that we are powerless to save ourselves from an evil world. Only a Savior from outside this world can liberate us from sin.

What is called the liberal view attempts to humanize Jesus by softening the radicalness of his teachings. The radical element is understood as applicable only in the context of an expected end of time. For those of us in the late twentieth century, Jesus is more of a commonsense reformer, someone who frees us from the burden of law. In this view, the Sabbath is a prime case of legalistic observance from which the Christian has been delivered. Each of us is liberated to be a reasonable, responsible, and upstanding citizen of today's nation-state.

In both liberal and conservative views, the Jewishness of Jesus is neglected or is implicitly denied. Both of them lack any sense that Jewish ethics is built around the Sabbath (and the Sabbath of Sabbaths) and that Jesus approaches the ethical situation from his Jewish perspective. Jesus was very much concerned with the practical questions of everyday ethics. For a Jew this could not mean a casual dismissal of Sabbath observance in the name of reasonable convenience. In fact, if the meaning of Sabbath is properly understood, Jesus can be seen to be demanding a stricter observance of Sabbath. The freedom that Jesus proclaims is not a freedom from Sabbath but a Sabbath freedom. And an ethic built around Sabbath and Jubilee is more relevant to today's world than an ethic of otherworldly idealism or liberal realism.[19]

Jesus' teaching might be called radically liberal by being radically conservative. An ethic in which Sabbath and Jubilee are central implies a recognition that everything is a gift. Everything can be enjoyed, but only when received with gratitude and shared with those in need. Thus the dominant theme of Luke's Gospel, as Yoder interprets it, is the oppression of the poor by the rich. The economic upheaval in first-century Palestine bears some resemblance to our own time and place. At the end of the twentieth century the United States is one of the richest nations in all history, but one where the gap between the rich and the poor is continuing to grow.

Most of the solutions to the problem of poverty were the same in the first century as they are in the present. (1) The poor will get their reward in heaven; preach patience to them. (2) The poor have to imitate the successful lives of the rich; enforce on them the discipline of hard work. (3) The poor need to acquire what the rich have; give them guns. In his bitter diatribe, *Slouching Toward Gomorrah,* Robert Bork identifies the main problem in the United States as envy on the part of the poor.[20] The poor being desirous of wealth may be one problem in our country. However, it seems not to cross Bork's mind that the unlimited greed of the rich may be a bigger problem. An acquisitive attitude intent on possessions can cause moral obtuseness for rich people, poor people, and the people in between.

The preaching of Jesus paradoxically demands a "political" solution, but one that does not follow from politics as usual. A transformation of the economic order requires a change of heart. In Jesus' view the rich are more likely to need the greater change, but there is no romanticizing of the poor. Everyone is called to examine his or her attitude to other people, to property, to the nonhuman world, and to the Creator of all.

Jewish ethics was and is built around the symbolic meaning and weekly practice of Sabbath. By stopping all business (busy-ness) the Jew is reminded that we own nothing when we come into the world and we leave in the same condition. In the interim, whatever we have is ours only on loan. The land as the source of vegetables and fruit, the animal as the source of meat and fur, the buildings erected by previous generations as the source of shelter and beauty are gifts that no individual owns. Human beings inevitably begin to forget that customary gifts are still gifts. Human beings are not the inventors or owners of sunlight, air, and oceans; fruits, vegetables, and meats; land, wood, and stone.

Sabbath observance is a time of freedom for all, but especially for those who carry the heaviest burdens of labor: the cultivator of fields, the beast of burden, the serf in the factory, the woman caring for home and child, the stranger eking out a living in solitariness. As Maria has indicated previously, the Jubilee is simply the most emphatic Sabbath. Twenty-four hours may not be enough time to change one's outlook on debt, forgiveness, and re-creation. There may have to be more dramatic Sabbaths, the Jubilee being the culminating year of re-creation.

Modern systems of ethics struggle along, determined to base everything upon rational self-interest. The main division of ethical systems is between utilitarian concern for large numbers of people and a human rights concern for individuals. These competing systems are more alike than different, focused on calculative thought and choice. While thought and choice are obviously human goods, modern ethical systems tend to neglect the place of emotion and ritual in life, as well as the human relation to the world of the nonhumans. The ecological movement has begun to reveal the shortsightedness of assuming a world of rational calculators.

Biblical ethics is more enlightened and more realistic than modern ethics has been.[21] It does not assume people act for their own benefit. People are regularly confused about their own self's good, failing to understand the relation of the human self to time, to land, and to other creatures. People need rituals to guide them through confusing and difficult times. That is especially true of situations in which the humans fail each other, times when confession and forgiveness are called for. The ethic that had developed by the time of Jesus had rituals that would defuse hostile situations. Jesus called for an intensifying of these practices and a more universal scope for their application.

Christianity's success at spreading this biblical ethic has been limited, in part by a misunderstanding of what is to be spread. The New Testament itself is at times part of the confusion, seeming to make Jesus' teaching a contradiction of the Bible on which he was brought up. For example, Matt. 5:38–39 has Jesus say: "You have heard that it was said 'an eye for an eye and a tooth for a tooth,' but I say to you, do not resist one who is evil." The reference in the first half of the statement is to Ex. 21:24. The Christian reader assumes that the Exodus text says *take* an eye for an eye, but the command is addressed to the one who has offended. The text says to the offender, "*Give* an eye for an eye." The command is about returning what has been taken; it encourages forgiveness and reconciliation, not revenge. Jesus' addition is not a contradiction of Exodus but a furtherance of reconciliation through the renunciation of violence, as in the command to "overcome evil with good."

When Jesus argued with religious teachers of his day about the observance of the Sabbath, it was on the basis that those teachers were missing the more important aspects of the Sabbath. Rituals are always in danger of obscuring a deeper level of engagement. The answer is not to do away with ritual but to reform and re-create it. The Pharisees, contrary to the impression conveyed by the Gospels, were the liberal reformers of the day. The Jesus movement drew upon Pharisaic reform along with several other reform movements of the time to prepare for a Jubilee that is still in the future.[22]

Much of the ecological movement of today tragically misunderstands its historical enemy by attacking something called "the Judeo-Christian tradition." The use of the phrase is nearly always a giveaway that the writer is unacquainted with Jewish tradition, Christian tradition, or the complex relation between the two traditions. The presumption is that the Bible placed "man" above "nature" and created an exploitive relation in which "nature" was abused.

Environmentalists attack "anthropocentrism," a human-centered world. If what is meant is that "man"—the rational, acquisitive, controlling, oppressive individual—should not be the center of things, I would agree. But the ethical alternative is the humans at the center—men and women and children who receive creation as a gift, respond to their vocation as caregivers, and share the good with one another and with other species. Sabbath and Jubilee are the needed periodic reminders of what a human being is: the one who must labor in the garden of earth for sustenance and must regularly stop to celebrate life and share it with the less fortunate.

Jesus tells his followers: "You therefore must be perfect as your Heavenly Father is perfect." As I noted above, this text seems to offer an impractical ideal, which can lead either to an obsessive perfectionistic striving or else to a pious passivity in the face of evil. However, the last word in the original text could be read as either "perfect" or "repay." In an ethic based on Sabbath and Jubilee, the second reading is the more likely: repay as your Father repays. The parallel text in Luke reads: "Be merciful as your Father is merciful" (Luke 6:36). What is called for is that humans forgive their debts, just as God forgives debts, and that enemies be won over by acts of compassion and kindness.

FOR REFLECTION AND RESPONSE

1. Have you ever experienced a year of Sabbath? What circumstances might make such a year possible in your life?

2. What are some practices that might be part of your letting the land lie fallow in daily life?

3. What debts do you need to forgive or be forgiven? What debts does your community (family, parish, congregation) need to forgive or be forgiven? What other kinds of forgiveness do you need to grant as well as to seek?

4. What do you think it means that the Liberty Bell—with the command to proclaim freedom engraved on it—is cracked and flawed?

5. Is there any area in your life or in your community's life that needs to be "returned" to others? If so, how might this return happen?

6. Why does Maria say we must give thanks and *be* thanks or perish from ingratitude? Do you agree with her? Why or why not?

7. How is the freedom that Jubilee proclaims a Sabbath freedom, in contrast to a freedom from Sabbath?

part four

TOWARD A WIDER WORLD

Chapter 10

WHAT CHRISTIANS CAN LEARN FROM JEWS

With Sherry Blumberg

GABRIEL: A few years ago we were invited to address students in a summer school program for religious educators. After our presentations, the director of the program said that he had been puzzled by our references to Jewish stories and traditions until he remembered where we were from: New York City. Although we agreed that living in the city with the largest Jewish population in the world keeps both of us aware of Jewish issues, that was not an explanation for our regularly citing Jewish history and Jewish authors. We regularly refer to Jews and Judaism because for us the Christian religion is unintelligible without its inherent relation to Jewish religion.

That principle—Christianity's necessary dependence on Judaism—is the basis for this chapter and its title.[1] Our main interest is what Christian religious educators could and should learn from their Jewish colleagues. Most of the time religious educators who are Christian are engaged in educating Christians, while Jewish educators are devoted to Jewish religious education. But the very existence of the term "religious education" implies that one religious group can learn from another.

Religious groups are not related to each other according to one set of abstract principles. One group may have almost no historical relation to another particular group; in some cases, however, one group may have grown up in reaction to another so that much of the later group only makes sense when considered in light of the earlier group. Judaism and Christianity stand in a special relation because of Christianity's historical indebtedness to Judaism and the subsequent interaction of the two religions. The relation is not entirely mutual. A Jew learning from Christianity is similar to a Christian learning from Islam; that is, there is much that might be of interest, especially when the two religions exist in close proximity. However, there is a stronger reason why a Christian has to study Judaism: Christianity makes sense only in relation to Jewish religion past and present.

In citing this historical connection we may seem to be stating an obvious fact. Have not Christians always acknowledged that their religion grew out of the Old Testament and the religion of the ancient Israelites? From the first century onward, Christianity has indeed acknowledged this link. But in much of that history the relation of Christians and Jews has been burdened with distortion and stereotype. In the second half of the twentieth century, the Christian churches have taken long strides to reestablish the relation on a sound historical basis. What we still need is for Christian educators to acquire more knowledge of Jewish history, not only up to the first century of the Common Era but to the end of the twentieth century. That can be accomplished by reading Jewish literature and talking with Jewish people.

What we therefore propose in this chapter is an image of a proper relationship between the Christian and Jewish religions. We have chosen examples from areas where Christians can learn from Jews. Both of us have had experience with these examples, although not equally so in each case. It also seemed fitting to include a Jewish perspective and response. Sherry Blumberg, a professor of religious education at Hebrew Union College, concludes this chapter with a response to our proposal.

The metaphor we use for the relation of Christian and Jewish religions is that of siblings.[2] Rabbinic Judaism and the Christian church have a common ancestry. Both trace their origins to ancient Israel and to reform movements from about two thousand years ago. Siblings have different viewpoints and can sometimes have severe disagreements, but ultimately they have to find a way to live within the same family. (This two-sibling family could be expanded to include Islam as another sibling, but we do not attempt to address that concern here.)

The synagogue and the church split apart in the first century C.E. and became two different religions. However, both retained the same body of sacred writings, although they disagreed over the inclusion of particular books and the ordering of the books in the canon. The Jews supplemented their Hebrew scriptures with Talmudic writings and later commentaries; the Christians added a New Testament to what they henceforth called the Old Testament in order to constitute the Christian Bible. Christianity also developed elaborate theological systems that do not play such a central role in Judaism.

What has often functioned as the Christian image of Jewish-Christian relations is that of mother to daughter. Daughterhood is a beautiful metaphor for capturing the Christian relation to ancient Israel, but it can suggest that

Jewish religion is only that of the "Old Testament" and that the Jewish religion essentially ended with the coming of Christianity. Using only the framework of mother and daughter, there were two ways for Christians to view Jews and Judaism. In one, Judaism was seen as the negative pole to Christianity's positive concepts. One extreme version of this showed up in heresies that contrasted a harsh and judgmental God of the Jews with the love and compassion of Jesus and his Father. The more common Christian attitude toward Judaism is that it prepares the way for Christian fulfillment.

This latter perspective has parallels in the history of religion. When a reform movement breaks off into a new religion, it is almost inevitable that the new religion looks with polite condescension upon the old. The attitude conveyed is: "You have many good things in your religion, but our religion includes all of those things and more. Not only are we free to incorporate any elements of your religion that we choose to, but you should feel flattered by our borrowing." No one should be surprised that the "unfulfilled" one in this relation does not look kindly upon such a patronizing attitude.

Can Christians avoid conveying such an attitude about and to Judaism? Only if Christians talk to Jews and discover both ancient Judaism and Jewish life today. However, Christians find when they speak with and listen to Jews that the development of a new relation is not a simple step. Any Christian attempt to reverse ancient stereotypes is always threatened by an uncritical appropriation by Christians of Jewish terms and Jewish practices. In an admirable desire to be positive about Jewish religion, Christians may unwittingly continue to appropriate what Jews believe is properly theirs.

Some Christians may therefore decide that it is easier to avoid the whole issue, but that is not a solution. Most Christian practices are not Jewish-neutral; they are either pro-Jewish or anti-Jewish. Attempts to be pro-Jewish do not always work out that way. There is no simple formula here to distinguish between Christians legitimately sharing in what was originally Jewish and Christians seizing what is mainly, if not exclusively, Jewish. The line between these two may shift, and some choices of language and practice are genuinely debatable. Only out of conversation between trusted partners can misunderstandings be avoided.

For example, Jews are largely responsible for the religious use and meaning of the word "covenant," but it is an idea that implies participation by all creation (as suggested in the story of Noah). That Christians, and other peoples, might claim some share in the covenant is not offensive to Jewish religion. The same could be said of revelation, faith, grace, commandment, prophecy, redemption, and other ideas that are mainly Jewish in origin. The Jewish voice should never be forgotten by Christians in discussing the meaning of these ideas but—even from a Jewish perspective—these terms are not the exclusive possession of the Jews.

The issue is more problematic where Christianity took over a Hebrew term and gave it a distinctively new twist. In some cases, a Greek or Latin term took on a specifically Christian meaning. Parallel to the development of Christian doctrines, the Jewish terms have retained their meanings within Judaism. Two thousand years after the split of synagogue and church, Christians have to be careful about reappropriating Jewish terms. For Christians to start using the term "Yahweh" frequently is not the way to be respectful of Jewish usage and sensibilities. For Christians to replace the term "Christ" with "Messiah" is not to bring Jews and Christians into a better relation. "Messiah" continues to be a Jewish term with a history distinctly different from the Christian history of "Christ."[3]

We also question a practice that has grown to be common in the last few decades: Christians holding what they call a "Seder" during Holy Week. Christianity took over much of the Jewish paschal meal in the celebration of the Eucharist. To recognize the origins of the Eucharist is commendable, and that recognition has led to a reform of the eucharistic liturgy in the Roman Catholic church. If Christians are invited by Jews to participate in their Seder, the experience can be illuminating and profound. However, Christians have no more right or ability to perform a Seder than would Jews—though not inclined to do so—have the right or ability to celebrate the Eucharist. Christians show their greatest respect for Jewish religion by acknowledging the autonomy of Judaism and by allowing Jews to teach them.

The most fundamental question in Judaism and Christianity is human beings' relation to God. This can also be the point of fundamental division between Jews and Christians. Jews brought into human history an experience of the Holy One, Creator of heaven and earth. This powerful king and ruler of the whole world made all other claims to divinity shrink to insignificance. God is not to be trifled with; God's mercy and justice are to be trusted; humans are not in ultimate control of the world.

With the advent of Jesus of Nazareth, Christians brought heaven to earth in the image of an individual human being. The image of father that had arisen in Pharisaic Judaism was given more prominence and greater concreteness in Jesus' discourse. Christianity thereby achieved an intimately personal religion whose power cannot be denied. But Christians have to be regularly reminded not to sentimentalize their religion by reducing the divine to human dimensions. Christians have to remember that they, like the Jews, worship One who goes beyond all names. While Jewish prayer shows a confidence based on long experience, it never presumes a chumminess with the Creator of all. Praying the Psalms can be a Jewish gift that Christians are partial heirs to. Being invited to take part in prayers greeting the Sabbath can be for Christians a reminder of the God who rules all and requires every creature to find its proper place.

On the human side of this relation is the person within a community. Jews had a large part in developing the idea of community. It most properly refers to the small human group intimately bound by history, ritual, and common action, often surviving in the face of dehumanizing powers. In today's overuse of the term, "community" refers to any disparate group of individuals who have *anything* in common. Christianity is partly responsible for this overuse and misuse of "community." The Christian movement broke from one small community in order to reach every nation. Such missionary movement can be a good thing. Some Jewish thinkers have even viewed Christianity as having a role to play among the nations in preparing for the Messiah. The twelfth-century poet and philosopher, Judah Halevi, wrote: "These people [Christians] represent a preparation and preface to the Messiah for whom we wait, who is the fruit of the tree which they will ultimately recognize as the roots which they now despise."[4] But Christians have to be careful about overreaching, so that they become a collection of individuals who call themselves Christian rather than a "Christian Community."

The Jewish sense of community has always been based on the rituals of family life; the synagogue is not the center of Jewish life in the way that church is for Christians. Most parishes and congregations are too large to be "a community," but they can be umbrella organizations under which many small communities help one another. Families need help both from other family units and individuals who are part of the larger organization.

One of the tests of a community, as the Bible shows on many occasions, is how it accepts the stranger, the one who is not a member of the family but is welcomed on occasions of need or celebration. Both Maria and I have had the experience of being welcomed into Jewish family celebrations. That experience forces us to think about how churches operate and how they might be more welcoming to outsiders.

MARIA: Whenever someone asks me where my initial interest in Jews and Judaism came from, I describe the family next door that was part of my growing-up years. When I was still a small child, my father died suddenly, and almost immediately the phrase "the widow and her children" took on very significant meaning for me. Much of this meaning came from the way other people treated us. Among these other people were our Jewish next-door neighbors, whose thoughtfulness and care in the form of friendship, food (especially baked goods—I can still recall the taste of the gingerbread), compassion, and kindness have never faded from my life. We were the strangers to whom Gabriel has already alluded, welcomed and warmed because of our need.

At the same time, I was growing up in a Catholic parish where priests and nuns treated us with similar compassion and where the liturgical practice was extremely rich, the latter a rare experience in the 1940s. One of the most powerful weeks of the year was Holy Week, the sacred time between Palm Sunday and Easter where all over the Catholic world the events of Jesus' suffering and death were remembered in a set of ancient forms, and during which, besides the Sundays, the weekdays had special names too: Spy Wednesday; Holy Thursday; Good Friday. On each of four days of Holy Week, a different Gospel account of Jesus' betrayal and death was read, and special prayers marked the ceremonies—the prayers no less special for their once-a-year inclusion in the liturgy.

Among these prayers were a set called bidding prayers, offered on Good Friday. These were prayers that directed attention to travelers, to those at sea, and to those suffering famine and flood, as well as to those closer to home including the church as a whole, its clergy, and all its people. Notable in this list of supplications was a prayer for the Jews. I prayed that prayer as I did the others, but it was only with Vatican II and the publication of *Nostra Aetate*—when the Catholic church publicly offered its first act of atonement to the Jews after centuries of anti-Jewishness—that I too learned to lament the paradox of that Holy Week prayer in my own life. For on all the Good Fridays of my childhood, even as I was succored by the family next door, I prayed not just for the Jews, but for the "perfidious" Jews. And I recognized a further wrong that attended that prayer. When we came to the prayers as a whole, we *knelt* as we offered each of them—with one exception. We *stood,* stiff-kneed and stiff-necked, when we prayed for the Jews.

That practice has left a permanent scar in my soul that surfaces whenever I reflect on what Christians can and should learn from Jews. Blessedly, we do kneel today as we pray for our Jewish sisters and brothers, and the word "perfidious" is long gone. But the references to "the Jews" that remain in the Holy Week readings from the New Testament continue to trouble me and remind me to be alert to lingering bias toward Jews in Christian religious education materials. Even as I now conduct a yearly session on anti-Semitism for *Facing History and Ourselves*[5] I am aware that I carry anti-Semitism's scar in my own person—as too many Christians do—and I mourn the centuries of loss that for too long characterized the relations between Christians and Jews.

Out of such experiences, the importance of Christians learning from Jews has become crucial for me as an essential part of *Christian* religious education. Because our traditions are so intertwined, we cannot know ourselves if this learning is ignored. Nor can we know each other. For me, this learning has crystallized around law, around Sabbath, and around the Holocaust.

Law. I have taught courses on women's spirituality for several years. One of the most memorable of those courses was at New York University, where the class included one or more Buddhists, Muslims, Protestant and Catholic Christians, and Reform, Orthodox, and secular Jews—all women. During one session, we were exploring practices of spirituality that each of us owned as having particular meaning in our spiritual lives. Most of us chose not only to talk about but to demonstrate the practice that held richness and meaning for us: the repetition of a particular word; a way of breathing; a specific bodily posture. Finally we came to Linda, who is an Orthodox Jew. She paused, hesitant. But eventually she told us that she was feeling uncomfortable with the way our session was going, because for her, the importance of a practice did not depend on its congeniality to her personally. Instead, she went on, she prayed and worshiped and fasted in the ways she did because these ways were *commanded.* They were practices that made her who she was as a Jew. They were the *law.*

I was recently reminded of that course during a class in California where I was teaching a group with a similar breadth of religious background. One of the participants, a Swede who described himself as having no religious affiliation, remarked to me that my presentation—on the five traditions of the biblical Jubilee—was "very Christian." That comment surprised me because I was relying on the prophet Isaiah and on Torah, especially the book of Leviticus, to lay out the Jubilee traditions. I wondered why he perceived my work as especially Christian. So I checked out the perception with my friend David Blumberg, who happened to be in the group. He thought for a while and then answered, "Well, Maria, you do use language a bit differently. You speak of Jubilee as a set of *traditions* or *teachings.* As a Jew, those wouldn't be the words I'd choose. For me, Jubilee is, quite simply, a set of *commands.*"

Both of those incidents had, and continue to have, the same effect on me: a change in my perception of the religious meaning of law. I have come to love the law, even as the psalmist did. And I have come to understand from Judaism that the laws of God are not rules the way traffic laws are; not a set of required good manners toward God, like "please" and "thank you." They are, instead, constitutive of who and what we are as human beings. We are the beings who worship One God, the God who is God. We are the ones who do not adore idols. We are the beings who honor parents; who do not cheat and lie and bear false witness against one another; who do not murder. We are the beings who practice marital fidelity. And it is the law that commands us to do (or to not-do) these things. "Breaking" those laws, those commands, does violence to us: to our humanity, to human community. "Keeping" them enables us to become ourselves.

Sabbath. Among these commands, observing the Sabbath holds a primary place of honor. As I mentioned in chapter 9, my own conviction is that Sabbath—certainly in the Western world and in Western religious traditions—is the cornerstone and centerpiece of spirituality and religious practice: its primary source. Initially, we learn the practice of this command from Jewish observance. Living in New York, one is never far from the example of Jews for whom Friday evening and Saturday are hallowed times. But I have lived in Boston too, and one of the most powerful memories I have of that city comes from Saturday mornings spent in Brookline, where Jews by the hundreds can be observed walking to synagogue to honor the Sabbath.

That honoring is, for Christians, a reminder and a challenge to our own religious observance of Sabbath. As much as it is about doing particular things, Sabbath is also about *not-doing* particular things, so that we might engage in Sabbath rest. For when the Sabbath comes, as Rabbi Abraham Joshua Heschel has written, we devote ourselves to sanctifying time. "All week long," he writes, "we are called upon to sanctify life through employing things of space. On the Sabbath it is given us to share in the holiness that is in the heart of time. Even when the soul is seared, even when no prayer can come out of our tightened throats, the clean, silent rest of the Sabbath leads us to a realm of endless peace."[6] That is as true for Christians as it is for Jews. But in practice, the example of being a Sabbath people is one that is a preeminently Jewish teaching from which Christians might learn their own relation to God. It is a teaching that will assist us in regularly turning from the world of creation to the Creator of the world.

The Holocaust. On the same Brookline streets where I was regularly reminded of Sabbath, I discovered a curriculum that I would argue is essential for all religious educators, but especially for those educators who are Christian. The curriculum is entitled *Facing History and Ourselves,* and its central focus is the events of the twentieth century that culminated in the Holocaust of European Jews, events that also include the Armenian genocide, as well as the terrible things that go on today, notably racism in the United States. The particular meaning of the phrase "facing history" as well as the additional "and ourselves" arises from the curriculum's centering on the present and alerting students and their teachers to those issues and experiences that can help them interpret the history that culminated in Auschwitz.[7]

In other words, *Facing History and Ourselves* is a curriculum that leads to responsibility. Students learn to read the newspapers and to monitor their own social settings, and through those "readings" to recognize their own responses to the times. They keep journals of personal reflections on history. In school and classroom, they grapple with issues such as hatred and prejudice not only in their neighborhoods but in the schools and classrooms where they are gathered. They discover their own contributions to present history and, in facing it, learn to face themselves. All of this is aided by art and by visual aids: propaganda of the Third Reich, children's books, the careful study of texts, films, videotapes, site visits.

I am disappointed that this curriculum, although now used worldwide, is still not a staple in Christian religious education—although it is present in several public and private school systems, including a number of Catholic diocesan schools. Twenty years ago, when I began studying the curriculum myself, my first foray was to an adult education program on Facing History that met on six successive Tuesday nights. There were thirty-six of us who gathered over the course of those sessions, and I can remember the night I discovered that only four of us were non-Jews. The power of that discovery came from my recognition that the other thirty-two—all Jews—needed this curriculum far less than I did. They and their families knew its story in ways that I never could, although I was part of that story too. For I was, first, a Christian and an heir to traditions that had made the Holocaust possible. Even more to the point, I was—and am—a religious educator whose own responsibility is to raise with my students the meaning of the central religious events, issues, and questions of our time. For me, to leave out this history and its contemporary implications is to betray that vocation.

Response

SHERRY: I have thought long and hard about the best way to respond to Gabriel Moran and Maria Harris. I wondered whether to write a response to their ideas, or to frame my response in terms of "what Jews can learn from Christians," despite Gabriel's statement that there is a significant difference in the relationship between Jews learning from Christians and Christians learning from Jews. I choose to combine the two in these remarks, although I am aware that each of these possibilities deserves its own discussion.

As a liberal Jewish woman living in the United States, I am aware of the many changes that have shaped the Jewish community. Ours is a community in flux, held together by centuries of tradition, a community that has partially been shaped by the fear of the "other" who often persecuted Jews.

TOWARD A WIDER WORLD

Many Jews have defined themselves in opposition to Christians, and in some ways even Jewish thought has been defined in contrast to Christian thought and modern secular thought.

When I read the ideas that both Gabriel and Maria presented I was struck by the fact that while the differences between Christians and Jews still exist, their openness to learning from Judaism and Jews would not be trusted by some Jews because of the fear of the "other." Thus, the genuine dialogue that could change the patronizing attitude of which Gabriel speaks would not be considered a priority by much of the Jewish community. I feel saddened by this because I believe that the dialogue is crucial, and not only for Christians to learn from Jews, but for Jews to learn about Christians, and, in truth, about themselves.

I believe that Christians do have to understand what Judaism was when Jesus lived; Jesus was a Jew. His life was shaped by Jewish teaching and Jewish texts. If Christians are to understand their foundations, they must study their foundations. To say that Christianity has a dependence on Judaism by using the metaphor of siblings is exciting for me. Siblings can come to love each other even as they compete with each other.

True, the Judaism of today is not the Judaism of two thousand years ago. Centuries of newer commentary, the whole Oral Law as found in Mishna and Talmud, and the creation of communities all over the world (bound together by their traditions and by fighting anti-Semitism) created different expressions of Jewish life. Jewish life and Jewish thought have always adapted to the places that Jews lived, but the threads that bound us—Torah, One noncorporeal God, and a longing for Israel and a reign of peace—have remained the same.

Judaism is a vibrant, diverse, and living religious tradition. It is often a difficult religion to follow because of our retention of Law and *Mitzvah* (Commandment). We are a people of action and of a faith that grows from those actions and those texts. Much of what Maria describes is true—but only for some of us. Similar forces that reformed and changed Christianity have been at work in the Jewish tradition. Many Jews chose a secular and ethnic Judaism rather than struggle to define a religious position. Jews gave up the requirements of law in order to move into a modern lifestyle. Jewish celebrations, practice, and education were transferred from the home to the synagogue. Thus there are many Jews today who also need to learn the basics of practice for the Jewish way of life. Jewish educators are struggling to return Jewish learning and celebration to the family and to empower the family with a sense of its own power in the transmission of our traditions. We are a people in search of its own "spirituality" and definitions of faith.

And this brings me to my second point. We Jews have a lot to learn from Christians. We can learn from the courage of some Christians to honestly examine the implications of their literature, liturgy, and history and to attempt to change and erase those things that cause persecution of the other. Jews also have texts that lead to a patronizing attitude toward the non-Jew. While we have survived the Holocaust and other persecutions, we need to use a curriculum like *Facing History and Ourselves* to examine our own tendency to oppress the stranger—despite all of our texts that remind us that "we were strangers in Egypt."[8]

Perhaps it is understandable that Jews have lived with the fear that they always would be persecuted; unfortunately, this fear is grounded in the reality of history. But it is this fear that creates a vicious circle in which Jews have responded to persecution by "circling the wagons" and isolating themselves from others. This separation then creates the mistrust and appearance of arrogance that fuels the flames of mistrust and hatred and can lead to persecution.

So, while I am conscious that Christians must confront their own responsibility for the persecution of the Jews, Jews need to be in dialogue with history as well. Together we can learn to move on, to guard against arrogance and bigotry so as to break this vicious circle of fear, isolation, and oppression. Jews can learn to really hear when Christians have grown beyond being those who would harm us.

In addition, Jews can learn a lot from Christians in how to educate for religious experience. While our task is different, being a minority in the midst of a majority culture, we have not been very good about educating for faith and belief.

When Jews lived in communities that supported the Jewish way of life—despite the persecution and limitations—the Jewish way of life (*Halacha*) kept Jews involved in Jewish life on a daily basis. As Jews moved into the mainstream and began to live among non-Jews, it became harder to maintain the "religious experience" of community. More and more emphasis was placed on the synagogue and liturgy. Jews who did not follow ritual practices in their everyday life and who had little support from the community soon found that the rituals were meaningless. They needed to ground their actions in faith and belief. Discussions about beliefs, commandments, and ritual practices were often missing from their education as Jews, and thus they often lacked a vocabulary that was understandable in the modern world. The debate about "spirituality" and "religious experience" is one such dilemma. Today the movement towards *Ruchanioot* (Spirituality) on the part of some Jews is viewed suspiciously by others.

When Judaism separated from Christianity, concepts that were similar in both religions became less likely to be seen as part of the Jewish mainstream. Ideas such as *Chayn* (grace of God) and *G'ulah* (personal salvation) were downplayed in Judaism. Mystical Judaism retained some of them, but Jewish tradition placed more emphasis on the doing of commandments without the need for faith. While Jews' faith in the system of *mitzvot,* and their faith in God, created a history of passion and tragedy, the modern Jew was often unequipped to deal with the intellectual dilemmas created when science and religion were in conflict. Faith and belief were often lost in the battle. Even if the Hebrew meaning of *Emunah*—faith as trusting God—was used, there were rabbis and educators who found no reason to speak about such topics.

By learning how Christians speak about and teach about faith, Jews can explore ways within their own context and texts to do the same. The fact that there have been three modern pop songs speaking about God in the last few years[9] tells us that it is a topic that demands our attention in a Jewish educational context.

I am aware that I have only touched on some of the important points that Gabriel and Maria raised. I have tried to identify a Judaism that is vibrant and changing and struggling with its own issues. I want to highlight the concept of the sibling relationship of which Gabriel speaks—I want to encourage the siblings to keep speaking and loving and learning from each other.

I am not naive enough to think that all Christians are as open to acknowledging that Judaism is a vibrant and authentic path to God, just as I know that not all Jews would acknowledge Christianity as a legitimate path. What I do know is that in this world, if we do not learn to acknowledge the other, to celebrate our own and yet not denigrate the other, we are going to be in serious trouble. Our world has grown very small; we can kill each other in many new ways, or we can find ways to work together to improve life for the other.

I want to close with a story. It relates to Gabriel's statement that the most fundamental question in Jewish and Christian religions is the humans' relation to God. I was at a meeting of the Association of Professors and Researchers in Religious Education when Yitzhak Rabin was killed by a Jewish man who believed that he was doing God's bidding. There were three Jews and 190 Christians (and a few Baha'i) at the meeting. I was very conscious of the love and concern that surrounded the three Jewish members. I was also very conscious of the irony. Here were "strangers" who treated us as cherished friends; yet one of "us," the killer, would have oppressed us even to the point of taking our life because we disagreed with his interpretation of "truth."

Both Christianity and Judaism have within them the possibility to assert their own truth and to trample upon the lives of others; yet both traditions teach that it is God who gives life and God who should take it away. Together we can help each other to grow beyond the arrogance in which we place our vision of truth above God's into a relationship of reverence between God and human beings that is one of love, compassion, and justice.

Ken Yehi Ratzon. . . . May It Be God's Will.

FOR REFLECTION AND RESPONSE

1. Why do Gabriel and Maria believe the Christian religion is unintelligible except in relation to Jewish religion? Do you agree or disagree with them, and why?
2. Why do the authors say that the image of siblings is a better one for understanding Christian-Jewish relations than is the image of mother and daughter?
3. If you are a Christian, spend some time identifying what you have learned from Jews; if you are a Jew, what is something you have learned from Christianity? If you belong to another tradition, what have you learned from both? Finally, what is at least one thing you hope people would learn about your religion?

Chapter 11

INTERNATIONAL CONVERSATION

With Friedrich Schweitzer

GABRIEL: As it has been described in this book, religious education can be a daunting endeavor. Indeed, the various lines of development suggested in previous chapters may seem to present an impossible task. Who could possibly master not only religion in its history, nature, and practice, but also education's nature, forms, and techniques? Ambitious attempts to expand the boundaries of religious education may have an opposite effect on many church educators. The attempts may cause a higher barrier to be erected around the area in which an educator works with some confidence.

Thus we are aware that this chapter, which affirms the need for international dialogue, could have the effect of discouraging people who do not feel prepared for such a conversation. What may be comforting is that no one is fully prepared for this dialogue and that international conversation about religious education is still at a beginning stage. But given the world of the jet plane and global communication systems, we are not going to be able to avoid the task. Even those who resolutely block out of their minds what is going on in other countries are still absorbing influences from places far as well as near. The preferable stance is to take a step in the direction of mutual understanding from wherever we are at present.

This chapter parallels in some ways the previous chapter, in which we urged Christians to learn from Jews. In that case, too, some Christian educators would say that they have enough work trying to instruct their pupils in the Christian religion. How can they be expected to add the study of Judaism to the curriculum? Our response has been that awareness of Judaism and Jewish concerns can provide an intelligibility to Christianity that might eventually simplify the work of Christian religious education. Admittedly, the initial step in that direction might be experienced as complex and confusing.

In an international conversation the initial partner is not as clear-cut as Judaism is for Christianity. However, the religious and educational patterns of Western Europe profoundly influenced the United States in the past, and the influence remains a predominant one even today when the

United States is shifting its vision to the east and south. As a Christian-Jewish dialogue must soon include Islam and be open to any conversants who wish to join in, the United States–Western European dialogue has to leave the door open to every nation. In this chapter, to provide a microcosm of international conversation, we have invited a response from a European scholar, Friedrich Schweitzer of Tübingen, Germany. He is one of the few people today who has the skills, the experience, and the interest to do comparative study of religious education in two countries.

It should be admitted at the start that international dialogue for people in the United States presents special difficulties. The United States has always considered itself an exception among the nations; an unfortunate result of this belief is that the United States has a scandalous record of not keeping international treaties. Events in the last decade have, at least temporarily, exaggerated the claim to exceptionalism. With its military power and its economic size, the United States tends to see itself as an arbiter between nations rather than one among equals.

In some ways the United States is in fact exceptional. From the beginning it has been a nation of nations, the child of Western Enlightenment. Religiously, it was founded as a paradoxical mix of eighteenth-century deists and apocalyptic-minded evangelicals. It tried to avoid religious conflict by putting religion, along with most other things, on the open market. Religion in the United States is an entrepreneurial business. The country's near obsession with religion, together with an intense interest in education, has continued to the present.

One can expect that the United States, as an experiment in the mixing of humanity, would have useful lessons for other nations. The lessons, however, will not be effectively conveyed unless people in the United States are willing to engage in real dialogue, that is, in a process of mutual learning. Because the United States thinks of itself as the tip of the arrow of human history (the term "America" has always been a synonym for the future), it is assumed we do not have to learn from other nations; we simply have to wait for them to become like us. Whether or not that might be true of basketball and rock music, that cannot be the presumption in religious education.

While the United States has brought together a mixture of humanity, the result has never been a "melting pot," an image that was created in the first decade of the twentieth century. The actual United States was less a smooth liquid and more a stew of meat and vegetables. For example, Catholics and Jews have remained distinctive in the culture, despite the great influence of the American ideal. The Jews have trusted in the family and in tradition while making use of the public schools. The Catholic church, partly in reaction to and partly in imitation of the culture, began building its own educational system which eventually reached gigantic proportions. One result is that for Catholics in the United States "religion" is assumed to be a course of study in school.

While the U.S. Jewish population has remained a small and constant minority, the Roman Catholic population has swelled to sixty million. The relation of the Catholic church to the culture and politics of the United States has undergone extraordinary change since the early 1960s. That change became evident with the election of John Kennedy in 1960 and was accelerated by the Second Vatican Council. Catholics began a dialogue both with their Protestant co-religionists and with secular culture. On most political, moral, and economic issues Roman Catholics fit the national profile. Even on such a divisive issue as abortion, Catholics (in contrast to their church leaders) are only slightly different.

One area where the Catholic-Protestant difference has not disappeared is education. Protestants still discuss Christian education, and Catholics refer to catechetics. Perhaps it is unrealistic and undesirable that there would be a total blending of educational practice in Protestant and Catholic churches. There is an intramural aspect to education in religious matters that will last as long as separate institutions exist. But there is also a value in dialogue between separate communities, and such dialogue requires a common set of categories. The term "religious education" might serve as an umbrella under which Catholics, Protestants, Jews, Buddhists, and Muslims could discuss similarities and differences of religion. But Catholics still regularly use "religious education" as synonymous with the CCD (or its parish-based successors) and Protestants sometimes refer to "religious education" as a movement that ended at mid-century.

A proposal for international discussion may seem premature if the national tongue is so divided. But similar to the Jewish-Christian dialogue, which can help Catholics and Protestants to recognize their differences, an international dialogue might also throw light on the differences closer to home. United States participants would discover that catechetics/Christian education is not the only way to divide the universe of religious education. They might also find that in some places catechetics does not exclude Protestants and that Christian education in some countries is biased toward Catholicism. The immediate effect may be disconcerting, but the lasting effect can be a more thoughtful conversation.

International conversation has the complicating factor of translation between languages. When no term is immediately and obviously available for translation, the introduction of a new term is problematic. Religious terms usually have deep roots in the language. The terms "catechetics" and "Christian education" go back many centuries; equivalents to them exist in most European languages. The term "religious education," in contrast, was artificially invented at the end of the last century. The equivalent of "religious education" in other languages is often unclear.

Nineteenth-century Unitarians in the United States are probably responsible for the invention of "religious education." The term then served as the basis for an ambitious and idealistic movement at the beginning of the twentieth century.[1] Those who chose the term had as an aim four sets of conversations between: (l) Catholic, Protestant, and Jewish educators; (2) secular and church-based education; (3) professional church workers and laity; (4) Canadian and U.S. populations. Logically, "religious education" was not owned by any of these groups, which means it is free of bias, but it also was (and is) lacking in passionate investment by any of these same groups.

Measured by the enthusiastic expectations of the movement's founders, religious education in the United States and Canada has been a disappointment. The "movement" ran out of energy when the conversations did not take place. The Catholics did not trust the movement and founded their own organization, the National Catholic Educational Association. Conservative Protestant groups remained skeptical of the movement and have not generally joined the Religious Education Association and its professional offshoot, the Association of Professors and Researchers in Religious Education. As for a bridge between the public school system and religious organizations, none has ever been achieved. And the hope for professionalizing education in every Protestant congregation collapsed with the economic depression of the 1930s.

It may seem quixotic to continue arguing for "religious education" when the votes have gone against it. But what the United States was not ready for in the twentieth century may be unavoidable in the twenty-first. The fact that particular coalitions did not develop in the past does not prove that efforts at coalition building are useless. Religious education as a movement in the first half of this century had early absorbed some naive elements of a religious liberalism. A more critical approach to religious assumptions can better situate an education in religious matters today.

No other country offers a ready-made model for the United States to use. The peculiar history of religion here, as well as the complicated system of education we have, must be acknowledged. The United States is a very young country in relation to the human race's history of religion and education. We could try out some new ways of speaking or at least stop repeating slogans that obstruct thinking ("religious instruction is a form of indoctrination" or "religion does not belong in the classroom").

For those of us in the United States the obvious first step in an international discussion is on our own continent. Although that should include countries to both south and north, whatever dialogue has existed previously has been with Canada. As I have indicated above, the religious education movement in the United States made a very conscious effort to include Canada, something quite unusual in U.S. practice. Partnership with Canada is actually very complicated, in part because the Canadian and U.S. educational systems are very different. The most interesting challenge would be to study Quebec, with its long history of tension between English-speaking Protestants and mostly French-speaking Catholics. If one tries to understand the Protestant system in Quebec and the educational systems of some other provinces, one is led, among other things, to the meaning of religious education in England and the British Commonwealth countries.

England has a better defined and more professionalized meaning of religious education than does the United States. At least since the 1940s, religious education has been closely associated with teaching in the state schools.[2] The term "religious education" had existed in England for several decades previously, but in the 1940s it was consciously chosen as a term that could indicate both serious academic purpose and religious tolerance. Whatever "religious education" means in the United States, it *excludes* the British meaning of a subject taught in state schools.

Thus the first step in a U.S.–British conversation reveals not just a difference but a near contradiction in the meaning of religious education. A conversation—or at least a search for some common ground of conversation—would seem worthwhile for both England and the United States, but there has been very little comparison of differences and similarities. I believe that if a fully developed theory of religious education in the English language is to emerge it will probably come from Canada, Australia, New Zealand, or Ireland. Those countries read literature from both the United States and England; and they also do not entirely accept either one.

In *Religious Education as a Second Language*[3] I attempted to lay out a comprehensive meaning of religious education by incorporating the contrast of religious education in England and the United States. That is, religious education has to include both academic instruction in religion and teaching people to practice a particular religious way of life. The main participants in my dialogue were the U.S. state school, the Catholic parish, and the British state school. I could have chosen other starting points but these three offered fruitful possibilities for developing a complete meaning of religious education. I also noted the limitations of language in all three cases: each of the three could be clarified by being viewed in the light of the other two.

What makes religious education in the United States different from Europe (and most other nations) is its peculiar language of "a wall of separation between church and state." The supposition that church and state are the two entities to be discussed was imported from Europe in the seventeenth century. That the two should be in separate spheres was proposed by Baptists (who were concerned that the government not intrude in the "garden" of the church) and was ratified by Thomas Jefferson (whose concern was a "wall" to keep the church out of the government). In a country that today has 20,000 local governments and more than a thousand religious denominations, "a wall of separation between church and state" is a misleading fiction. More accurate ways of speaking could have been chosen (for example, James Madison's "line between civil and religious bodies").

In U.S. discussions of religious education, church-state language is an obstacle to thinking about what is educationally and politically appropriate. Supreme Court decisions in the 1960s seemed to open a new window, but the Court's language proved inadequate to initiate any large-scale rethinking. This country prides itself on keeping religion and politics separate, while in fact the nation and its politics are saturated with religiosity. We do almost everything with religion except examine it educationally. It would be difficult to name a journal or a forum where a national discussion of education in religious matters even occasionally surfaces.

Would dialogue with Sweden, Spain, or Germany provide us with a better perspective? No quick fixes are to be expected, but the point would be to understand other countries on their own terms. Eventually that might help us to find new distinctions and new emphases. The work of Mary Ann Glendon in comparative law offers a possible model. The United States discusses abortion and divorce as if those two problems existed nowhere else. Glendon has shown how we could develop some different policies if we were aware of how European nations deal with divorce and abortion.[4]

The United States is not going to remove religion from the open market. Having the government play a larger role is always going to be met with suspicion and resistance. Nevertheless, to assume that all education in religion should occur in the local congregations of Jews, Protestants, and Catholics is an illusion. Without relinquishing the degree of religious tolerance we have, we also have to engage our different religions in serious conversations among themselves and with the secular government. Other countries with longer histories might have something to teach us while they also learn from our experience.

MARIA: My contribution to this dialogue with Gabriel and Friedrich takes the form of a brief exploration of how we in the United States might engage in international conversations on religious education. I think it is important to note that many of us are already involved in this enterprise, and my own contribution here is to name and describe some of the ways it already goes on. I will do that by (1) referring to the work of ISREV, the International Seminar on Religious Education and Values, which has been in existence for over twenty years; (2) noting the fairly common experience of U.S. Americans teaching in countries other than the United States—an experience that sometimes has been one's own, but at other times is that of close colleagues; (3) observing the (again common) situation of religion teachers who, although never leaving the States, are engaged in international religious education through work with nationals of other countries. Among these nationals are those who come here as immigrants planning to become U.S. citizens and those who arrive as students planning to return to their own countries. The existence of each of these groups is already reshaping our understanding of international religious education.

The International Seminar. In 1976, John Hull of Birmingham, England, and John Peatling of Union College in Schenectady, New York, invited a group of colleagues to consider meeting in Birmingham in order to begin a conversation among friends on common issues in religious education, a conversation that would extend beyond our own national borders. Both Gabriel and I were asked to be part of this conversation, and that was the beginning of our participation in ISREV, which has continued to meet every two years. The sites of the meetings have alternated between the two sides of the Atlantic, but the format has remained remarkably similar and wonderfully workable. The planners (usually from the host country) choose a theme, and then five plenary sessions are held where the theme is presented from differing angles of vision and by members from different countries. At the 1996 meeting, for example, the theme was visual culture: its imagery and its impact on religious education. The plenaries dealt with television images; literary arts and imagery; critiquing the visual culture; and the experience of blindness in such a culture, the final plenary offered by John Hull.[5] Following the plenaries, small response groups meet daily—across national borders—and in these sessions members draw out implications for their own religious education settings. The afternoons and the evenings are devoted to "collegial" papers, where each member, or a team of members, presents work in progress—again in smaller, multinational groupings. The greater part of one day is always spent on an outing, offering experience of another culture.

I want to pass on at least two learnings from the seminar. First, the social and cultural location in which religious education goes on has remarkable implications for understanding others' religious realities. In Ireland, for example, the entire membership visited New Grange, the site of an ancient religious shrine that was built by hand, stone upon stone, five thousand years ago. At New Grange, the sun lights up the interior of this hallowed place on the occasion of the winter solstice. The Celtic setting and origins of New Grange speak loudly of values, learning, and religious understanding as it exists among the people of Ireland.

Similarly, a journey together to the Columbia Ice Fields of northern Canada and to Banff in western Canada taught us something fundamental about that country and its relation to space and place. But as a group, we have also culled learnings about the United States from a week in Los Angeles together—learnings no less powerful for being implicit in contrast to explicit curriculum. We have learned about Denmark by visiting Tivoli as well as the Little Mermaid who symbolizes Denmark's nearness to the sea; about the Netherlands from praying in Amsterdam's house of the Beguines and climbing the staircase to the hiding place of Anne Frank's family; and about Germany from participating together there in a concert of Hebrew music. Not only do we understand social and cultural locations as a result of such outings, however. After we return from them, we *hear* one another's papers differently because we have been with one another on such journeys.

The second learning I will highlight is the ease with which others can create similar seminars. We may not be able to travel overseas, but in every state of this union and in every province in Canada, it is possible with a little imagination to design our own seminars. Start small with a few friends; choose a topic; ask the friends to bring other friends; and be sure the group includes national, ethnic, and cultural diversity. If you need to, begin with a meeting that lasts only one day; it can grow—as ours has—to a weeklong experience.

Teaching in Other Countries. As a variation on this theme, many of us can find and then take the opportunities that come our way to teach in another country and learn that country's religious education patterns from the inside. Let denominational, judicatory, academic, and diocesan offices (as well as foundations willing to fund educational projects) know you are interested in foreign study and teaching, and then, when you get there, take note of the different visions of religious education that exist. I have, for example, taught in Australia four times and been immeasurably enlightened by the practical wisdom in that country while at the same time being educated in aboriginal art and spirituality; I have taught in Korea and been tutored by the serenity and listening power of Buddhist students; I have taught and been taught in Wellington and Auckland, New Zealand, and have learned the particular genius of international education in that country. In one parish setting, for example, parishioners serenaded Gabriel and me in the Maori language, while in one of Auckland's grade school classrooms, the children greeted us in 17 different languages! However, we need not travel to other countries to learn. I have never taught in Costa Rica or in Mexico, but I learned from my colleague Jane Cary Peck's yearlong sabbatical in Costa Rica where some of that Central American country's educational power lay. And from Professor Joanmarie Smith's ongoing involvement with indigenous Mexican peoples in the state of Oaxaca, I too have come to understand the importance of liberation education among the poorest of the poor, and discovered that the impulse of people in rich, first-world countries to redistribute capital often begins with assessing the capital represented by education.

Education with Immigrants and Non-U.S. Students. At Our Lady of Victory Parish in the South Bronx section of New York City, I have had the opportunity over a four-year period to be involved, as an educator and on a regular basis, in a setting where many if not most of the parishioners are Central and South American and native African. They come from Colombia, from Puerto Rico, from Guyana. They worship in their own native languages, especially in Spanish. But they also worship in English with English-speaking co-parishioners who are not new to the parish. Almost necessarily, the most powerful educational medium is the liturgy, which draws on music that is both English and Spanish. The pastor describes the parish as a place where many stay for a while and then move on, an initial starting place for new immigrants.

Responding educationally to their multinational situation, the parish team has brought many of their parishioners together in small groups as part of the RENEW process, and through the small groups international identities are shared and understood. Many such places now exist in the United States, and they represent fallow seedbeds for still another form of international education.

In a distinct but related enterprise here in the United States, but in other countries as well, persons are coming together across national boundaries in unprecedented ways in colleges, seminaries, and graduate schools, usually—but not exclusively—in large cities. When I began teaching in graduate school over thirty years ago, I recall that every class was made up of at least 10 percent who were in the United States to study religious education; I met them at Fordham, at New York University, at Princeton Seminary, at Andover Newton Theological School. Now, however, it is not surprising when 50 percent of the students are from nations other than the United States. The opportunity for the rest of us to draw on their wisdom, their ways of learning and understanding, and the intersection of their religious with their national identity is an invaluable resource for all those who are part of these classes.

Finally, a word on resources: In our midst are agencies who are sensitive to the divergent perspectives brought about by the international settings in which many of us now work, even in our own countries. Church World Service, through its Office on Global Education (P.O. Box 968, Elkhart, IN 46515) is a pioneer here, offering study-action guides on issues—such as land mines and their destructive consequences—which demand response of North Americans to their worldwide partners. The Children's Defense Fund, especially through its yearly "Children's Sabbath," offers resources appropriate to particular national groups, notably Anglo and Latino, even as it brings persons together across religious lines (CDF, 122 E Street, Washington, DC 20001); Masao Takenaka and Ron O'Grady's edited collection, *The Bible through Asian Eyes,* has made religious, Bible-based art from many Asian countries available throughout the world (published in Auckland, New Zealand in association with the Asian Christian Art Association, 1991). Poet Carolyn Forche's edited collection, *Against Forgetting: Twentieth-Century Poetry of Witness,* draws on powerful expressions from people in countries as diverse as Nigeria, Vietnam, Pakistan, Palestine, and Austria. Finally, the Arts and Lectionary Resource entitled "Imaging the Word" published by the United Church Press (700 Prospect Avenue East, Cleveland, OH 44115; 216-736-3706) has few peers in international understandings that are also interreligious.

Response

FRIEDRICH: I am glad to participate in this conversation. From an American perspective, I am one of those others who may become partners in international dialogue. I am working at the Protestant Faculty of Theology at the University of Tübingen, as an academic religious educator, training pastors and teachers for their future work in school or congregation. In Germany we have religious education as a subject in state schools. In most cases this means Catholic or Protestant religious education, but there are also a growing number of students who are not part of any denomination and who attend ethics classes, the compulsory alternative for those who do not participate in religious education. In addition to this, there is a considerable group of children from non-Christian backgrounds, mostly Muslim, who do not receive religious education at school.

Actually, this is not the first occasion for me to participate in international exchange and cooperation. Like Maria, I have been part of ISREV, the International Seminar on Religious Education and Values, for more than a decade, and I have organized international consultations, which I found very stimulating. More recently, I have been able to do some comparative work on religious education in Germany and the United States, working with Richard R. Osmer of Princeton Theological Seminary. One of our starting points for this project was the fascinating discovery that something like the religious education movement, which in the United States began around the turn of the twentieth century, existed not only in the United States. There were parallel movements in Germany and in other European countries, all happening at about the same time. So a first question that may be asked in international cooperation and research is what such parallels might tell us and what they could mean for our understanding of these movements that were so important for modern religious education. At this point, we are trying to understand these movements as paradigmatic responses to the challenges of modern society, which we consider was the common situation in Germany and the United States at the time when the reform movements emerged.[6]

Through all the situations of international exchange in which I have been involved, it has become increasingly clear to me that international perspectives could and should play a much bigger role in religious education. Why do I think so? In my view, at least three reasons can be mentioned:

First, international work may strengthen our ecumenical awareness. It makes us familiar with other countries, with other cultures, with other denominations, or with other religions. So I consider international exchange as a type of ecumenical, intercultural, and interreligious learning. It involves me in praxis, which I perceive as a very important part of the educational work I expect of my students.

Second, the fact that more and more cultural and social developments are of an international scope makes it necessary to consider them at an international level. They cannot be understood, and even less responded to, as long as we look at them solely from our national perspective. If, for example, secularization and pluralization are problems that are encountered by religious educators all around the world, we should look not only at what people are doing in our own countries. We should also become aware of the global backgrounds if we are to reach an adequate understanding which may guide our educational activities. And why shouldn't we listen to others from abroad who are facing similar challenges? Why shouldn't we learn from their stories?

Third, international cooperation allows for comparisons between similar situations, institutions, policies, and programs of religious education.

Looking, for example, at the situation in Germany with religious education in the state school, we can compare it to the United States' situation where there is no religious education in public schools. And through this we may gain new insights into the advantages and disadvantages of both systems.

However and alas, Gabriel is right when he says that international dialogue is especially difficult in our field. Gabriel refers to the terminology problem, suggesting that catechetics and Christian education are terms which are used either by Catholics or Protestants in the United States and which make it hard to converse across denominational borderlines. And he wonders if the term "religious education" might help the conversation. How is it in Germany? In one way it is the same; in another it is different. It is also true for Germany that the terminology varies with the denominational background. Many Catholics speak of "catechetics" when they refer to educational activities in the parish. Most Protestants consider "catechetics" to be a type of religious instruction which was part of a different time and which is now of only historical interest. Both Protestants and Catholics speak of "religious education" when they think of school-based religion classes. It may also be said that school-based religious education has become a very important field for cooperation between the denominations. While the Catholic church hierarchy is slow to acknowledge Protestants as equal partners, individual religion teachers have been unwilling to wait for their superiors. So in the schools and in the training of teachers within or without the university, there is a fair amount of ecumenical cooperation—a hopeful sign of people overcoming prejudice, tension, and hostility. But is this due to a common term "religious education," or to a cultural and educational situation in which denominational differences appear to be of secondary importance?

And even if there is interdenominational cooperation and mutual understanding in one country, this does not necessarily mean that the terminological problems that arise in international dialogue would be solved as well. The longer I work in this field, the more I feel and see that the main terms which we use, be it "catechetics," "Christian education," "nurture," "religious education," or any conceivable term, always have a different ring in every country. These terms seem to assume the meaning they have in a specific context of persons, policies, institutions, learning materials, and so forth. So if we want to really understand each other when we communicate about matters of religious education, we also have to learn about the cultural backgrounds, the traditions, and histories, and whenever possible we should simply go to another country and see for ourselves.

Germany is part of Europe, and Western Europe is more and more becoming one "country," at some point possibly even with a common government and a common currency. So teachers also have started to look at other countries, at least within Europe. There are a number of European associations of education or religious education, some of them founded by high school teachers, others located at a university level. The many international conferences and consultations which are organized by such associations have become an important part of our ongoing work in religious education. For example, I was recently invited to do a seminar with junior religious education researchers in the Netherlands where we looked at empirical studies on religious education, and I was part of an international consultation on "Youth and Religion in Europe," one of the first conferences in this field to bring together people from former Eastern Bloc countries and from Western Europe.

Some other forms of international exchange in Europe and beyond should also be mentioned here even if I have not been part of them myself. There are exchange programs for religion teachers and educators who are invited to work in another country for some time, be it in the school or in the parish. It is fascinating to see that these programs seem to be very attractive. Many people must experience it as enriching and even as invigorating to teach in a new country and to find out about the different ways in which one's own work may be done there.

If, in conclusion, I ask myself the question of what might have been the most important point for me in international dialogue, I realize that there is no simple answer. Too many things come to mind—mostly individual persons who have left a lasting impression on me, unknown contexts that made me see things differently, new insights into the nature of religious development and education that otherwise would not have been available to me. But maybe in the end, there is one thing that I want especially to emphasize and that may be the core of intercultural and ecumenical learning and exchange. Many times I have been struck by the realization that my own familiar ways of seeing certain questions concerning the nature and tasks of religious education proved to be quite inappropriate when I tried to apply them in a different context. The relationship between religious education and theology is one example of this.

In Germany, a lot of tension exists around this topic. Quite often educators feel that theologians do not take educational work seriously and that religious educators are controlled rather than supported by theology. In my own work, I have attempted to build bridges between religious education and practical theology—by giving educational questions a place within theology on the one hand and by drawing on theological analysis for educational work on the other. It was quite a surprise to me when I learned that something like practical theology does not really exist in England, or that practical theology is an almost exclusively Protestant concept in the United States.

Again, different terminologies make dialogue difficult, while similar terms with different meanings in different countries may cause misunderstanding. But this should not discourage us. Because whenever we come across such differences and whenever we realize their existence, we are likely to see ourselves in new ways. And this, of course, is the way that all learning takes place, especially in religious education—through encounters with other people and with other things which allow us to see ourselves anew.

FOR REFLECTION AND RESPONSE

1. Where are you already engaged in international religious education?
2. Try to think of at least three reasons why religious educators in the United States would benefit from conversation with religious educators in Europe.
3. In addition to European educators, what other peoples of the world are necessary as partners in conversations about religious education?
4. Why—and how—is international religious education also quite often interreligious?

Chapter 12

THE YEARS AHEAD

Throughout the previous chapters, we have written about religious education as a combination of religion and education. In the Introduction, we discussed educational and religious changes in the past that have influenced the present. In this conclusion, we turn to what we see in the future as religious and educational changes that might affect religious education.

Q. In the years ahead, what religious issues are likely to emerge within the Christian churches?

MARIA: Among Orthodox and Catholic churches, I think that issues of identity will continue to be important. Roman Catholicism, for example, will continue to be strong in an identity shaped by sacrament, doctrine, and liturgy, even as it continues to become a church in and for the modern world. This will probably take the form of an increased emphasis on community and empowered laity, and although resistance to change, silencing, even excommunication may continue in some parts of the church, more bishops will be eager to redistribute the capital of power and eager to act collegially. I hope this will happen. If it does, I believe it will be bolstered by the continuing influence of feminism, liberation, small Christian communities, and the choice of a fundamental option for the poor.

I also think that mainline Protestant churches—at least in the United States—will continue moving toward federation, union, and permeable identity borders, as they have been, and especially if their denominational identity continues to break down. And I believe evangelical churches will continue to prosper as they have over the last twenty years.

I would also guess that the Catholic church will ordain women—perhaps as deacons first—and begin to foster, officially, the ministry of married priests that is already going on unofficially. This might even lead to temporary terms of ordination such as four- or eight-year terms, or to ordination to specific ministries, although it might also lead to constricted understandings of priesthood. Still, if positive changes occur they will break open unimaginable creativity throughout the world and will draw on sources that have not been used, or used only marginally. I can see many benefits from such movements, although I would be dishonest if I did not also express some fear of an increased rigidity in church structures.

Related to wider ordination, I think it possible that the Catholic church might celebrate sacramentality even more richly by permitting an African-American rite that could stand alongside other already existing rites such as the Ukrainian, Byzantine, Coptic, and Ethiopian. I believe all of the churches would benefit by drawing on the richness of such rites. The source of my hope? The Holy Spirit. Who would have dreamed that as the third millennium of the Common Era begins, the Berlin wall is down, apartheid is outlawed in South Africa, and the Soviet Union has collapsed? Whether in the churches or beyond them, the Creator Spirit is never outdone in surprises.

GABRIEL: I believe that Western and Eastern Christianity have their best chance in a thousand years to restore good working relations, if not complete reunification. When the Soviet Union was collapsing, it was amazing to watch the resurgence of the churches, as if Communism had been a scab that was now being pulled back. Both Eastern Orthodoxy in Russia, Ukraine, or Romania, and Roman Catholicism in Poland, Lithuania, or the Czech Republic, which had not been part of a worldwide conversation, were caught in a time warp. So we could see the resumption of old battles, as seemed to be the case in Yugoslavia. But I am hopeful that serious conversation and Christian service will tip the scales toward cooperation and understanding.

Within the Western church I expect that the progress of the past thirty years will continue. The Roman Catholic church is being invigorated by a more evangelical energy and individual commitment. Protestant churches are having to confront structural realignments and the development of adequate patterns of authority. I view the sixteenth-century Reformation as, on the whole, a positive step in the church's history, so I am not anxious to see the restitution of one pattern of authority, liturgy, and outreach. There could be healthy competition between Christian denominations in Russia, Latin America, or Africa, without Protestant and Catholic missionaries being enemies.

The question in the United States as well as other countries is whether the church is a liberator of the best in humanity—that is, whether it understands its mission to speak on behalf of the silenced and whether the church embodies a united human-nonhuman community before God. I think the changing relation of women and men is at the heart of all the other changes that are important in the church's future. Christianity, along with Judaism and Islam, is ineluctably tied to its past, which includes a God imagined as male. That can change and to a small degree already has, but much bigger changes may be on the way. It is not clear to me how much Jewish, Christian, and Muslim religions can change themselves on this point.

Changes in the relating of men and women are a crucial part of how the church will look when most of it is in the southern hemisphere. The shift from a church shaped by European culture toward a church of real cultural diversity will bring about unimaginable changes in liturgy, community life, and scholarship. I do wish that the U.S. Catholic bishops would take the lead in arranging for a discussion of what an American (in contrast to a United States) church will be in the future. The United States government is unlikely to be so farsighted in the political arena. The Catholic church, in alliance with Protestant churches, is the only institution I can see that might address not only the church issue in North, South, and Central America but other issues as well. The linguistic problem is a major one, but every U.S. bishop should learn Spanish just as every Latin American bishop should be given help in learning English.

Q. What religious changes are likely in the world beyond the churches?

GABRIEL: I indicated earlier that "spirituality" is a worldwide movement, with the main energies of interest being non-Christian, sometimes anti-Christian. Or as perhaps has been true for several centuries, a kind of scavenging goes on, people taking ideas that Christianity helped to germinate—often with prolific praise for Jesus of Nazareth—while attacking any institutional framework called "church." Such attacks are more often than not ill-informed and unfair; but they do indicate that the church or churches still have considerable private and public power. The attack is part of a mistrust of all institutions, an attitude that is traceable as far back as the twelfth century's Joachim of Flora, who proclaimed the beginning of the third age, the age of the spirit. Joachim has had many descendants (Karl Marx most prominently), but the belief in a new age, a final age, an age of the spirit, has never been as strong as it is now, and I expect that it will grow even stronger.

I am enough of a conservative to think we still need institutions and historical traditions to ground spiritual thirsts and mystical feelings. But just as the churches had better talk to each other so as not to waste their energies in foolish conflicts that ultimately serve no one, so also the major religious traditions need such conversation and understanding lest they undermine each other.

Islam offers a good reference point for what is happening religiously. Islam is a religion that swept across Asia, Africa, and Europe in the early Middle Ages and is now experiencing an extraordinary resurgence. This development includes the United States, where Islam shows great vitality and Muslim leaders are open to cooperation with Christians. On most issues in the world, Islam and Christianity should be standing on the same side. But in the United States there is still an inexcusable ignorance of Muslim religion and blatant prejudice against Muslim religion and Arab people (most Arab people in the United States are Christian). This ignorance extends to foreign policy where a country such as Indonesia—the largest Muslim nation and fourth most populous country in the world—is almost totally unknown in U.S. perception.

I do hope that as the Muslim population increases in the United States we will have fruitful exchanges between Christians and Muslims. In addition, the Muslim presence can give new life and different perspectives to Jewish-Christian exchanges. Islam never underwent the modern Western Enlightenment, so it is a challenge to carry on dialogue with Muslims. But in a world now said to be "postmodern," Islam may offer a route that differs from our liberal-conservative opposition. The language of liberal and conservative, left and right, comes from the French Revolution and has never been adequate to religious discussions.

MARIA: We already have significant clues to what is probable in the wider religious world. The rise of and the impact of fundamentalism—in all religious bodies—will continue to be a challenge to opening religious worlds to one another. But at the same time, the commitment to ecumenism begun in the twentieth century and the extraordinary speed and extent of communication and world travel in our times has already erased boundaries we once thought rigid. As Friedrich has already testified in his description of the situation in Germany, every country in the world, in greater or lesser degree, is now multireligious and will only become more so.

Therefore, my educated guess is that within national boundaries, and not only across national boundaries, we will be face to face with peoples of other religions on a daily basis. This will be particularly true for the United States, Canada, and Australia which are not only multicultural countries, but ones where reverence for native peoples' spiritualities and practices have been hallmarks of the late twentieth century. In many if not most countries of the world, however, awareness of a wide range of religious being-in-the-world will exist. In the United States, for example, instead of one Muslim or Buddhist or Hindu family on the block or in the neighborhood, there will be several.

Given this multireligious context, one tendency will be even greater imitation and appropriation of traditions that ring true as humanly and religiously valid: traditions such as Sabbath, love for the land, declaring no person a stranger. It will not be "odd" for the next generations to go to school in this multireligious setting, and therefore, as kids often do, our children and grandchildren will become our teachers in understanding other religions. Another continuing tendency will be for religious leaders to seek out one another for conversation and collaboration at the local community level. In other cases, religious leaders will seek out a group for conversion (I think of conservative Southern Baptists vis-a-vis the Jews) although that in itself may also contribute unexpectedly to conversation and collaboration.

Q. What technological changes do you see occurring in education?

GABRIEL: In addressing this issue, I think it is important to distinguish between the classroom and the non-classroom parts of education (a more relevant distinction than school and non-school). Television and computers are revolutionizing education, and most of the change is for the good. Of course, any technology can be overused. The average household in the United States has the television turned on for six hours a day; that seems excessive. After fifty years, parents are still learning to live with television and now are having to cope with the computer. Whatever the problems, however, television can be a source of entertainment and education. The computer, now in the process of merging with television, extends the information available in the home beyond imaginable lengths.

The computer has fast become an indispensable tool for every student in school. It is transforming what libraries can do; for those brought up on the computer, the access to material has become simpler and quicker. The Internet can be misused and overused, similar to the way television has dominated some lives during the past half-century. I can recall conferences in the early 1980s where MTV was denounced as the end of civilization and the ultimate seducer of the young. These days MTV is struggling for its market share and is introducing other programming to attract an audience. We probably need at least fifteen years to get perspective on what the Internet is going to mean.

For the classroom, I remain unpersuaded that any technology should be central. That children spend many hours with the television and/or computer is not proof that the classroom should be dominated by these machines. On the contrary, I think the classroom should be a retreat, resistant to the technologizing of life. The classroom should have its own time and style that sets it off against the rest of education. The central fact of the classroom should be face-to-face conversation that leads to understanding. The classroom is not a place to be fed information; it is a place to learn how to read better, to write better, and to speak better. That happens when students meet teachers who read well, write well, and speak well. I have no objection to television and computers being present in the classroom for judicious use. The VCR has been a terrific addition, replacing the old 16 mm projector. But film segments should be auxiliaries to classroom talk, not substitutes for it.

MARIA: I agree with Gabriel concerning the power of both television and computers. Their power and their influence will not go away. At the same time, I am concerned with the limited availability of computers and of computer literacy, which ought to belong not just to the richer, more "developed" nations of the world and to the richer and more developed segments of the population in these nations. I am also concerned that reliance on the computer and entree to the Internet have a tendency to overshadow other modes of knowing that are *not* technological: moral, aesthetic, and religious modes that depend on non discursive and nonverbal semantics.

However, the technological problem here is not with the computer or with the modes of knowing it fosters. Actually, if there is a problem it is with our understandings of education and of who deserves it. And here I can only applaud the technological advances that make computers less and less expensive and therefore able—as the television has been able—to bring the peoples of the world into daily contact with one another. And I can only applaud the artistic advances brought by both computers and television as they give access to the funded creativity of the human race to both older and younger generations.

Q. What about the political and economic contexts for educational change?

MARIA: I've already alluded to some of this in my response to the previous question. Here let me enlarge on it by advocating political and economic attention to one group who has little political power and less economic power globally, nationally, and locally: children. In a *global* context, the United Nations, through UNICEF (the United Nations Children's Fund), has brought attention to the plight of children throughout the world in ways that few religious bodies have been able to do, including almost single-handedly eliminating death through dysentery for the world's children. As I indicated in chapter 5, UNICEF has insisted on the peoples of the world giving attention to those children who are too often hidden victims of our political and economic systems and lacking in proper nutrition, medical care, and schooling.

The political and economic context is also *national.* In the United States, no advocacy group is more worthy of religious educators' support than the Children's Defense Fund (headquartered in Washington, D.C.), whose work on the Children's Sabbath has already been noted in these chapters.[1] This yearly observance offers an opportunity to raise voices of concern for children by exploring the religiously based imperative to speak out on behalf of the vulnerable, and to encourage commitment in addressing the political and economic plight of children. CDF makes rituals, lesson plans, and suggestions for community action available for doing this not only through service and advocacy, but through prayer and schooling as well.

One year, for example, the Children's Sabbath program was directed to stopping gun violence among children: in the United States, a child dies from gunfire every two hours. Along with community action, CDF suggested that from sundown on Friday—the beginning of the Jewish Sabbath—until Sunday afternoon, a siren or gong or church bells be sounded every two hours as a memorial to such children. In another year, the CDF focused attention on the plight of children in poverty. In still another it centered on political advocacy. But every year this agency has brought people together across religious boundaries to address children's political and economic contexts at the national level.

Programs akin to CDF's and UNICEF's programs can be implemented on the *local* level, and again, we have religious bodies in our midst who are already doing this. One local community of which I am aware is Our Lady of the Miraculous Medal Parish in Wyandanch, New York, which, although a low-income parish itself, has discovered ways to support a dance program; provide computer literacy for neighborhood children after school, on weekends, and during the summer; keep families from fragmenting by ensuring adequate housing; be advocates for health care; and generally, to follow the biblical mandate to seek justice, love kindness, and walk humbly with God (Micah 6:8). As such, it is a model for other religious congregations that have far more resources to do the same in their own local contexts.

GABRIEL: I agree with Maria about computers widening the split between rich and poor in the United States and the world. The repeated promise of technology from the seventeenth century onward has been that technology would liberate mankind. The language of "man and nature" embodies the problematic character of the promise. Who is the enemy? Who is to be liberated? The power relation expressed in this language places "man" on top of all that is not man, that is, "nature." But the introduction of technology into a world already divided into haves and have-nots exacerbates the division. What was hidden in the man/nature dichotomy was the awareness that some men oppress other men, some men oppress women, some men's minds oppress their own bodies.

Our modern political reforms since the eighteenth century show some success in freeing people from oppressive governmental regimes. But democracies do not last long if there is a chasm between rich and poor. Educational opportunities are radically different between rich and poor countries. Technology is not the enemy, but political will is needed to see that appropriate technology will serve the educational needs of the poor. For example, the radio can be a very useful educational tool in many parts of Africa or Asia, rural outposts where television makes no sense. And the telephone must precede the use of fax machines or the Internet. If a culture jumps unilaterally and too quickly to the latest machinery, the benefit will be to a very small elite and the solidification of their power.

Combined with other political and economic changes, technology has the potential to finally narrow the gap educationally, but I am not optimistic about this happening. Even within the United States we have had a continuously widening gap between rich and poor since 1980. Although schools are not necessarily better because they spend more money per student, if a school in suburban Connecticut spends $18,000 per student per year and a school in Alabama spends $1,800, the chances of equal opportunity are slight. And when the problem of poverty overlaps our unresolved problem of race, we have a terrible tangle of educational failure. Television has contributed to racial progress by giving visibility to black entertainers, politicians, reporters, and athletes. And if the black middle class continues to expand, this will offer hope to black families trapped in urban poverty. But I fear any racial progress may get overwhelmed by despair on the side of blacks and moral obtuseness on the side of too many whites.

Q. Who and what are your greatest allies as you face the future of religious education?

MARIA: My previous answer is a partial response: my—and the reader's—allies are *everywhere.* They are global, national, and local, and a reminder that we are never alone. But I would also add that our allies, and my own, are individual and personal too, and Gabriel, my husband, is First Ally in my life. As an example of an ally on the personal level, he reminds me that it is an extraordinary support, as well as one of life's great privileges, to be able to examine political, economic, and religious issues at the breakfast table with your closest human companion. To him I add the many personal friends who have been my support through the decades, and with particular affection and gratitude I add the women and men of my religious communities—from the many women in religious orders who have taken me in, to the DREs and DCEs and pastoral personnel of local churches, to the retreatants here and abroad with whom I have prayed many a prayer over the last three decades.

I also rely on poets and poetry as allies, and I believe with Coleridge that if we spend enough time with poets, they make us poets too. I've already named some of my favorites in the pages of this book: Jenny Joseph, who by her "Warning" has helped me make up for the "sobriety of my youth" and Carolyn Forché, who has taught me that always, always, in the face of life and death, we must be "against forgetting."[2] To them I would add Marge Piercy, Mary Oliver, and Anne Sexton in her "awful rowing toward God."[3] I also rely on Wisdom, on "She Who Is," to use Beth Johnson's radiant phrase. That is, I rely on the Great Spirit in our midst who never ceases to remind me that the world is forever charged with the grandeur of God. She is the Spirit who will never let us go, even as She continues to brood over the bent world with "warm breast and with Ah! bright wings."[4]

GABRIEL: My main allies are the many people of intelligence and good will who share our interests. It is easy to forget the goodness and dedication of ordinary people if one's outlook is too much determined by the nightly news with its laundry list of today's murders and scandals. Reformers of any institution have to stir up indignation and passion to correct the injustices within that sphere of life. Churches have a lot wrong with them, and a religious education has to be critical of failure. But churches continue to be remarkable places where intelligent and generous people do daily acts of kindness and occasionally heroic acts of service. I am especially struck these days by older priests and nuns, people who have made the long journey across diverse terrain, people who are well aware that they are at the end of an institutional history but who continue to do their work with enthusiasm, dedication, and good cheer.

Both Maria and I have mentioned contacts we have in other countries, cultures, and religions. It is always heartening and never ceases to be surprising that a colleague half a world away is interested in similar ideas, reading the same literature, trying out projects of mutual concern. The fact that we meet face to face once a year or once every three years does not prevent the person from being in one's community. This worldwide solidarity can also be chastening to one's prejudices. In recent years I have been taken to task by Unification Church members and by Iranian Muslims for offhand comments made in my books about Sun-Myung Moon and Ayatollah Khomeini.

I find support for religious education in journals such as *Religious Education* or *The Living Light.* I also find help in religious and educational journals, ranging from *Commonweal,* to *Harvard Educational Review,* to *Tikkun,* to *The New York Review of Books,* to *The Responsive Community.* I think everyone in religious education owes a debt of gratitude to James Michael Lee and his commitment to the publications of Religious Education Press. Other publishing houses are still often skeptical of attempts at theorizing about religious education.

Universities and seminaries continue to be indispensable allies in any future for religious education. The university has a responsibility to maintain an academic seriousness in preparing people for religious education. Several good master's programs still function. I think the university has to resist a clericalizing of all education in the church. Seminaries are closer to the problem, which can be an advantage or a disadvantage. We have to keep aiming at a language that widens the circle of conversation while drawing more deeply on our particular traditions. Professional organizations, such as the Association of Professors and Researchers in Religious Education, are a needed arm for this conversation. Through such organized contacts, as well as the accidents of one's personal history, a small group of people come to have invaluable importance in one's life. As years have turned into decades the support and friendship of these people—and Maria first of all—have come to have for me an importance surpassing all measure.

FOR REFLECTION AND RESPONSE

1. In the years ahead, what religious issues do you see as likely to emerge within the Christian churches?
2. In the years ahead, what religious changes do you see likely in the world beyond the churches?
3. What technological changes do you see occurring in education in the future?
4. What do you have to say about the political and economic contexts for educational change that might develop in the future?
5. Who and what are your greatest allies as you face the future in religious education?

Notes

INTRODUCTION

1. Maria Harris, *Theology of Revelation* (New York: Herder & Herder, 1966), and *Catechesis of Revelation* (New York: Herder & Herder, 1966).
2. See Howard Gardner, *Frames of Mind: The Theory of Multiple Intelligences* (New York: Basic Books, 1983). Gardner names seven intellectual competencies: linguistic, musical, logico/mathematical, spatial, bodily/kinesthetic, interpersonal, and intrapersonal.
3. There are a significant number of Catholic dioceses and individual Catholic schools that do teach the Holocaust, however, especially through using *Facing History and Ourselves*, the superb curriculum available from the group of the same name (16 Hurd Road, Brookline, Mass. 02146-6919).
4. Maria Harris, *Teaching and Religious Imagination* (San Francisco: Harper & Row, 1987) both develops and draws on this earlier work which was published in 1972 under the title *The Aesthetic Dimension in Redefining Religious Education* (Ann Arbor, Mich.: University Microfilms).
5. Maria Harris, *Showing How: The Act of Teaching* (Valley Forge, Pa.: Trinity Press International, 1997).
6. Maria Harris, *Religious Education as a Second Language* (Birmingham, Ala.: Religious Education Press, 1989).

1. THE CURRICULUM OF EDUCATION

1. Bernard Bailyn, *Education in the Forming of American Society* (New York: Vintage Books, 1960).
2. Ibid., 14.
3. Edmund Morgan, *The Puritan Family* (New York: Harper & Row, 1966).
4. John Dewey, "The Child and the Curriculum," in *Dewey on Education,* ed. Martin Dworkin (New York: Teachers College Press, 1959), 96–106.
5. Eugene Boyer, *High School* (New York: Harper & Row, 1983).
6. See Gabriel Moran, *Education Toward Adulthood: Religion and Lifelong Learning* (New York: Paulist Press, 1979), and idem, *Religious Education Development* (Minneapolis: Winston Press, 1983).
7. The letters CCD stand for the Confraternity of Christian Doctrine, the official organ of instruction for Catholic laity throughout the world. In 1935 it was set up in the United States to provide catechetical instruction to young people who were not students in Catholic schools.

8. Maria Harris, *Fashion Me a People: Curriculum and the Church* (Louisville, Ky.: Westminster/John Knox Press, 1989).
9. See Edward Schillebeeckx, *Christ the Sacrament of Encounter with God* (New York: Sheed & Ward, 1963), 47ff.
10. In "The Tasks of the Curricular Theorist," in *Curriculum Theorizing: The Reconceptualists,* ed. William Pinar (Berkeley, Calif.: McCutchan, 1975), 276ff. See also Maria Harris, "The Grace of Power," in *Teaching and Religious Imagination* (San Francisco: Harper & Row, 1987), 78–96.

2. THE AIMS OF RELIGIOUS EDUCATION

1. Friedrich von Hügel, *The Mystical Element in Religion* (London: James Clarke, 1961), 46.
2. Mary Douglas, *Natural Symbols* (New York: Vintage Books, 1970), 59–76.
3. The typology was originally proposed in Alan Race, *Christian and Religious Pluralism* (Maryknoll, N.Y.: Orbis Books, 1983); see also John Hick, *A Christian Theology of Religions* (Louisville, Ky.: Westminster John Knox Press, 1995).

3. TEACHING THE WAY

1. The word *catechesis* is derived from the Greek *katechein,* "to echo." In Vatican II's Dogmatic Constitution on Divine Revelation, it is considered a ministry of the word. Originally, the term applied to the oral instruction given adults and children before Baptism. In the 1979 National Catechetical Directory of the United States, catechesis is referred to as "the efforts which help individuals and communities acquire and deepen Christian faith and identity through initiation rites, instruction, and formation of conscience. It includes both the message presented and the way in which it is presented." Ultimately, catechesis is the responsibility of the whole community. See Beverly M. Brazauskas in the *HarperCollins Encyclopedia of Catholicism,* ed. Richard P. McBrien (San Francisco: HarperSanFrancisco, 1995), 235.
2. NCCB/USCC, "Called and Gifted, The American Catholic Laity" (Washington, D.C.: USCC, 1980) and NCCB/USCC "Called and Gifted for the Third Millennium" (Washington, D.C.: USCC, 1995), 56.
3. See the following: Division for Ministry, Task Force on the Study of Ministry, and Department for Ministry in Daily Life, *On Assignment from God: The Ministry of the Baptized* (Chicago: Evangelical Lutheran Church in America, 1991). Also see *The Book of Discipline of the United Methodist Church* (Nashville: UMC Publishing House, 1996), paragraphs 101–109, pp. 107–9.
4. See Richard J. Beauchesne, "Yves Congar Leaves Rich Legacy," quoted in *National Catholic Reporter,* July 14, 1995, 2.
5. John R. Donahue, "Biblical Perspectives on Justice," in *The Faith That Does Justice,* ed. John C. Haughey (New York: Paulist Press, 1977), 69.
6. Antonio Machado, "Moral Proverbs and Folk Songs," in *Times Alone,* trans. Robert Bly (Middletown, Conn.: Wesleyan University Press, 1983), 147; quoted in Robert Bly, *Iron John* (Reading, Mass.: Addison-Wesley Pub. Co., 1990).
7. Quoted in Ada María Isasi-Díaz, "To Live Is to Struggle: Education for a New World Order," *PACE* 23 (March 1994), 15.

8. Small Christian communities are communal by definition; RENEW is a communally-based program used by Catholic parishes throughout the world. See *RENEW: An Overview* (Ramsey, N.J.: Paulist Press, 1984) and *RENEW 2000* (National Office of *RENEW International,* 1232 George Street, Plainfield, New Jersey 07062; [908] 769-5400). RCIA is the acronym for the Rite of Christian Initiation of Adults. See James B. Dunning, *New Wine: New Wineskins: The Rite of Christian Initiation of Adults* (New York: William H. Sadlier, 1981).
9. Quoted by Adam Gopnik in "The Virtual Bishop," *The New Yorker,* March 18, 1996, 61.
10. Renato Kizito Sesana, "Priest-parched in Sudan," *National Catholic Reporter,* December 1, 1995, 14.
11. Sara Ruddick in Mary Belenky et al., *Women's Ways of Knowing* (New York: Basic Books, 1986), 217–19.
12. From *The Corn Is Green*, by Emlyn Williams, in *The Collected Plays,* vol. 1 (New York: Random House, 1961), 263.
13. "Sensus Fidelium," *HarperCollins Encyclopedia of Catholicism,* 1182.
14. *Lumen Gentium,* note 12.
15. See Gerard Sloyan, *Jesus in Focus* (West Mystic, Conn.: Twenty-Third Publications, 1983), 146.
16. See Herbert McCabe, *What Is Ethics All About?* (Washington, D.C.: Corpus, 1969), 132.

4. THE ROOTS OF MODERN DEVELOPMENT

1. John Dewey, *Democracy and Education* (New York: Macmillan Publishing Co., 1916), 49.
2. Edward Thorndike, *Educational Psychology,* 2d ed. (New York: Teachers College Press, 1910).
3. James Fowler, Karl Ernst Nipkow, and Friedrich Schweitzer, eds., *Stages of Faith and Religious Development* (New York: Crossroad, 1991).
4. James Fowler, *Becoming Adult, Becoming Christian* (San Francisco: Harper & Row, 1984).
5. William Perry, *Forms of Intellectual and Moral Development* (Cambridge: Harvard University Press, 1947), 44.
6. See "Diakonia: The Curriculum of Service," in Maria Harris, *Fashion Me a People: Curriculum in the Church* (Louisville, Ky.: Westminster/John Knox Press, 1989), 144–63.
7. See John Haught, "Theological Aspects of Ecology," in *HarperCollins Encyclopedia of Catholicism,* 449–50.
8. See Maria Harris, *Jubilee Time: Celebrating Women, Spirit and the Advent of Age* (New York: Bantam Books, 1995), 42. See also René Dubos, *A God Within* (New York: Charles Scribner's Sons, 1972) for a classic statement on Franciscan and Benedictine spiritualities as they relate to ecology.
9. Thomas Berry, *The Dream of the Earth* (San Francisco: Sierra Club Books, 1988), 72.
10. Wendell Berry, "Christianity and the Survival of Creation," in *Sex, Economy, Freedom and Community* (New York: Pantheon Books, 1993), 109.

11. Ibid., 110.
12. Sharon Deloz Parks, "Household Economics," in *Practicing Our Faith: A Way of Life for Searching People* (San Francisco: Jossey-Bass, 1997), 50–51.
13. Thomas Kelly, in *Quaker Spirituality,* ed. Douglas V. Steere (New York: Paulist Press, 1984), 302–3.
14. See *Proclaim Jubilee!* 84–87.
15. This example comes from an editorial entitled "Palms Down," in the *New York Times,* Oct. 12, 1994, sec. A 14.
16. See Marian Burros, "Eating Well," *New York Times,* December 11, 1996, sec. C 8.
17. Available by calling (800) GLEAN-IT. Businesses that want additional information may call (800) 845–3008.

5. DEVELOPMENT AND GENDER

1. See Lyn Mikel Brown and Carol Gilligan, *Meeting at the Crossroads* (Cambridge: Harvard University Press, 1994).
2. (Cambridge, Mass.: Harvard University Press, 1982). See also Carol Gilligan, "Women's Place in Man's Lifecycle," *Harvard Educational Review* 47 (winter 1984): 431–46; Carol Gilligan, Nona P. Lyons, and Trudy J. Hammer, eds., *Making Connections: The Relational Worlds of Adolescent Girls at Emma Willard School* (Cambridge, Mass.: Harvard University Press, 1990). For the research presented in Cleveland, see Lyn Mikel Brown, *Narratives of Relationship: The Development of a Care Voice in Girls Ages 7 to 16* (Cambridge, Mass.: Harvard University Press, 1989) and her *Meeting at the Crossroads,* co-written with Carol Gilligan (Cambridge, Mass.: Harvard University Press, 1992).
3. Erikson, Piaget, and Fowler did use female as well as male subjects, and I do not wish to be misread in saying they did not. The issue of gender bias, however, and the possible biases of the researchers only became important in recent years.
4. See *Shortchanging Girls, Shortchanging America* (Washington, D.C.: AAUW, 1991) and *How Schools Shortchange Girls* (Washington, D.C.: AAUW, 1992).
5. Ibid., 9.
6. *A Capella* (Ottawa: Canadian Teachers' Federation, 1990).
7. "The Girl Child" (New York: UNICEF Programme Division), 1990.
8. I am indebted to Judith Dorney for suggesting this metaphor to me.
9. See Maria Harris, *Dance of the Spirit: The Seven Steps of Women's Spirituality* (New York: Bantam Books, 1989).
10. See Erik H. Erikson, *Childhood and Society* (New York: W. W. Norton & Co., 1963), 266–68.
11. For a report on a group of teachers involved in such work, see Judith A. Dorney, "Educating Toward Resistance: A Task for Women Teaching Girls," in *Youth and Society,* 27, no. 1 (Sept. 1995): 55–72.
12. See my *Jubilee Time: Celebrating Women, Spirit and the Advent of Age.*
13. One of the best known of these studies has been reported by George Vaillant in *Adaptation to Life* (Boston: Little, Brown & Co., 1977); and in the follow-up volume, *The Middle Years* (New Haven: Yale University Press, 1989).
14. Myra Sadker and David Sadker, *Failing at Fairness: How America's Schools Cheat Girls* (New York: Charles Scribner's Sons, 1993).

15. See Peter Harrison, *"Religion" and Religions in the English Enlightenment* (Cambridge: Cambridge University Press, 1990).
16. Daniel Levinson, *The Seasons of a Man's Life* (New York: Alfred A. Knopf, 1978); Homer Figler, *Overcoming Executive Mid-Life Crisis* (New York: John Wiley & Sons, 1978); Michael Farrell and Stanley Rosenberg, *Men at Midlife* (Boston: Auburn House, 1981).
17. Bly, *Iron John.*
18. David Gutmann, *Reclaimed Power: Toward a New Psychology of Men and Women in Later Life* (New York: Basic Books, 1987).
19. Richard Rohr, in *Commonweal,* December 20, 1996, 2. See also Richard Rohr, *The Wild Man's Journey* (Cincinnati: St. Anthony Messenger Press, 1992).

6. DEVELOPMENT AND DEATH

1. Elisabeth Kübler-Ross, *On Death and Dying* (New York: Macmillan, 1969).
2. See Elisabeth Kübler-Ross, *On Life After Death* (Berkeley: Celestial Arts, 1991).
3. Sherwin Nuland, *How We Die* (New York: Alfred A. Knopf, 1994).
4. Karl Rahner, *Theology of Death* (New York: Herder & Herder, 1961); *The Tibetan Book of the Dead* (San Francisco: HarperCollins, 1992).
5. Helen Prejean, *Dead Man Walking* (New York: Vintage Books, 1993).
6. Kübler-Ross, *On Death and Dying,* 40.
7. Ibid., 112.
8. Miguel de Unamuno, *The Tragic Sense of Life* (New York: Dover Publications, 1954), 39.
9. Nuland, *How We Die,* 58, 70.
10. *National Catholic Reporter,* September 16, 1996, 10.
11. *New York Times,* October 5, 1996, 29.
12. Dietrich Bonhoeffer, *Ethics* (New York: Macmillan Publishing Co., 1974), 79.
13. *Tibetan Book of the Dead,* 169–70.
14. Ruth Benedict, *The Chrysanthemum and the Sword* (Boston: Houghton Mifflin Co., 1946), 186.
15. Erich Lindemann, "Symptomology and Management of Acute Grief," in *Death and Identity,* ed. Robert Fulton (New York: John Wiley & Sons, 1965), 186–201.
16. Mark Twain, *The Autobiography of Mark Twain,* vol. 1 (New York: Harper & Brothers, 1934), 234.
17. Harold Kushner, *When Bad Things Happen to Good People* (New York: Avon Books, 1980), 90.
18. John Keats, "Hyperion," in book 3 of *The Complete Works of Keats* (Boston: Houghton Mifflin Co., Cambridge Edition, 1899), 211–12.
19. Lindemann, "Symptomology and Management of Acute Grief."
20. The book is Terrence Real's *I Don't Want to Talk About It: Overcoming the Secret Legacy of Male Depression* (New York: Charles Scribner's Sons, 1996); the review is in the *New York Times Book Review,* February 16, 1997, 24.

7. SPIRITUALITY AND ITS ROOTS

1. Paul Tillich, *Systematic Theology* (Chicago: Univ. of Chicago Press, 1963), 3:22.
2 I think this point can be confirmed by consulting the twenty-five-volume series, *World Spirituality,* published by Crossroad in the 1980s.

3. There are books on spirituality that try to borrow from modern physics, such as Fritjof Capra, *The Tao of Physics* (New York: Bantam Books, 1977). There are also books by physicists, mathematicians, and biologists such as Robert Sheldrake, *The Rebirth of Nature* (New York: Bantam Books, 1981) and Werner Heisenberg, *Physics and Philosophy* (New York: Harper & Brothers, 1958).
4. See Basil Mitchell, *Morality: Religious and Secular* (Oxford: Clarendon Press, 1980); Basil Willey, *The Eighteenth Century: Studies in the Idea of Nature in the Thought of the Period* (Boston: Beacon Press, 1961).
5. *The Essential Plotinus,* ed. Elmer O'Brien (Indianapolis: Hackett Publishing Co., 1964). For the influence of Plotinus, see Denys Turner, *The Darkness of God* (Cambridge: Cambridge University Press, 1995); Arthur Lovejoy, *The Great Chain of Being* (Cambridge: Harvard University Press, 1936).
6. Bernard McGinn, *Meister Eckhart: Teacher and Preacher* (New York: Paulist Press, 1986).
7. Thomas Moore, *Care of the Soul* (New York: HarperCollins, 1992).
8. On this point, see *The Cloud of Unknowing,* edited with an introduction by James Walsh (New York: Paulist Press, 1981).
9. See my *Dance of the Spirit,* 62.
10. Nathan Scott in *The Wild Prayer of Longing* (New Haven, Conn.: Yale University Press, 1971), 49.
11. Rosemary Crumlin in *Aboriginal Art and Spirituality,* ed. Rosemary Crumlin and Anthony Knight (San Francisco: HarperCollins, 1991), 15.
12. In my *Jubilee Time: Celebrating Women, Spirit and the Advent of Age* I draw on the implications of age for the years after 50, citing the biblical command to count up seven years of seven years so that the total is forty-nine years, and then to hallow the fiftieth year (Lev. 25:8–12).
13. The Beguines were lay groups who led lives of prayer, community, and Christian service, especially in times of plagues and epidemics. They flourished in the Low Countries from the twelfth to the fourteenth centuries and focused on the religious experience of women. Hildegard of Bingen (1098–1179) was a German nun, mystic, and scholar who did not become prominent and influential until her early forties. She is known as a theologian, physician, and composer and has been a significant figure in today's ecological and feminist spiritualities. Julian of Norwich (ca. 1342–ca. 1420) was an English mystic who lived a life of solitude and received a series of mystical visions described in her *Book of Showings.* She has influenced twentieth-century figures as diverse as T. S. Eliot and Annie Dillard.
14. See Matthew Fox, *Original Blessing* (San Francisco: Bear & Co., 1983).
15. The phrase "God who arrives" comes from the work of Elizabeth A. Johnson. See her *Women, Earth, and Creator Spirit* (Mahwah, N.J.: Paulist Press, 1983), 41. See also her brilliant and prize-winning *She Who Is: The Mystery of God in Feminist Theological Discourse* (New York: Crossroad, 1993).
16. Charles Taylor, *Sources of the Self* (Harvard University Press, 1989), 115–42.
17. Hannah Arendt, *The Life of the Mind: Willing* (New York: Harcourt Brace Jovanovich, 1978).
18. St. Augustine, *Confessions* (New York: Penguin Books, 1961), 114.
19. *The Compact Edition of the Oxford English Dictionary,* vol. 2 (New York: Oxford University Press, 1971), 2968.
20. Taylor, *Sources of the Self,* 139–40.

21. G. K. Chesterton, *St. Francis of Assisi* (Garden City, N.Y.: Image Books, 1957), 87.
22. See for example Kathleen Norris, *Dakota: A Spiritual Geography* (Boston: Houghton Mifflin Co., 1993), and *The Cloister Walk* (New York: Riverhead Press, 1996).
23. This list is not, of course, exhaustive. For further sources see Richard Foster, *Celebration of Discipline* (New York: Harper & Row, 1978); Anthony de Mello, *Sadhana* (Garden City, N.Y.: Doubleday & Co., 1984); Dorothy C. Bass, ed., *Practicing Our Faith* (San Francisco: Jossey-Bass, 1997); Marva Dawn, *Keeping the Sabbath Wholly* (Grand Rapids: Wm. B. Eerdmans Publishing Co., 1989); Padraic O'Hare, *Busy Life, Peaceful Center* (Allen, Tex.: Thomas More Publishing, 1995); and Maria Harris, "Nourishing," in *Dance of the Spirit,* 114–41.

8. DOING JUSTICE

1. See Rabbi Abraham Joshua Heschel, *The Prophets,* vol. 1 (New York: Harper & Row, 1962), 3.
2. For a brief but powerful reflection on the essentials of justice, see Daniel C. Maguire, "Doing Justice to Justice," in *Keeping PACE* (Dubuque, Iowa: Brown-Roa, 1996), 155–59.
3. See "Just/Justice," in *Anchor Bible Dictionary,* vol. 3 (New York: Doubleday, 1992), 1127–28.
4. From Judy Chicago, *The Dinner Party* (Garden City, N.Y.: Doubleday & Co., 1979), 256.
5. For development of these forms, see Maria Harris, *Fashion Me a People: Curriculum and the Church* (Louisville, Ky.: Westminster/John Knox Press, 1989), 147–55.
6. See Carol Gilligan, *In a Different Voice* (Harvard University Press, 1982).
7. Nel Noddings, *Caring* (Berkeley, Calif.: University of California Press, 1984).
8. Helen Prejean, *Dead Man Walking,* 246–41.
9. Maguire, "Doing Justice to Justice."
10. Plato, *Republic,* 455e.
11. Ibid., 540e.
12. John R. Donahue, "Biblical Perspectives on Justice," in *The Faith That Does Justice,* ed. John C. Haughey (Mahwah, N.J.: Paulist Press, 1977), 69.
13. For this meaning, I draw on the work of Walter Brueggemann; see his "Voices of the Night—Against Justice" in Walter Brueggemann, Sharon Parks, and Thomas H. Groome, *To Act Justly, Love Tenderly, Walk Humbly* (Mahwah, N.J.: Paulist Press, 1986), 5–28.
14. Richard Ford, *Wildfire* (New York: Atlantic Monthly Press, 1990), 123.
15. Jenny Joseph, "Warning," *Selected Poems* (Newcastle-upon-Tyne: Bloodaxe Books, 1992).
16. For the development of these ideas on responsibility, see my *A Grammar of Responsibility* (New York: Crossroad, 1996).
17. Plato, *Republic,* 433b.
18. Carol Gilligan, "Justice and Responsibility," in *Toward Moral and Religious Morality,* ed. Christiane Brusselmans (Morristown, N.J.: Silver Burdett, 1980), 248.
19. Gilligan, *Social Science as Moral Inquiry,* ed. Norma Haan (New York: Columbia University Press, 1983), 40.

20. Arthur Adkins, *Merit and Responsibility: A Study in Greek Values* (Oxford: Oxford University Press, 1960).
21. Bonhoeffer, *Ethics*, 234.
22. *Contract with America* (Washington, D.C.: Republican National Committee, 1994), 9–10.

9. PROCLAIMING JUBILEE

1. Returning home—to your place and to your people—is itself a primary Jubilee theme. See Lev. 25:10, 13, 41.
2. See André Trocmé, *Jesus and the Nonviolent Revolution* (Scottdale, Pa.: Herald Press, 1983); John Howard Yoder, *The Politics of Jesus* (Grand Rapids: Wm. B. Eerdmans Publishing Co., 1972); J. Massyngbaerde Ford, *My Enemy Is My Guest: Jesus and Violence in Luke* (Maryknoll, N.Y.: Orbis Books, 1984); and J. A. Sanders, "From Isaiah 61 to Luke 4," in *Christianity, Judaism and Other Greco-Roman Cults,* 4 vols., ed. Jacob Neusner (Leiden: E. J. Brill, 1975).
3. See Emilio Castro, *Your Kingdom Come* (Geneva: WCC, 1980); Mortimer Arias, "The Jubilee: A Paradigm for Mission Today," in *International Review of Mission* (Geneva: Commission on World Mission and Evangelism of WCC), January 1984, 33–48; Dorothee Soelle, "God's Economy and Ours: The Year of the Jubilee," in *God and Capitalism: A Prophetic Critique of Market Economy,* ed. J. Mark Thomas and Vern Visick (Madison, Wis.: A-R Editions, 1991); and Sharon H. Ringe, *Jesus, Liberation, and the Biblical Jubilee* (Philadelphia: Fortress Press, 1985).
4. John Paul II, "On the Coming of the Third Millennium: Tertio Adveniente Millennio" (Washington, D.C.: USCC, 1994).
5. See *National Catholic Reporter,* July 29, 1994, 8.
6. For information, contact ELCA Division for Congregational Ministries, 8765 Higgins Road, Chicago, IL 60631.
7. Herman E. Daly, "A Biblical Economic Principle and the Steady-State Economy," *Epiphany Journal* 12 (winter 1992): 6–18; Alvin Schorr, *Jubilee for Our Time: A Practical Program for Income Equality* (New York: Columbia University Press, 1977).
8. See "New Evangelization: 1992 the Year of the Lord. The Bishops and Missionaries of Panama Propose the Celebration of a Continental Jubilee Year," *SEDOS Bulletin,* May 15, 1991, 139–41.
9. See Arthur Waskow, "From Compassion to Jubilee," *Tikkun,* March-April 1990, 78–81; and Richard Cartwright Austin, "Jubilee Now! The Political Necessity of the Biblical Call for Land Reform," *Sojourners,* June 1991, 26–30.
10. Two such parishes in the United States are Blessed Sacrament Catholic Community of Alexandria, Virginia, celebrating its Jubilee over the year that extended from September 1995 to September 1996, and St. Frances Cabrini Parish of Allen Park near Detroit, which celebrated its Jubilee in 1997.
11. See my *Proclaim Jubilee!* (Louisville, Ky.: Westminster John Knox Press, 1996), especially chap. 2. See also my *Jubilee Time: Celebrating Women, Spirit, and the Advent of Age.*
12. On amnesty, see Ringe, *Jesus, Liberation, and the Biblical Jubilee,* 22ff.
13. See John Howard Yoder, *The Politics of Jesus,* 66. Yoder writes, "Accurately, the word *opheilema* of the Greek text signifies precisely a monetary debt, in the most

material sense of the term. In the 'Our Father' then, Jesus is not simply recommending vaguely that we might pardon those who have bothered us or made us trouble, but tells us purely and simply to erase the debts of those who owe us money; which is to say, practice the Jubilee."

14. Stephen B. Oates, *The Fires of Jubilee: Nat Turner's Fierce Rebellion* (New York: Harper & Row, 1975).
15. David W. Blight, *Frederick Douglass' Civil War: Keeping Faith with Jubilee* (Baton Rouge, La.: Louisiana State University Press, 1989).
16. Margaret Walker, *Jubilee* (New York: Bantam Books, 1966).
17. Sidney Callahan writes of "The Capital That Counts," in *Commonweal,* November 22, 1996, pp. 7, 8.
18. Carol Lakey Hess, "Becoming Mid-wives to Justice: A Feminist Approach to Practical Theology," in *Feminist Practical Theologies,* ed. Riet Bons-Storm and Denise Ackermann (forthcoming). In making this point, Hess draws on Iris Young in *Justice and the Politics of Difference* (Princeton: Princeton University Press, 1990), 16.
19. Pinchas Lapide, *Sermon on the Mount* (Maryknoll, N.Y.: Orbis Books, 1982).
20. Robert Bork, *Slouching Toward Gomorrah* (New York: HarperCollins, 1996).
21. Larry Rasmussen, *Earth Community, Earth Ethics* (Maryknoll, N.Y.: Orbis Books, 1997).
22. John Bowker, *Jesus and the Pharisees* (Cambridge: Cambridge University Press, 1973).

10. WHAT CHRISTIANS CAN LEARN FROM JEWS

1. This chapter would be incomplete if we did not acknowledge the pioneering work in this area by two religious educators: Mary C. Boys of Union Theological Seminary in New York and Sara S. Lee of Hebrew Union College-Jewish Institute of Religion in Los Angeles. They are joined by a significant number of colleagues in two important issues of *Religious Education.* The first issue (vol. 90, no. 2 [spring 1995]) includes a Forum entitled "Protestant, Catholic, Jew: The Transformative Possibilities of Educating Across Religious Boundaries," 254–301. The second issue is subtitled "Religious Traditions in Conversation" (vol. 91, no. 4 [fall 1996]). See also Mary C. Boys, *Jewish-Christian Dialogue: One Woman's Experience* (Mahwah, N.J.: Paulist Press, 1997). We also wish to note the significant work of Padraic O'Hare on the same and similar issues. See his *The Enduring Covenant: The Education of Christians and the End of Antisemitism* (Valley Forge, Pa.: Trinity Press International, 1997).
2. Hayim Perelmuter, *Siblings: Rabbinic Judaism and Early Christianity at Their Beginnings* (Mahwah, N.J.: Paulist Press, 1989).
3. For a further development of these ideas, see my book *Uniqueness: Problem or Paradox in Jewish and Christian Traditions* (Maryknoll, N.Y.: Orbis Books, 1992), chaps. 4 and 5.
4. Quoted in Robert Gordis, *Jewish Ethics for a Lawless World* (New York: KTAV, 1987), 144. The development of this idea can be found in the great work of the twentieth-century thinker Franz Rosenzweig, *Star of Redemption* (New York: Holt, Rinehart & Winston, 1970), 336–79.
5. See note 7 below.

6. Abraham Joshua Heschel, *The Sabbath* (New York: Farrar, Straus & Giroux, 1995), 101. (First published in 1951.)
7. For information on this curriculum, write to: *Facing History and Ourselves,* 16 Hurd Road, Brookline, MA 02146-6919.
8. Exodus 22:20 (NRSV 22:21): "And a stranger thou shalt not wrong, neither shalt thou oppress him, for ye were strangers in the land of Egypt." Leviticus 19:34: "The stranger that sojourneth with you shall be unto you as the home born among you, and thou shalt love him as thyself; for ye were strangers in the land of Egypt."
9. The songs are *From a Distance* sung by Bette Midler, *What If God Were One of Us?* sung by Joan Osborne, and *Blue Cars* by Dishwallah.

11. INTERNATIONAL CONVERSATION

1. Stephen Schmidt, *A History of the Religious Education Association* (Birmingham, Ala.: Religious Education Press, 1983).
2. John Hull, *New Directions in Religious Education* (London: Falmer, 1982); W. Roy Niblett, "The Religious Education Clauses of the 1944 Act: Aims, Hopes and Fulfillment," in *Religious Education 1944–84,* ed. A. G. Wedderspoon (London: George Allen & Unwin, 1964).
3. Maria Harris, *Religious Education as a Second Language* (Birmingham, Ala.: Religious Education Press, 1989).
4. Mary Ann Glendon, *Divorce and Abortion in Western Law* (Cambridge: Cambridge University Press, 1987).
5. For further understanding of this theme, see John Hull, *Touching the Rock* (New York: Pantheon Books, 1990), an account of John Hull's experience of blindness.
6. A first article on this will be published in 1997–98 in the new *International Journal of Practical Theology.*

12. THE YEARS AHEAD

1. Children's Defense Fund, 122 E Street, Washington DC 20001, (202) 628-8787. Write to them for information on the Children's Sabbath.
2. See Jenny Joseph, "Warning," in *Selected Poems* (Newcastle-upon-Tyne: Bloodaxe Books, 1992); and Carolyn Forche, ed., *Against Forgetting: Twentieth-Century Poetry of Witness* (New York: W. W. Norton & Co, 1993).
3. See Anne Sexton, "Not So. Not So," in Anne Sexton, *The Awful Rowing Toward God* (Boston: Houghton Mifflin Co., 1975), 83.
4. Gerard Manley Hopkins, "God's Grandeur," in *A Hopkins Reader,* ed. John Pick (Garden City, N.Y.: Doubleday, 1966), 47–48.

Index

Index

Index

Index

Index

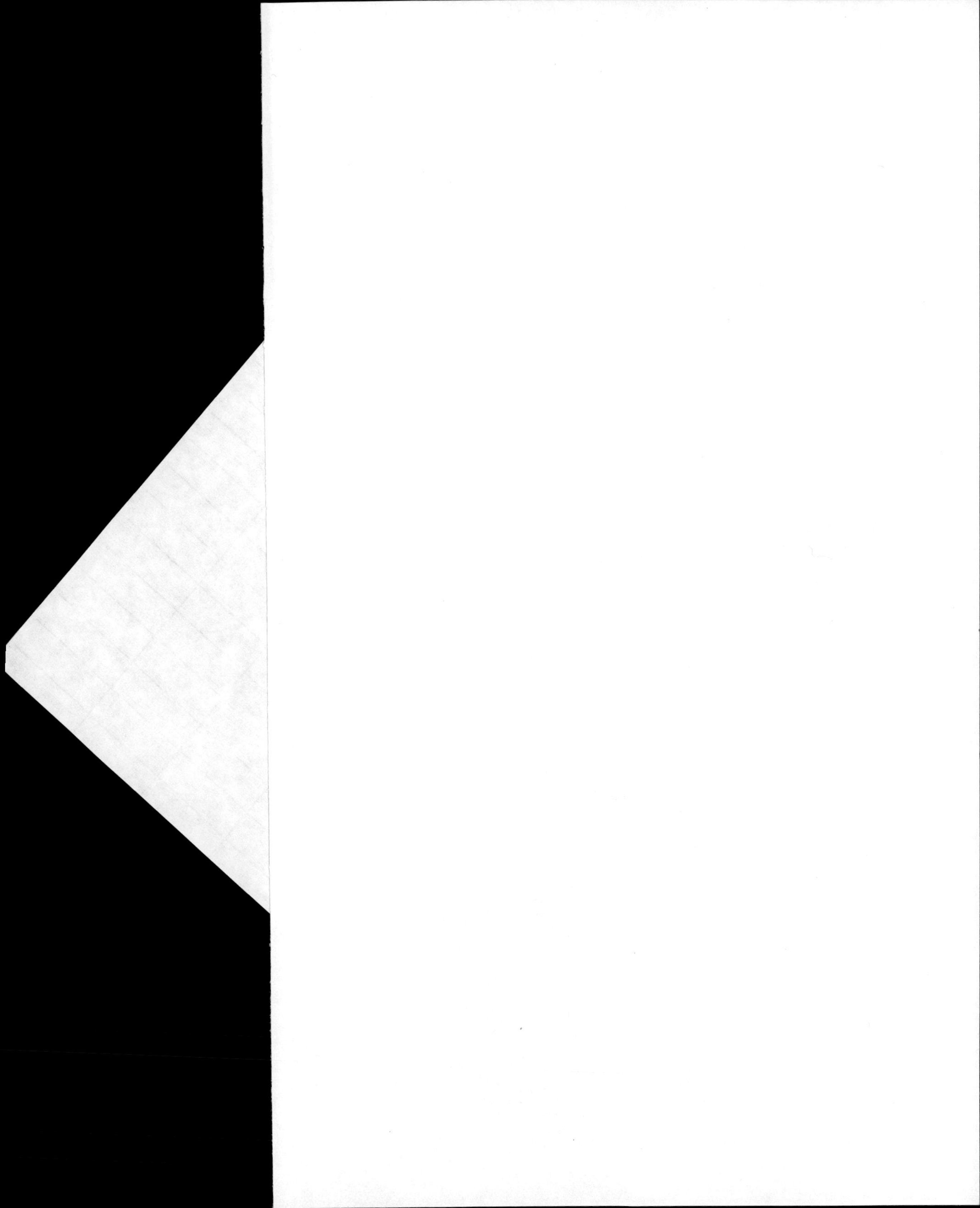

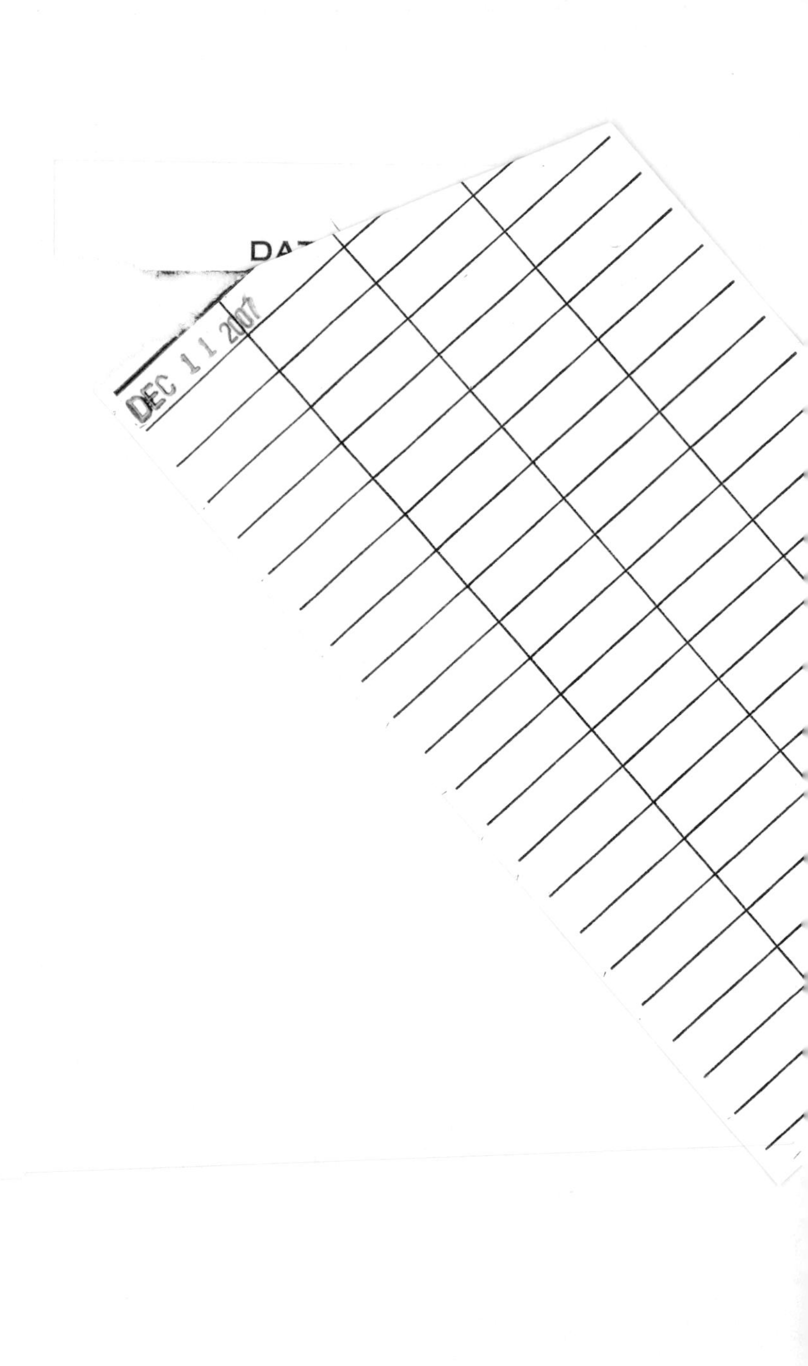
DA
DEC 1 1 2007